Jonathan Edwards on Worship

Jonathan Edwards on Worship

Public and Private Devotion to God

Ted Rivera

PICKWICK *Publications* · Eugene, Oregon

JONATHAN EDWARDS ON WORSHIP
Public and Private Devotion to God

Copyright © 2010 Ted Rivera. All rights reserved. Except for brief quotations in critical publications or reviews, no part of this book may be reproduced in any manner without prior written permission from the publisher. Write: Permissions, Wipf and Stock Publishers, 199 W. 8th Ave., Suite 3, Eugene, OR 97401.

Pickwick Publications
An Imprint of Wipf and Stock Publishers
199 W. 8th Ave., Suite 3
Eugene, OR 97401

www.wipfandstock.com

ISBN 13: 978-1-60899-256-0

Cataloguing-in-Publication data:

Rivera, Ted.

Jonathan Edwards on worship : public and private devotion to God / Ted Rivera

xii + 176 p. ; 23 cm. Includes bibliographical references.

ISBN 13: 978-1-60899-256-0

1. Edwards, Jonathan, 1703–1758. 2. Worship. I. Title.

BX7620.E3 R65 2010

Manufactured in the U.S.A.

To Barbara

Proverbs 18:22

Contents

List of Illustrations | *viii*
Foreword by Kenneth P. Minkema | *ix*
Abbreviations | *xi*

one   Introduction | 1
two   Public Worship | 20
three The Practice of Self-Examination | 75
four Private Devotion | 117
five Conclusion | 159

Bibliography | *167*

Illustrations

The Oldest Extant Order of Worship in North America | 9

Foreword

Jonathan Edwards spoke of worship of the living God as both a duty and a pleasure. Glorifying God was the "main business" of human life, the reason we were created. But for the believer, who is illumined by the gift of grace, glorifying God or seeking divine excellency was "pleasant." For Edwards, worship and praise were ways of participating in the beauty of God, enjoying union with God as a member of the body of Christ. True followers hungered and thirsted after that beauty and that union.

Worship was a many-faceted activity that reached into every nook and corner of human life. Certainly, Sabbath observance was central. But the elements of public worship—prayer, singing, reading and hearing the Word—were also to fill daily life. Individually, in family, and in community with friends, neighbors, and strangers, daily devotion, prayer, meditation and self-examination, reading edifying literature, and other "means," helped the soul to progress on its journey of faith. "Heart worship," Edwards called it.

Edwards is often regarded for his metaphysics, his philosophy. But his philosophical thought welled out of a deep piety and spirituality. His personal writings reveal to us the struggles he had, as well as the rapturous moments—all too fleeting—for which he lived. Alongside the enduring image of the great logician, and, for that matter, of the stern preacher, we must hold that of Edwards sitting on a hillside watching an approaching thunderstorm, weeping, singing, and chanting praises to the God he adored.

Ted Rivera's study is the first that systematically attempts to show us Edwards' views of worship, and so represents an important resource for scholars and religious practitioners alike who are interested in liturgy, "the practice of piety," and spiritual growth. Through an engagement with Edwards' own words—in letters, notebooks, and sermons—we learn of Edwards' own spiritual life and of the nature of private and corporate devotion.

But, as Rivera points out, Edwards was not content with worship and navel-gazing for their own sakes, cut off from life. As Edwards made clear in his essays and sermons, there was a vital connection between piety and action. Religious affections, he famously argued, exhibit themselves in enduring and explicit Christian behavior and practice. In acts of worship as in acts of charity, true virtue consisted in having *God* as our object. When that is the case, then acts of charity, and their fruits, *are* acts of worship.

Kenneth P. Minkema
Jonathan Edwards Center
Yale University

Abbreviations

BL *The Blessing of God: Previously Unpublished Sermons of Jonathan Edwards*, edited by Michael D. McMullen, (Nashville: Broadman & Holman, 2003)

WJE *Works of Jonathan Edwards*, edited by Perry Miller (vols. 1–2), John E. Smith (vols. 3–9), and Harry S. Stout (vols. 10–25) (New Haven: Yale University Press, 1957–2006)

*Works*² *Works of Jonathan Edwards*, edited by Edward Hickman, 2 vols. (Edinburgh: Banner of Truth Trust, 1987)

one

Introduction

What part did worship play in Jonathan Edwards's thought and in his preaching? How central a concern was worship to Edwards? Was worship even in some way an organizing principle or an essential motif for him? The answers to such questions will offer potentially profound insights into what drove Edwards. Such considerations have remained virtually unexplored in Edwardsean scholarship, and Edwards himself never devoted a full treatise to the topic. And yet, for Edwards, worship was that end for which man is created, that lofty purpose that must fill both the present life and eternity. He writes, "all things are from God as their first cause and fountain; so all things tend to him, and in their progress come nearer and nearer to him through all eternity: which argues that he who is their first cause is their last end."[1] At some point between the summer of 1722 and the spring of 1723, Edwards, still shy of twenty years of age, settled on the text of Psalm 89:6 for his message entitled "God's Excellencies," which reads, "For who in the heaven can be compared unto the Lord, and who among the sons of the mighty can be likened unto the Lord?" In his message, with words that in retrospect form something of a purpose statement for his ministry, Edwards preached, "My design . . . [is] to endeavor, by God's help, to exhibit and set forth the greatness, gloriousness, and transcendent excellency of that God who made us, and whom we worship and adore."[2]

As poignant as that might be, a key objection to be faced is that of irrelevance. How can Edwards, the preacher of such sermons as "Sinners in the Hands of an Angry God," "The Eternity of Hell Torments," and "The Justice of God in the Damnation of Sinners," be relevant in any contemporary theological discussion, much less a discussion of worship, a topic that has begun to enjoy such freedom and variety of expression? Despite this, the value of

1. Edwards, *Concerning the End*, 8:444
2. WJE 10:416.

a study of Edwards's approach to worship appears evident. Given Edwards's strong biblical orientation, at a minimum, two primary constituencies would appear to benefit from his insights on the subject. First, those who share Edwards's view of the Bible, and who therefore are likely to esteem his insights relating to other matters, will likely be interested in taking seriously his counsel on matters relating to public and private worship. Second, students of Christian worship may well be spurred to renewed reflection and consideration, and to potentially consider the possibility that Edwards's views may positively inform contemporary dialogue. As such, Jonathan Edwards, by virtue of his thoroughgoing dependence on Scripture and his unique insight, offers counsel that may prove perceptive with respect to Christian worship today, through his preaching and teaching on public and private devotion to God.

In this introductory chapter, representative background will be provided on the different positions held with regard to the value of Edwards's contributions, as there are widely divergent estimations now prevalent, with seemingly little middle ground. Next, the Puritan pattern for worship will be reviewed in order to identify the elements of public and private worship that were customary, given the likely connection between the Puritans and Edwards in this crucial respect. Finally, an initial glimpse into Edwards's view of worship will be provided by means of the review of a key sermon, and some preliminary implications will be observed. In the chapters that follow, Edwards's insights into the components of public and private worship will be considered in turn, focusing first on public worship, next on self-examination as the bridge between public and private worship, and then on private worship itself. Last, some tentative conclusions will be noted, and potential areas for further study will be highlighted.

Background

At one extreme end of the critical spectrum, with all of the extraordinary effort that has been expended to analyze and psychoanalyze Edwards, one wonders why one simple word has not more consistently been used by his detractors to describe him—*neurotic*. Patricia Tracy, for example, speaks of Edwards's "Resolutions"[3] as "the urgent gropings of a depressed man toward

---

3. Found in WJE 16:753–59.

some sense of emotional stability."[4] Consider just a few easily observed details from the vast warehouse of oddities that could be brought to bear in order to build a portrait of Edwards that would forever cast him as history's archetypical neurotic. Edwards was the introverted only son of a strong mother and controlling father—not to mention grandson of the so-called "pope" of New England, Solomon Stoddard—and fifth in birth order amidst a slew of ten doting sisters. The case can plausibly be made that he had few if any meaningful relationships with any man throughout his life. Possible exceptions to this contention might be David Brainerd, a much younger man some might think was easily manipulated, with personal habits similar to Edwards's that might be labeled excessive; or perhaps Samuel Hopkins, a man we would say was mentored by Edwards, and also arguably easily influenced. Edwards, for his own part, referred to Joseph Bellamy as "one of the most intimate friends I have in the world."[5]

That compulsions ravaged Edwards seem readily evident; while many would point to his lifelong habit of thirteen hours of study a day as evidence of incomparable devotion, others could easily see in such behavior a pattern of obsessive compulsion that bordered on self-destructiveness. In a related vein, Edwards's celebrated gauntness, a near walking cadaver in the eyes of some, can either be explained away as a man preoccupied with spiritual matters to the point of self-neglect, or perhaps as evidence of anorexia to a more jaundiced eye. Consider this diary entry by Edwards:

> I find that when eating, I cannot be convinced in the time of it, that if I should eat more, I should exceed the bounds of strict temperance, though I have had the experience of two years of the like; and yet, as soon as I have done, in three minutes I am convinced of it. But yet, when I eat again, and remember it, still, while eating, I am fully convinced that I have not eaten what is but for nature, nor can I be convinced that my appetite and feeling is as it was before. It seems to me that I shall be somewhat faint if I leave off then; but when I have finished, I am convinced again, and so it is from time to time.[6]

Given the more dark and extreme characterizations of Edwards that have been set forth, one marvels that even more sensationalistic theories, such as that Edwards was perhaps as a sufferer of Munchausen syndrome—or

---

4. Tracy, *Jonathan Edwards, Pastor*, 85.
5. WJE 16:348.
6. WJE 16:784.

worse, Munchausen by proxy, lived out through his daughter Jerusha or even his protégé Brainerd—have not seriously been proposed. In one of the more spectacular examples of dark characterization, Struthers Burt "blamed Edwards for the violent gangsterism of the Prohibition Era."[7] In "The Anachronism of Jonathan Edwards," H. Richard Niebuhr adds, "A highly popular, widespread impression of Jonathan Edwards is the one expressed in verse by Phyllis McGinley: 'Whenever Mr. Edwards spake / In church about Damnation, / The very benches used to quake / For awful agitation.'"[8]

At the far opposite end of the spectrum, even hagiolatry seems too weak a word for some of the characterizations that many have made, with Edwards in "nearly messianic terms" portrayed as a man of unassailable virtue of whom the world was not worthy.[9] Consider some of the glimpses that proponents of Edwards might offer. Edwards can be represented as a titanic spiritual force and a true Biblicist, embodying self-control to a degree that must invariably strike awe in others, modeling a spiritual rigor that can and must inspire even a self-absorbed and seemly insatiable age. It could be argued that Edwards, though ever severe, was rightly so; were others to take seriously his contention that there was a literal heaven and hell, an eternal reward or punishment, they too would drastically alter the pattern of their own lives in favor of the views he espoused.

Consider the many possible calls to emulate this man that can and have been made. Some would suggest that teenagers should follow the impulse of his "Resolutions," and at an early age unreservedly devote themselves to God. Others might urge that congregations must shake free of their materialistic impulses in favor of devoted obedience to the word of God. And still others might desire that pastors should speak the uncompromising truth of Scripture even to the risk of their own comfort and security. Perhaps supremely, many might hope that evangelistic and missionary impulses would once again rise with fervor, even now, in response to the challenge of this great visionary father of the church. John Piper is illustrative of contemporary authors who have pointed to Edwards as a motivating example for evangelism, missions, preaching, and devoted faith.[10]

7. Stout et al., *Jonathan Edwards at 300*, vii.
8. Niebuhr, "Anachronism of Jonathan Edwards," 480.
9. Moody, *Jonathan Edwards and the Enlightenment*, 162.
10. Piper, *Let the Nations Be Glad*; *Supremacy of God*; *Godward Life*; and *God's Passion*; Davies, "Jonathan Edwards: Missionary Biographer."

What might tip the scales in favor of one representation over the other? With the continuing publication of the works of Edwards—requiring the agonizingly painstaking labor of transcribing his unique form of writing, which one could interpret as either neurotically bizarre or as a benign paragon of humility—a permanent polarization of opinion about his place in the history of religion seems inevitable. On the one hand, as difficult as it may seem for some to consider, it appears impossible to ignore the psychological baggage that Edwards in fact carried; his seemingly unceasing inner turmoil, his *angst*, forever wrestling against the world, the devil, and perhaps most especially, his pride, his own flesh. On the other, the earnestness of his inner spiritual life seems indisputable. As a consequence, it is especially tempting to bring to the dialogue about this man works one's own predilections and attitudes about what is true and real. But if it is difficult to know another man or woman fully, how much more difficult is it to fully know a man from whom one is removed by centuries and by high cultural walls? It might be tentatively set forth that while Edwards was marked by habits of behavior some might view as neurotic, and at the very same time by intense spirituality, the one may have fueled the other.

While this dual perspective provides an intriguing backdrop, the primary focus of the present study ultimately builds on these notions but lies elsewhere, on Edwards's understanding of worship. Imagine for a moment: What would it have been like to be a part of Edwards's congregation? In a far less transient age, what would it have been like to sit under this man's indisputably austere leadership, to hear his meticulously crafted sermons for long years? Might it not prove well-nigh unavoidable that his personal strengths (e.g., his fervent spirituality) and weaknesses (e.g., his suspected neurosis) would be transmitted? Depending on one's attitude, this transmission might potentially sound like an either terrifying or marvelous proposition—but might it not have been both?

For many, "Puritan" is a word dripping with pain and repression and restriction, a decaying straightjacket that nevertheless still smothers out life even now—and Edwards was arguably the consummate child of the Puritans. For others, "Puritan" is a word that calls us back to a simpler time, when hard work was rewarded with a fair profit, when sin was an omnipresent reality to be confronted, and when all was done to the greater glory of God. J. I. Packer writes, "Horse racing is said to be the sport of kings. The sport of slinging mud, has, however, a wider following. Pillorying the Puritans, in particular, has been a popular pastime on both sides of the Atlantic, and most people's image of Puritanism still has on it much disfiguring dirt that needs to be scraped off."[11] In an essay entitled "Puritanism Lives," David Gelernter adds, "Hatred of Puritanism happens to be one of the best established bigotries of modern times. 'Puritan' has been an insult for hundreds of years. It suggests rigidity, austerity, and censoriousness—exactly the kind of religion secularists love to hate." He continues, "We ought to know Americanism for what it is: the form in which Puritanism still survives and inspires peoples who dream of moral freedom."[12]

The temptation in answering the question as to what it would have been like to be a part of Edwards's congregation is to bring to bear one's own outlook on the subject. As a result, this book will studiously seek to let Edwards speak for himself and in particular, to allow the reader to hear his portrayal of the various facets that constitute Christian worship. For this description of worship, rather than relying primarily on his theological treatises, which have formed the basis for much of the academic study of Edwards (e.g. *The Freedom of the Will* or *Religious Affections*), it seems more appropriate to start elsewhere: with a consideration of Edwards's preaching, where worship was practiced rather than merely described.[13] And, in the preaching of Jonathan Edwards, a full-orbed vision of worship will be discovered. It is at once thoroughly consistent with and likely the pinnacle of the Puritan understanding of public and private worship, while at the same time it anticipates some of the sea changes in worship that would follow. At this point, then, it is necessary to understand the Puritan approach to worship with which Edwards would have been familiar from his earliest days.

Worship in Puritan New England

In the late seventeenth and early eighteenth century, public worship was marked by a very narrow, almost formulaic profile in New England. The regulative principle to which the Puritans rigorously adhered stipulated

---

11. Packer in Ryken, *Worldly Saints*, ix.

12. Gelernter, "Puritanism Lives," 25.

13. While Edwards's sermons will provide the basis for the majority of the information brought to bear on this subject, important insights from other relevant primary sources will also be included as appropriate. In particular, his letters and personal writings will be consulted closely in the section in chapter 4 entitled "Morning and Evening Family Devotions."

that all elements included in corporate worship must be explicitly taught in Scripture. Private worship, or devotion, was also delineated by consistent patterns and expectations. Such manuals as Lewis Bayly's *The Practice of Piety* were virtually reprinted constantly, so profound was their influence. Joel Beeke, in his introduction to *The Practice of Piety*, notes, "First published in the early 1600s (the exact date is unknown, but was probably 1611) . . . by 1643 it had reached its thirty-fourth English edition; by 1714, its fifty-first English edition; by 1792, its seventy-first English edition!" Horton Davies describes "the form and order of Puritan Worship" in this manner:

> On each Lord's Day there were two services, one in the morning commencing about nine o'clock, and the other in the afternoon beginning around two o'clock. Each service was arranged in the following order and we may assume that what was done in Boston was also done elsewhere in New England:
>
> > Opening Prayer of Intercession and Thanksgiving
> > Reading and exposition of a chapter of the Bible
> > Psalm singing
> > SERMON
> > Psalm singing
> > Prayer
> > Blessing
>
> The sole modification in morning worship was a monthly or bi-monthly celebration of the Lord's Supper. The only occasional changes in the afternoon service were baptism, a collection (called the "Contribution"), and, occasionally, the admission of new members.[14]

Charles Hambricke-Stowe confirms this pattern of public worship and, importantly, illustrates how this corporate duty was to be augmented with private devotional habits.[15] He writes, "These exercises included reading of Scripture and other devotional books, various types of meditation, prayer, psalm singing, the keeping of a diary or other spiritual records, and 'conference,' or consultation, with a spiritual counselor."[16] Significantly, the private devotional life was intended to undergird and build on the experience of public worship: "Secret exercises were the most powerful channels through which grace might flow, whereby New Englanders attained their highest reaches of spiritual experience. . . . They provided the crucial point of

14. Davies, *American Puritans*, 8.
15. Hambrick-Stowe, *Practice of Piety*.
16. Ibid., 136.

connection between the believer and God; without them, the outward forms of public worship and family devotions could become hollow and hypocritical performances."[17] William Spohn summarizes this situation well:

> The first generation Puritans rejected monasticism while transferring its religious intensity to "the affirmation of ordinary life." They repositioned asceticism and regular religious disciplines in the daily world of work and family. A high sense of calling was maintained by regular recourse to the means of grace, which were divided into two main groups. The ordinances of public worship consisted of reading and preaching the Scripture, the sacraments, and prayer, fasting, community discipline, collections for the poor, and special days of prayer and thanksgiving. Private devotions included examination of conscience, keeping spiritual journals, morning and evening family prayers, private reading of Scripture, "conference" with another Christian, and a comprehensive observance of the Sabbath.[18]

Against this backdrop, Edwards must be seen as largely conforming to Puritan formulations of public and private devotion. This is not to suggest he was not an innovator even in this regard; for example, Edwards endorsed his congregation's acceptance of the hymns of Isaac Watts long before it became fashionable to do so. In a letter to Benjamin Colman, written in 1744, Edwards writes, "It has been our manner in this congregation, for more than two years past, in the summer time, when we sing three times upon the Sabbath, to sing an hymn, or part of a hymn of Dr. [Isaac] Watts', the last time, viz.: at the conclusion of the afternoon exercise. I introduced it principally because I saw in the people a very general inclination to it."[19] Still, one would be hard pressed to make the case that Edwards deviated markedly from either the pattern of worship he learned at the feet of his father Timothy or that of his grandfather Solomon Stoddard (with the obvious exception being the communion controversy that led to Edwards's ultimate expulsion from his Northampton pulpit).[20] What is more, the external forms for worship in New England remained largely unchanged even well into the beginning of the nineteenth century, as illustrated by the order of worship

---

17. Ibid., 156.
18. Spohn, "Spirituality and Its Discontents," 253–76.
19. WJE 16:144.
20. WJE 12:1–90.

pictured in figure 1 below.[21] It is therefore safe to conclude that the structure of the form of worship that Edwards inherited and employed remained intact, although his points of emphasis will warrant close consideration, especially when private devotion is analyzed as an effective extension of public corporate worship. Prior to a consideration of the various aspects of public and private worship identified as customary features in Puritan worship, and of Edwards's attitude toward each of these aspects of worship, it is essential to catch a glimpse of the big picture first.

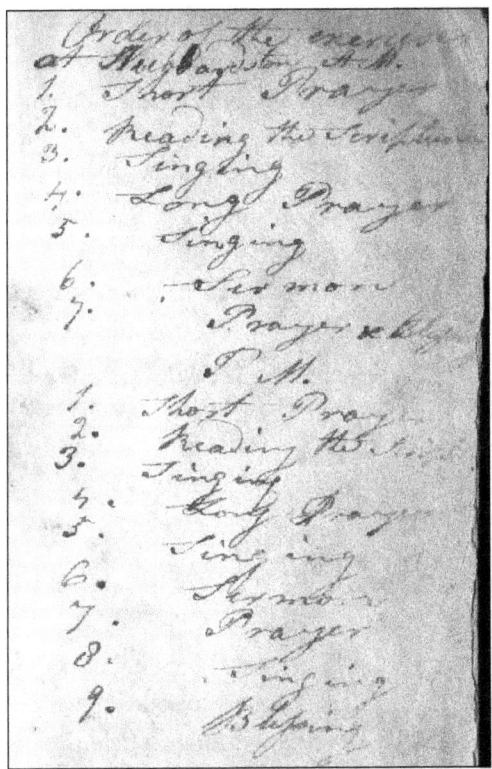

FIGURE 1. The oldest extant order of worship in North America. The image is reproduced with the permission of Wilson Kimnach and the office of the Works of Jonathan Edwards at Yale University.

21. The oldest extant order of worship in North America is handwritten in the front pages of *The Psalms of David* (Boston, 1801), a double volume that also includes *Hymns and Spiritual Songs*. Both of these volumes are by Thomas Watts, and printed by Samuel Hall. The book was the pulpit hymnal of the church in Hubbardston, Massachusetts, and is now the possession of Wilson H. Kimnach of the University of Bridgeport. Its order remains very much in line with the Puritan patterns presented from even the early seventeenth century, revealing the staying power of these forms.

"Mercy and Not Sacrifice"

During the second period of revival at Northampton, Edwards preached what is arguably his most focused sermon on the subject of worship, "Mercy and Not Sacrifice." It may not be too strong an assertion to suggest that this sermon represents his most concise and representative teaching on the subject of worship in the whole of his vast written corpus. It is noteworthy also that this sermon was preached in January of 1740, when concerns for revival would soon burn more brightly. Only one month later, Edwards would invite Whitefield to preach at Northampton, an offer Whitefield accepted, arriving at Northampton in October of that same year.[22] In this way, the subject of worship appears prominently at a vital moment in the life of the congregation at Northampton, when concerns for revival were undoubtedly on Edwards's mind, and a review of this sermon will help prevent a study of the parts of worship according to Edwards without understanding first their contribution toward the larger whole.

"Mercy and Not Sacrifice" is based on Jesus' statement as recorded in Matt. 12:7: "But if ye had known what this meaneth, I will have mercy, and not sacrifice, ye would not have condemned the guiltless." The sermon follows Edwards's customary pattern of text, doctrine, and application, and was preached in two installments. The doctrinal section, while rarely brief in Edwards's preaching, is even more prominent than usual in this particular sermon.[23]

Text

Edwards very narrowly pinpoints the subject he will examine in Matthew's Gospel. Matthew 12:1–7 recounts an episode in which Jesus' disciples plucked heads of grain while walking through a field to satisfy their hunger. This ostensibly innocent act, though, represented a profound offense to the Pharisees, because in their estimation this action constituted a clear violation of Sabbath regulations. Edwards by his selection of a portion of Matthew 12:7 hones in on the key rebuttal offered by Jesus to the Pharisees, the prophetic insight from Hosea, "I will have mercy and not sacrifice." These few words constituting the precise subject of his sermon, Edwards explains, "Two kinds of duties [are] compared, mercy and sacrifice, the one a moral

22. WJE 16:79–81.
23. WJE 22:113.

duty towards men, viz. that of mercy. . . . The other duty is a duty of external religion towards God, viz. offering sacrifice."[24]

These two duties, while each important, have a relative priority: "We may observe to which of these the preference is given, viz., to mercy, which is a moral duty towards men. This God prefers before sacrifice, that is, an external duty of religion towards God."[25] While Edwards asserts that Jesus uses this text to justify the actions of his disciples, it should be noted that this in no way betrays a setting aside of Puritan sabbatarianism: "Christ seems to allow that their plucking ears of corn and rubbing them in their hands to get food to eat on the Sabbath day would be unlawful were it not that their own relief required it."[26] Edwards intimates, however, that it may be a defensible act to set aside some of the external requirements of worship in instances where mercy toward one's fellow man should be given priority.

Doctrine

Edwards jolts his hearers with his opening volley. The doctrinal essence Edwards distills from this text runs contrary to all religious conceptions of external worship as the epitome of human activity: "Moral duties towards men are a more important and essential part of religion than external acts of worship of God."[27] In fact, taken in isolation, this doctrinal formulation seems to run contrary to the emphasis many see in Edwards as preeminently preoccupied with the glory of God. Does not the Westminster Shorter Catechism, which Edwards was in agreement with, teach that "Man's chief end is to glorify God and to enjoy him forever"? In a letter to the Rev. John Erskine, Edwards writes, "As to my subscribing to the substance of the Westminster Confession, there would be no difficulty." The "Westminster Confession" in this context can for Edwards be considered a synecdoche for not only the Westminster Confession but also the Larger and Shorter Catechisms.[28] He elsewhere preaches, "So true repentance as the catechism teaches us is from

---

24. WJE 22:114. It is worth noting that throughout the course of this sermon Edwards moves between the phrases "external worship" and "external duties of religion" as essentially synonymous.

25. Ibid.

26. WJE 22:115.

27. Ibid.

28. WJE 6:355

an apprehension of the mercy of God in Christ."[29] Does this not seemingly run contrary to Edwards's assertion elsewhere that "It is manifest that the Scriptures speak, on all occasions, as though God made himself his end in all his works: and as though the same Being, who is the first cause of all things, were the supreme and last end of all things."[30] If it is the case that "moral duties" are "more important" than "external acts of worship," how can the glory of God remain the ultimate concern?

Edwards explains, "Whatever duties men perform not as subject to a deity or without any reference to him, what they do has no religion in it, nor is not to [be reckoned] as any part of religion: for God is the object of all religion."[31] In other words, one may perform good deeds toward others, acts of mercy, in one of two ways. On the one hand, "if a man is temperate only from regard to his health, or if he [is] liberal and generous only for the applause of men, his temperance and liberality are no part of religion."[32] On the other hand, "if he is temperate and charitable with conscience towards God, and the man performs these duties as subject to him, then they are performed as duties of religion."[33] In this light, then, there is no conflict between acts of mercy and acts of worship that glorify God. Rather, all religious activity, whether offered in service to others or pertaining to genuine worship, are subsumed in this notion that, finally, "God is the object of all religion."

As such, and consistent with the preceding review of Puritan formulations, worship is constituted by both internal and external dimensions. External worship consists of public and private elements, "such as outward prayer, singing psalms, going to the public assemblies of God's people, attending the sacraments, keeping days of fasting or thanksgiving, reading and hearing the word of God, attending private religious meetings, speaking respectfully of God, [and] talking much of God and Christ."[34] Inward acts of worship consist of such elements as "the inward actings of love to God,

29. Compare "The Shorter Catechism" in Presbyterian Church in America, *Westminster Confession of Faith*, 27. See also Edwards's sermon preached in 1752, "God Stands Ready to Forgive Every Sinner upon His Heartily Confessing and Forsaking His Sin," based on Prov 28:13 ("He that covereth his sins shall not prosper; but whoso confesseth and forsaketh them shall have mercy"), in BL 135.

30. Edwards, *God Created the World*, in WJE 8:467.

31. WJE 22:116.

32. WJE 22:117.

33. Ibid.

34. Ibid.

and inward fear and reverence towards God, acts of inward trust in God and submission to him."[35] Edwards in this way arrives at the sermon's key point of emphasis:

> The internal acts of worship, or the worship of the heart in inward acts of love and fear of God and trust in God, *are the most essential and important of all the duties of religion whatsoever*. Christ teaches us this; he tells us that the first and great command of the Law is to love the Lord our God with all our heart, {and with all our soul, and with all our mind} (Matt. 22:37–38). This is the very essence of true religion, the most fundamental part, the source.[36]

True religion, then, will be evident only in a heart directed toward God. In this way, God's glory remains preeminent, for whether or not a true Christian is engaged in external acts of worship or in works of mercy, the aim will be a life organized around loving God "with all our heart." Moreover, whereas in the Old Testament external acts of worship were litigiously specified, in the New "men are called upon to worship God in the Spirit."[37] It is in this way that acts of mercy rise to greater prominence: "Jesus Christ, when he was on the earth, did abundantly more insist on such duties than on the duties of external worship."[38] And the Apostle Paul "insists ten times so much on moral duties towards men as the external acts of worship."[39]

Edwards employs a battery of Scriptural references to bolster his case that moral duties are more important than acts of external worship, and to affirm that it is possible to "abound in acts of external worship . . . but not in duties of righteousness and charity."[40] Remembering the Pharisees, Edwards avers, "Hypocrites and self-righteous persons do much more commonly abound in the outward acts of worship of God than they do in the duties of righteousness and mercy towards their neighbors."[41] Pressing still further, Edwards adds, "External worship is of no use but only as a sign of something else, viz. a sign of internal worship."[42]

35. Ibid.
36. WJE 22:118; emphasis added.
37. WJE 22:119.
38. Ibid.
39. Ibid.
40. WJE 22:122.
41. WJE 22:123.
42. WJE 22:126.

[B]Application

Given Edwards's extensive doctrinal treatment in this sermon, his application is comparatively brief. Because internal worship is more important than external worship, and since acts of mercy are to be emphasized over against external worship, it is not surprising that Edwards urges his congregation to action by means of these two points of emphasis. The "best evidences" of "eminence in piety" will not be visible to others. In fact,

> the best evidences to others are not persons' abounding in outward acts of worship, in reading {the Scriptures}, hearing {the word preached}, or in shows of respect to God, to talk [much of the things of religion], or being exceeding strict and exact in these things, but their abounding in a Christian behavior, in deeds of righteousness, meekness, forbearance, peaceableness, love and mercy amongst men. These are the greatest evidences that men can have of others' eminency in religion, that is much to be preferred to man's being much in the religion of the tongue, as in external acts of worship.[43]

Edwards warns his congregation, in the midst of a cold Northampton January, that "we have declined" in acts of inward religion and in acts of mercy. In closing, he urges, "If you do truly love God, you won't be content not to express your love. Yea, you will want to express your love a great deal. You have now been told which is the most acceptable way of expressing love to God. Therefore seek to express your love much in this way, by being very much in such deeds of righteousness, faithfulness, mercy and love towards your neighbor."[44]

Heart Worship: The Pressing Concern

"God is the object of all religion" is by no means an ancillary concern expressed only in "Mercy and Not Sacrifice." Moreover, service to others as evidence of true conversion is similarly emphasized repeatedly by Edwards. The editors of the volume in which "Mercy and Not Sacrifice" appears rightly set the sermon in its larger historical context: "As in this sermon, the question of how to differentiate between genuine and false piety is central to Edwards' revival treatises, *A Faithful Narrative*, *Distinguishing Marks*, *Some Thoughts*, and *Religious Affections*."[45] In this regard, genuine, Spirit-inspired, inward

---

43. WJE 22:132.
44. WJE 22:135.
45. WJE 22:113.

religion—heart worship—might well be seen as the basis for personal and ultimately corporate revival, and at the core of his larger theological program.

At a surface level, it is worth noting that in other sermons preached also in 1740, Edwards echoes similar themes. Drawing on 1 Thessalonians 5:23, Edwards observes that the change wrought in the converted is so substantial as to transform all of life, even our very bodies. It is a "very unscriptural, lustful, and dangerous notion" to believe that "a man may be converted and live no better than he did before."[46] This sermon, preached in July of 1740, is entitled "In True Conversion Men's Bodies Are in Some Respect Changed as Well as Their Souls," and is based on 1 Thessalonians 5:23: "And the very God of peace sanctify you wholly, and I pray God your whole spirit and soul and body be preserved blameless unto the coming of our Lord Jesus Christ." It is pernicious to conclude that an "inward change" is required "but that there is no need of any external change."[47] Pressing the point to his congregation, he urges, "consider after what manner you used to employ the members of your body—your eyes, ears, tongues, and hands—in the service of sin before what you call your conversion."[48] In this way, one's actions must be thoroughly conformed to what one professes to believe.

Similarly, in a sermon preached in October of 1740, the same month in which Whitefield also preached at Northampton, Edwards drew out this relationship between belief and action: "If you know that Christ is your redeemer and know that he has loved you from eternity and that he has laid down his life for you, it will greatly fill your heart in love to him."[49] What will be the result of such faith? "It will cause you to do your duty with the greatest cheerfulness and will draw you on in the way of holiness that you may not only walk but run in the way of God's commandments."[50] More to the point, this is no optional outcome: "'Tis not a privilege attainable only by a few but that which in the use of proper means might ordinarily be attained by the saints."[51]

46. BL 306.
47. Ibid.
48. BL 307.
49. This is cited from a sermon preached in 1740 and 1755 entitled "It Is a Matter of Great Comfort and Rejoicing to Anyone in Whatever Circumstances He Is in, When He Can Say That He Knows His Redeemer," which was based on Job 19:25: "For I know that my redeemer liveth." See BL 62.
50. BL 63.
51. Ibid.

And, while such examples could be easily multiplied, they would provide only superficial connections between "Mercy and Nor Sacrifice" and the essence of Edwards's view of genuine heart worship. In order to probe into this further, consider once more the form of Puritan worship, public and private, that was previously outlined. On the one hand, there are a number of elements of public worship that have been mentioned: singing, the reading and preaching of the Scriptures, prayer, and so forth. Similarly, in private devotion, a number of other elements have been touched on: prayer, Scripture reading, private conversation, and the like. What is perhaps missing, however, in such a consideration, is the means by which public and private worship are *connected* in Edwards's program. How is it that public worship is to influence private devotion? How is it that private devotion is to enhance public worship? The practice of self-examination, so relentlessly prescribed by Edwards, may well provide a bridge between the two, given that it is a nearly constant point of application in his preaching, a practice to be meticulously and regularly undertaken in personal devotion.[52]

Moreover, it can be argued that self-examination is precisely that which is featured in "Mercy and Not Sacrifice." This is particularly noteworthy, given that in this sermon Edwards nowhere specifically calls upon his congregation to undertake the practice. Rather, it was already persistently in the groundwater, as it were. Here Edwards is calling upon his hearers to consider what Pharisaical religion would look like—a mere external adherence to forms and practices—and to assess their own approach to worship and to life as a whole. Has their worship been typified by adherence to outward customs of worship, but void of the marks of mercy toward others? Have they perhaps become adept at displaying an external piety that conceals an inner void? Such questions would call for self-examination in "Mercy and Not Sacrifice," and in this way the nature of true heart worship becomes more evident: all of Edwards's emphasis on the affections, on true and false religion, on inward and external religion, devolves on this matter of a heart sincerely inflamed by love for God.

So, for example, when Edwards in his sermon "The Importance and Advantage of a Thorough Knowledge of Divine Truth" urges a thoroughgoing understanding of the Scriptures, it is connected to such matters as have been considered: "Seek not to grow in knowledge chiefly for the sake of applause, and to enable you to dispute with others; but seek it for the benefit

---

52. The centrality of self-examination will be considered at length later in this work.

of your souls, and in order to practice."[53] So also when Edwards considers "Praying for the Spirit," all superficiality is thrown down. One must not ask "in words, but at the same time" resist "the bestowment [of the Spirit] in practice."[54] And in the same way, after waxing rhapsodic with regard to the benefits of seeking after Christ, he implores, "Be willing to lose all other things, that you may find Christ. Whatever has been dear or pleasant to you heretofore, if it seems to stand in the way of your finding Christ, be willing to part with it."[55] In each instance, Edwards conveys the view that spiritual realities can only be known by putting into practice the principles of Scripture, and that genuine affection for God results in a substantially altered life. Such insights are inevitably intended to evoke rigorous self-examination.

The Significance of Worship in Edwards's Thought

This brief review has of course scarcely scratched the surface in investigating the role of worship in Edwards's preaching. All told, there are more than 1,200 sermons preached by Edwards that remain extant. More to the point, his writings, and perhaps in particular his personal letters, have yet to be reviewed to determine the proper prominence of worship for Edwards. That said, one clear point seems evident even at this juncture: the Puritan pattern for worship may well serve as a kind of skeletal structure by which to more systematically reevaluate Edwards's larger program, as a means by which to determine the connection between worship in its public and private dimensions and the desired outcome in the life of the believer and the Christian community. It has been suggested that the practice of self-examination provides an essential bridge between these two dimensions.

There remains in research on Edwards a gulf; on the one hand, the vast majority of study that has taken place over the last hundred years is of an academic or scholarly bent,[56] on the other, there is the possible temptation toward hagiolatry. One point of contrast may help to provide perspective. In 2003, the year marking the 300th year since Edwards's birth, two collections of essays were produced. From the academic community, one finds *Jonathan*

---

53. WJE 22:102. This sermon was preached in November of 1739, and is also often referred to by the shorter title "Christian Knowledge."

54. Ibid., 22:221. "Praying for the Spirit" is a fast day sermon preached in November of 1740.

55. Ibid., 22:295. "Seeking After Christ" was preached in December of 1740.

56. Hart et al., eds., *Legacy of Jonathan Edwards*, 228–47.

Edwards at 300: Essays on the Tercentenary of His Birth.[57] While one sees much of value in the essays in this volume, there is a sense in which the research presented remains consciously at arms length from the Christian faith that Edwards espoused and sought to advance. In a slightly more popular vein (but largely avoiding charges of hagiolatry), another volume arose marking this occasion, entitled *A God-Entranced Vision of All Things: The Legacy of Jonathan Edwards*.[58] The essays in this volume are also of a predominantly scholarly bent, but the authors on the whole are open to not only observing Edwards but also to endorsing his views at points; the aim is to introduce readers "to Edwards, and more importantly, to his 'God-entranced vision of all things.'"[59]

This latter approach seems likely to more adequately comprehend Edwards aright. John Piper, one of the editors of the latter volume, draws attention to an obscure miscellany recorded by Edwards:

> So God glorifies himself towards the creatures also in two ways: (1) by appearing to them, being manifested to their understandings; (2) in communicating himself to their hearts, and in their rejoicing and delighting in, and enjoying the manifestations he makes of himself. . . . God is glorified not only by his glory's being seen, but by its being rejoiced in, when those that see it delight in it: God is more glorified than if they only see it; his glory is then received by the whole soul, both by the understanding and by the heart. God made the world that he might communicate, and the creature receive, his glory, but that it might [be] received both by the mind and heart.[60]

Edwards's statement could be viewed from a number of vantage points: its "aesthetic" dimensions could be admired, its philosophical roots explored, or its historical import examined. In truth, though, Piper is right to set forth such material as a means by which one is invited by Edwards to enter into *relationship* with Edwards's God.

This gap between academic and so-called devotional writing may help explain why, while hundreds of books and dissertations and thousands of articles have been written about Jonathan Edwards, virtually nothing in print has broached the topic of Edwards on worship. This is true despite the

57. Stout et al., eds., *Jonathan Edwards at 300*.
58. Piper and Taylor, eds., *God-Entranced Vision*. It should be noted that the essay on Sarah Edwards in this volume is an anomaly; it is hagiolatrous in the truest sense.
59. Ibid., 13.
60. WJE 13:495

fact that worship is a theme both readily discerned in his sermons and writings, as demonstrated by this brief survey, and by the fact that his sermons are themselves in reality an integral part of the worship that took place at Northampton and elsewhere.

In a sermon preached several times over the course of his ministry, Edwards declared:

> In heaven alone is attainment of our highest good. God is the highest good of the reasonable creature. The enjoyment of him is our proper happiness, and is the only happiness with which our souls can be satisfied. To go to heaven, fully to enjoy God, is *infinitely* better than the most pleasant accommodations here: better than fathers and mothers, husbands, wives, or children, or the company of earthly friends. These are but shadows; but God is the substance. These are but scattered beams; but God is the sun. These are but streams; but God is the fountain. These are but drops; but God is the ocean. Therefore it becomes us to spend this life only as a journey towards heaven, as it becomes us to make the seeking of our highest end, and proper good, the whole work of our lives; and we should subordinate all other concerns of life to it. Why should we labor for anything else, or set our hearts on anything else, but that which is our proper end, and true happiness?[61]

With such declarations, it should be evident that Edwards would desire that his extensive preaching and voluminous writings might produce not merely forensic, detached study, but would rather serve to point others to not only consider Edwards himself, but to worship his God. Would not Edwards have ultimately contended vigorously that it was the Holy Spirit, and the Holy Spirit alone, who was the instrumental cause for the revivals that took place in his day? Would he not desire that such insight fire the affections, inspire piety, and evoke heart worship?

---

61. WJE 17:437–38; emphasis original. Valeri notes that this sermon was preached first in September of 1733, but also "at New Haven, at Boston in October 1753, and at Stockbridge to the Indian Congregation on an unspecified date." WJE 17:428. This sermon was entitled "The True Christian's Life a Journey towards Heaven," and was based on Heb 11:13–14: "And confessed that they were pilgrims and strangers on the earth. For they that say such things declare plainly that they seek a country."

two

Public Worship

In the same way that there are dangers in esteeming Edwards too highly, or seeing him as riddled with flaws, there are similar dangers that can take place when one considering the congregations he pastored, most notably the congregation at Northampton where he was pastor for over twenty years. One might well be tempted to sanctify the congregation where "awakenings" and "revivals" were common, or on the other hand, to vilify as fools those who would drive out a godly pastor such as Edwards. While it is difficult to break through to all of the details of worship in Edwards's day, similarly, consider how difficult it might be to describe almost any contemporary church. The attitude of the congregants can be easily swayed by a substantial social event on any given week. An unusually powerful sermon can break through to individuals who appeared "sermon-proof," a term Edwards used to describe his own congregation at Northampton in the spring of 1729.[1] The music in worship, or prayer, or the observation of the sacraments might be especially meaningful in a given service. A late Saturday night could produce an inability to focus adequately on the proceedings. And week by week, the vicissitudes of the participants might affect one or many members of the congregation based on the birth of a child, the death of a loved one, an unfortunate incident, or countless other matters. If it would be difficult to articulate how a contemporary congregation might be characterized in its worship, how much harder might it be to three-dimensionally characterize Edwards's Northampton, or even harder still, his brief New York pastorate, or the mission outpost at Stockbridge?

There are aspects of life in Edwards's day, though, that are different enough from the contemporary situation as to warrant mention; reminders of eighteenth century New England that will help to move us back toward the historical reality. At Northampton, for example, while there may have

1. WJE 14:365.

been a tanner, a hat maker, a lawyer, a couple of blacksmiths, and the proprietor of a general store in the services of the church, by and large, almost every head of household was a farmer.[2] It might not be uncommon for riders to arrive on horseback in a manner that would terrify those nearby, as they made an effort to impress others with their new colt.[3] In Stockbridge, Native Americans might well worship alongside "pioneers." The danger of attack from "Indians" or foreign armies was sometimes real and imminent in both venues; Edwards's private letters often drift to such topics.[4] There was an earthquake in 1727 and a diphtheria epidemic in the mid 1730s.[5] And, for good measure there was the occasional bizarre incident, such as the account Edwards provides in March of 1737, after having "'just laid down his doctrines' for the text 'Behold, ye despisers, and wonder, and perish.'"[6] In private correspondence, he recalled that

> in the midst of the public exercise in the forenoon, soon after the beginning of sermon, the whole gallery—full of people, with all the seats and timbers, suddenly and without any warning—sunk, and fell down, with the most amazing noise, upon the heads of those that sat under, to the astonishment of the congregation. The house was filled with dolorous shrieking and crying; and nothing else was expected than to find many people dead, or dashed to pieces.[7]

The point is simple: it is an error to consider the worship of Jonathan Edwards without considering the flesh-and-blood people he ministered among. There was a reason Edwards preached a sermon series on love to the congregation at Northampton; there was often a real and profound "spirit of contention."[8] There was a reason he spoke periodically about drunkenness at Stockbridge; there was a real problem of alcohol abuse among the Stockbridge Native Americans. While it is possible to consider treatises such as Edwards's *The Nature of True Virtue* or *The End for Which God Created*

---

2. Tracy, *Jonathan Edwards, Pastor*, 97.

3. Earle, *Sabbath*, 248.

4. While these concerns were more frequent at Stockbridge (see, for example, Edwards's letter to Thomas Foxcroft dated October 9, 1756), they were by no means unknown in Northampton. See WJE 16:690–91.

5. Tracy, *Jonathan Edwards, Pastor*, 87.

6. WJE 16:64.

7. Ibid., 16:66. Remarkably, no one was killed, although one woman was seriously injured.

8. WJE 4:146.

the World or *The Mind* as pure, theoretical, theological documents, worship with real people proved to be a messy business at times. As just one example, consider the following warning Edwards presented during a sermon:

> The last thing I will mention is sleeping at meeting. This is a thing that has been found amongst us in times past, but it may well be expected that we should worship God with greater reverence and diligence since God has so remarkably poured out his Spirit amongst us. If there be many among us in our assembly who appear to be asleep in their seats in the time of divine service, this will be a thing that strangers will observe. When they come here, they will naturally take notice how people appear in their public worship, whether there seems to be an evident and remarkable difference between them and other people, whether they seem to give better attention or to attend with greater reverence and diligence. If they observe that we sleep at meeting as much as at other places, it will doubtless bring much to them in what they have heard of us.[9]

It might be tempting to consider the various facets of worship, then, as if they could be neatly excised from congregational life, but they can't. As a consequence, it is important to recall that what Edwards said was intended to confront specific sins and to offer comfort in the midst of real sorrows— and that as the congregation came together for worship, and participated in singing and prayer and the preaching of the Word, they often had mud on their boots.

Edwards's encouragement to worship could be simple: "'Tis in your power to attend to all ordinances, and all public and private duties of religion, and to do it with your might."[10] And at times, Edwards himself would worship, even as he preached. For the people of God,

> their God is a glorious God. There is none like him, who is infinite in glory and excellency: he is the most high God, glorious in holiness, fearful in praises, doing wonders: his name is excellent in all the earth, and his glory is above the earth and the heavens: among the gods there is none like unto him; there is none in heaven to be compared to him, nor are there any among the sons of the mighty, that can be likened unto him. Their God is the fountain for all good, and an inexhaustible fountain; he is an all-sufficient God; a God that is able to protect and defend them, and do all things for them: he is

---

9. BL 270.
10. WJE 19:283.

the King of Glory, the Lord, strong and mighty, the Lord mighty in battle: a strong rock, and an high tower. There is none like the God of Jeshurun, who rideth on the heaven in their help, and in his excellency on the sky: the eternal God is their refuge, and underneath are everlasting arms: he is a God that hath all things in his hands, and does whatsoever he pleases: he killeth and maketh alive; he bringeth down to the grave, and bringeth up; he maketh poor and maketh rich: the pillars of the earth are the Lord's. Their God is an infinitely holy God: there is none holy as the Lord. And he is infinitely good and merciful. Many that others worship and serve as gods, are cruel beings, spirits that seek the ruin of souls; but this is a God that delighteth in mercy; his grace is infinite, and endures for ever: he is love itself, an infinite fountain and ocean of it. . . . They have an excellent and glorious Savior, who is the only begotten Son of God; the brightness of his Father's glory; one in whom God from eternity had infinite delight; a Savior of infinite love; one that has shed his own blood, and made his soul an offering for their sins; and one that is able to save them to the uttermost.[11]

One final point warrants mention as preparatory to understanding Edwards's view of the different elements that constitute public worship. Whether because of the size of the towns Edwards was a part of, or because of the rigorous Puritan approach to religious matters, or because of the social or economic realities of life in the early eighteenth century, these communities were very tightly knit, and the church was the center of community life. There was a drumbeat to life. On Saturday afternoons and evenings, preparations for the Sabbath would be undertaken. Sunday would entail lengthy morning and afternoon exercises of worship. Still more, particular days would be set aside as days of fasting, or for times of thanksgiving and celebration. Discipline would at times be conducted in the context of the church. The poorer members of the community would have been seen as not only a social concern, but as a Christian one. As such, when one speaks of Edwards's view of public worship, it entails not merely the events that took place on Sunday, but this larger public context, and this fuller notion of what it means to be a worshiping people.[12]

---

11. Ibid., 19:310. his quote is taken from a sermon entitled "Ruth's Resolution," which was preached in April of 1735 and was based on Ruth 1:16: "And Ruth said, Entreat me not to leave thee, or to return from following after thee; for whither thou goest, I will go, and where thou lodgest, I will lodge; thy people shall be my people, and thy God, my God."

12. WJE 25:729. Alice Morse Earle's *The Sabbath in Puritan New England* offers rich

In the following, the main dimensions of public worship will be considered in turn, with an eye toward hearing Edwards's perspective on each of these features. These include the reading and preaching of Scripture, the sacraments, public prayers, fast days, community discipline, collections for the poor, and special days of prayer and thanksgiving.

The Reading and Preaching of Scripture

The reading of Scripture in the worship services conducted by Jonathan Edwards, while a consistent component in its order, is one for which there is little information. One engaging historical vignette does provide some limited information, however. Edwards was to preach at the ordination of Job Strong, but was detained while traveling there on horseback.[13] A minister was asked to fill in for Edwards and entered into prayer, during which time Edwards arrived and slipped into the service without notice. During the course of this prayer, the minister thanked God for Edwards, God's "eminent servant," but was surprised and apparently flustered to find Edwards standing behind him at the conclusion of the prayer. He said famously,

> Brother Edwards, we are all of us rejoiced to see you here today, and nobody, probably, as much so as myself; but I wish that you might have got in a little sooner, or a little later, or else that I might have heard you and known that you were here. I didn't intend to flatter you to your face; but there's one thing I'll tell you: they say that your wife is going to heaven by a shorter road than yourself.[14]

The account continues dryly, "Mr. Edwards bowed, and after reading the Psalm, went on with the sermon. His text was John xiii. 15, 16, and his subject, 'Christ the Example of Ministers.'"[15] Apart from the awkward humor of

---

details on all of these points and numerous others. Also, one sermon that may provide additional context for Edwards's views on the subject of public worship warrants further investigation. Edwards's unpublished sermon on Ecclesiastes 5:1, entitled "It greatly concerns persons to take heed to themselves how they behave when they go to the house of God and attend the solemn duties of God's public worship there," which was preached in October of 1746, is also likely noteworthy, but has not yet been transcribed.

13. This account is a distillation of the report of the event given by Sereno Dwight. See *Works* 21:cviii–cix.

14. *Works*² 1:clx.

15. Ibid. This sermon appears in WJE 25:333–48 under the title "Christ the great Example of Gospel Ministers."

the moment, and Edwards's apparent humility (or his lack of social grace), we see Edwards here reading from the book of Psalms, and not from the Gospel of John from which he was preaching, which he would normally read from during the course of his sermon. Beyond this, we have little insight into how Scripture was read during worship led by Jonathan Edwards.

But of far greater consequence, what of Edwards's preaching, and his approach to preaching? In the same way that the one portrait of Jonathan Edwards painted during his lifetime has been subtly revised by later artists—and yet likely all miss the mark—so also caricatures of Edwards in the pulpit are remarkably predictable.[16] Typically, they proceed this way: the gaunt, malnourished Edwards is speaking in a high-pitched monotone, straining to read the tiny, nearly illegible print of his manuscript while constantly looking down, ever so slowly flipping the pages during two-hour sermons delivered with insufficient volume. Such, some might argue, was the inevitable result of religious monopoly at a time when everyone was expected in church. If this portrayal is in any real way accurate, one is compelled to wonder how it was that Edwards's congregation at Northampton was moved into seasons of revival under his ministry, even long before the far more effusive George Whitefield arrived in town. Would some seek to argue that God worked despite Edwards, rather than because of him? Even more fundamentally, what characteristics mark Edwards's preaching?

Simply put, the preaching of the Word was the single most important aspect of worship to Jonathan Edwards. This, it must be emphasized, was biblical preaching, where Edwards saw himself as setting forth the very oracles of God. Richard Bailey writes:

> Believing that revelation contained the key to understanding the mysteries of religion, Edwards saturated almost every sermon, from text to doctrine to application, with Scripture. Given his understanding of revelation as the guide to instruct humanity in its relationship to a holy God, Edwards, almost without fail, interlaced every argument with Scripture. No better way existed than to employ Scripture to

---

16. Sean Michael Lewis writes, "Surprisingly, there are not many studies of Edwards as preacher. Four worthy of mention are Yarbrough's *Delightful Conviction*, Piper's *Supremacy of God*, Turnbull's *Jonathan Edwards the Preacher*, and Miller's essay "Rhetoric of Sensation." See Lewis, "Jonathan Edwards between Church and Academy" in Hart et al., *Legacy of Jonathan Edwards*, 234. Also of help are the editor's introductions to each of the volumes in WJE that contain his sermons: vols. 10, 14, 17, 19, 22, and 25.

explicate Christianity's intricate conceptions and doctrines, because Edwards saw Scripture as the legend to the map of religion.[17]

Similarly, George Marsden adds, "Essential to understanding Edwards as an eighteenth-century Reformed Protestant is his biblicism."[18] And according to Robert Brown, this is a point at which Edwards is often misunderstood: "Other than characterizing him as a rather traditional interpreter with a peculiar penchant for typology, modern biographers of Edwards have almost universally passed over the subject and materials of his interest in the Bible. . . . This is so despite the fact that his biblical writings constitute a large portion, if not the majority, of his literary output."[19] In short, to understand Jonathan Edwards *at all*, much less understand his approach to public worship, one must begin and end with an acknowledgement that the Bible determined the whole of his agenda.

As such, attention will first be given to Edwards's manner of preaching, but in far greater detail focus will be placed on his "hermeneutics" in an effort to adequately comprehend him at this crucial point. Edwards's method of interpreting the Bible is foundational to understanding the content of what was said in public worship and what should be practiced in private—matters that are ultimately far more central than how he said these things. In the end, one cannot rightly appreciate Jonathan Edwards at worship and fail to recognize how, in many ways, the preaching of the Word *was* worship.

Edwards's Manner of Preaching

It is often unnerving to be confronted with criticism regarding one's preaching. How much more unnerving would it be to be met with objections within one's own family, much less by a grandfather of the stature of Solomon Stoddard? Bear in mind: as has been noted, Stoddard has often been referred to as the "pope" of western Massachusetts, so great was his influence while serving as pastor at Northampton for perhaps sixty years.[20] Stoddard's view of the use of notes was unequivocal—they were anathema. In his sermon

---

17. Bailey, "Driven by Passion," 67.
18. Marsden, "Quest for the Historical Edwards," 8.
19. Brown, *Jonathan Edwards and the Bible*, 2. It must be added that given the paucity of references to the Scriptures in Brown's own work and the title of his book, Brown's words appear greatly ironic.
20. Stoddard, *Safety of Appearing*, vi.

"The Defects of Preachers Reproved," Stoddard raises a key question and provides his unwavering perspective:

> The reading of sermons is a dull way of preaching. Sermons when read are not delivered with authority and in an affecting way. . . . When sermons are delivered without notes, the looks and gesture of the minister is a great means to command attention and stir up affection. Men are apt to be drowsy in hearing the Word, and the liveliness of the preacher is a means to stir up the attention of the hearers and beget suitable affection in them. Sermons that are read are not delivered with authority; they favor the sermons of the scribes (Matthew 7:29). Experience shows that sermons read are not so profitable as others.[21]

The same congregation at Northampton where Stoddard preached this very sermon was the one to which Jonathan Edwards came in 1726, and "Solomon Stoddard, the patriarch, now eighty-three, though somewhat feeble and nearly blind was still sharp of mind, strong of opinion, and a formidable presence."[22] Unfortunately, for all of Edwards's remarkable abilities, free speech was evidently never a natural gift. Even late in life, Edwards wrote, "So far as I am able to judge of what talents I have, for benefiting my fellow creatures by word, I think I can write better than I can speak."[23]

Especially early on, Edwards was apparently closely tied to his notes: "There were none of the arts of the orator. During the first part of his ministry Edwards wrote out the sermons and read them from manuscript. . . . He would lean habitually upon the pulpit with his notes in the left hand, and his right hand was used to turn the pages."[24] It is very likely, if not certain, that Stoddard was there to offer "counsel." George Marsden, whose recent biography is now considered the standard presentation of Edwards's life, writes:

> Stoddard's publications were also full of advice to clergy, which he doubtless repeated to his young protégé. He urged ministers not to preach with notes, or if they must, to not let them hinder gestures. For the meticulously thorough Edwards, most comfortable writing in the privacy of his study, this was hard advice. He was not the animated natural conversationalist his grandfather was. Although he practically memorized his sermons, not until late in his career could

---

21. Stoddard's sermon was preached on May 19, 1723, on Matt 23:2–3.
22. Marsden, *Jonathan Edwards: A Life*, 114.
23. WJE 16:729.
24. Turnbull, *Jonathan Edwards, the Preacher*, 100.

he manage to abandon writing them out in precise detail and having the security of the text in front of him.[25]

While Edwards would have taken seriously Stoddard's advice, no immediate metamorphosis occurred. Years after the death of Stoddard, however, another episode would bring the matter to light once more: "The fervour ... generated during the Great Awakening called for something more dramatic than a discourse read out as if it were a treatise."[26] In particular, the arrival of George Whitefield, the young, remarkable, extemporaneous preacher, the fulcrum of fervor during the Great Awakening, represents a significant moment. Not only was Whitefield preaching to vast crowds and celebrated by the likes of Benjamin Franklin for his profound oratorical skills, but at the invitation of Edwards, Whitefield came to Northampton, preached in Edwards's own pulpit, and stayed in his home.[27] The effects of Whitefield's preaching were felt not only in a revival that Edwards saw as lasting for years at Northampton, but also by Edwards himself. In a letter to Whitefield, Edwards wrote, "I hope salvation has come to this house since you was in it, with respect to one, if not more, of my children."[28]

Evidently, however great the impression of Whitefield, any change in Edwards's manner of preaching was at best partial. Years later, in reflecting on Edwards's preaching to the Indians at Stockbridge, "Gideon Hawley recalled that Edwards was 'a plain and practical preacher' whose delivery was 'grave and natural.'"[29] Despite this, while historical caricatures may present Edwards as a merely wooden manuscript preacher, they are likely overstated. As one author suggests, "While it might be possible that Edwards, the manuscript preacher, encouraged others to develop an extemporaneous style that was not his own, it appears unlikely. Instead, contemporary accounts from students such as Hopkins indicate that Edwards himself provided the model for their extemporaneous preaching."[30] Nevertheless, coupling this with Gideon Hawley's report and Edwards's own self-admission, it appears reasonable to conclude that extemporaneous speech was never Edwards's strong suit.

25. Marsden, *Jonathan Edwards: A Life*, 119.
26. Smith, *Jonathan Edwards: Puritan, Preacher, Philosopher*, 139.
27. Marsden, *Jonathan Edwards: A Life*, 205–8.
28. WJE 16:87.
29. Wheeler, "Friends to Your Souls," 241.
30. Ehrhard, "Preaching of Jonathan Edwards."

While Edwards's manner of preaching is historically intriguing, *why* he said what he did remains the heart of the matter. One could have every other element of worship, but without the Word preached, such worship was hollow. And as has been stressed, what Edwards said was always biblical. Wilson Kimnach is correct in discerning change and development in Edwards's preaching, but Edwards never deviated from the absolute centrality of Scripture in that preaching. This assertion by Kimnach, then, appears overstated: "especially during the second half of his ministry, Edwards did tend to downplay the statement of doctrine—the keystone of the traditional sermon—by integrating it merely as a 'proposition' or 'thing to be considered' in the course of argument, making at least a gesture of accommodation to the trend of the times."[31] One can easily review sermons preached near the end of his ministry to mark Edwards's continuing reliance on the Bible. In one of the last full sermon manuscripts we have from his pen, Edwards quotes the Bible at no fewer than two-dozen points.[32] In this light, Edwards's interpretation of Scripture reveals the essence of his preaching, and the heart of worship.

Edwards's Hermeneutic

While biblical interpretation is as old as the Bible itself, the term "hermeneutics" did not appear in prominent theological usage until 1654, when the Lutheran theologian Johann Konrad Dannhauer published his *Hermeneutica sacra sive methodus exponendarum sacrarum litterarum*.[33] Since that time, the term has come to represent an entire field of often technical theological study, exploring a wide range of concepts related to the understanding and interpretation of Scripture.[34] To speak of Jonathan Edwards's hermeneutic, then, is essentially an anachronism; at the same time, Edwards has much to say about the Bible, about how to understand it, and most particularly, what to do with that understanding—and it is in this ultimate sense where the connection to worship is most evident. While many approaches could be taken to consider his method of interpretation, one model sermon will be considered as illustrative; it will provide the kernel of his teaching on un-

---

31. Kimnach, "Edwards as Preacher," 122.
32. WJE 25:701–12.
33. This section presents the revision of my article "Jonathan Edwards's 'Hermeneutic.'"
34. Vanhoozer, ed., *Dictionary for Theological Interpretation*.

derstanding Scripture, and also serve as a framework by which to consider Edwards's approach to preaching the Scriptures and to entering into worship. That sermon is "Christian Knowledge."[35]

It bears notice that the subtitle of this sermon is "The Importance and Advantage of a Thorough Knowledge of Divine Truth." This emphasis on an individual Christian's need for a thorough knowledge of Scripture, while clearly present in this particular sermon, is by no means unique for Edwards. Rather, it is a regular point of emphasis in many of his works, and a frequent point of application in his sermons. This was an extension of Edwards's own personal habits of Bible study: "It is impossible to overstate the significance of Edwards's study of the Bible for his preaching."[36] This emphasis did not rise accidentally from the ether of the eighteenth century; there was in Edwards himself a resolute personal habit of life, a fixed disposition, a determined and deliberate study of Scripture, grinding at intellectual and spiritual work in his study—work that revolved around Scripture thirteen hours a day for years on end.[37] His celebrated "Resolutions," penned for the most part in his late teen years, reveal this drive in even his early Christian experience: "Resolved, to study the Scriptures so steadily, constantly and frequently, as that I may find, and plainly perceive myself to grow in the knowledge of the same."[38] This same orientation persists through the whole of his life and is seen even in the approach used in his last work, *Original Sin*, completed in 1757 shortly before his death. Nearly half the length of the work is comprised of its second part, "Containing Observations on Particular Parts of the Holy Scripture, Which Prove the Doctrine of Original Sin."[39] Scripture was for Edwards never extraneous, never secondary; its consideration represented nothing less than a lifelong obsession. Ola Winslow writes, "His figures of speech were almost strictly scriptural."[40] One other author observes, "In a sense Edwards was dealing with the interpretation of Scripture almost ev-

---

35. WJE 22:83–102. The sermon will be referred to as "Christian Knowledge" throughout this section.

36. Stein, *Cambridge Companion*, 188.

37. For a thought-provoking consideration of Edwards's teachings regarding "habit," see Lee, *Philosophical Theology*, 15–75.

38. WJE 16:755. Resolution 28 of 70, all of which Edwards apparently reviewed meticulously throughout the course of his life.

39. WJE 3:221–349. By even a cursory examination, it is not difficult to see how the whole of this work is an examination of this doctrine in the light of Scripture.

40. Winslow, *Jonathan Edwards, 1703–1758*, 139.

ery day of his life. All his notes in all his writings were directly or indirectly involved in this enterprise. We have never encountered a sermon which did not begin with a text of Scripture and expound and apply it throughout."[41]

In considering Edwards's hermeneutic, then, it must be stated emphatically that Edwards's view of and use of Scripture can be categorized as decidedly in line with his Reformed forebears. George Marsden summarizes this perspective well:

> Edwards, like his Reformed and Puritan predecessors was "biblicist" in the sense of rigorously attempting to follow the Reformation principle of "the Bible alone" as an authority, particularly in matters pertaining to theology and the church. Many of their beliefs and practices were determined because, according to their scholarship, such were taught in Scripture. At the same time, every biblicist interprets the Bible through a tradition of interpretation, and Edwards' biblicism was refracted through the scholarship of his Calvinistic heritage.[42]

"Christian Knowledge" is in this way representative of Edwards's usual treatment of Scripture. The sermon's construction follows the familiar Puritan pattern of Text, Doctrine, and Application a:

> I have concluded that 'Text' is the most accurate term for the first section of the sermon, since it invariably beings with the reading of a Scripture text and there is frequently *no explication* . . . if the text seems clear enough without it. When JE [Jonathan Edwards] does refer to textual explication, he usually calls it the 'Opening of the Text.' 'Doctrine' and 'Application' are JE's customary terms for the second and third major divisions of the sermon.[43]

Before moving to consider these three elements of Text, Doctrine, and Application in "Christian Knowledge," one further horizon must be considered that dramatically underscores Edwards's singular focus on Scripture. It is just as important to observe what is *missing* from his sermons (and writings) as it is to take notice of what is *present*, as evidence of what he sought to accentuate. In this respect, his preaching is in no way "modern." His most

---

41. Gerstner, *Rational Biblical Theology*, 1:180. Gerstner claimed to be the only person to have read all of Edwards's more than 1,200 extant sermons—with the obvious exception of Edwards himself!

42. Marsden, *Jonathan Edwards: A Life*, 514n4.

43. WJE 10:32.

famous sermon, "Sinners in the Hands of an Angry God," is a deceptive point of contact in this regard; it is in some ways not at all representative of his preaching.[44] It seems wise to argue, however, against various authors who have defended Edwards in his use of so-called hellfire in "Sinners" by arguing that it is somehow atypical—Edwards in fact very often pronounces warnings about hell and its reality.[45] "Sinners" contains a number of potent images that we might call "illustrations." In this respect, the number, vivacity, and frequency of these illustrations is perhaps atypical. Edwards does often use metaphorical language and analogies, but they are most typically drawn directly from Scripture rather than from other sources, and are not at all like contemporary sermon illustrations. In many of Edwards's sermons, one will be hard pressed to find illustrations of any kind whatsoever. In addition, Edwards only very rarely quotes other preachers or authors in the course of a sermon. Lastly, humor is not a notion that Edwards is at all familiar with, so far as his preaching is concerned.[46]

The overall effect of these missing elements is that Edwards retains an unwavering focus on the text, on its doctrine, and supremely, on its application. In this way, Edwards would aim to have his hearers deal with God himself—the God his hearers had come to worship—as he has revealed himself in his Word. The overall impression can be most unsettling: there is nothing to distract the listener or ease the tension. Scripture and ultimately God himself remains the preeminent concern. This reveals a settled confidence in Scripture as sufficient—as far more persuasive than mere human wisdom.

The Text of "Christian Knowledge"

After reading Heb 5:12, the text for "Christian Knowledge," Edwards sets the verse in the fuller context of Hebrews 5 and 6, and articulates the occasion for its writing. He repeats the verse itself, as well as portions of it, frequently throughout the sermon as he emphasizes its various facets: "For when for the time ye ought to be teachers, ye have need that one teach you again which be the first principles of the oracles of God; and are become such as have need of milk, and not of strong meat." In all, Edwards makes forty-three references or clear allusions to Scriptural passages in the course

---

44. WJE 22:400–435.
45. For example, see the eleven sermons in Edwards, *Wrath of Almighty God*.
46. Gerstner, *Rational Biblical Theology*, 1:481.

of the sermon, with nearly a quarter of these citations taken from the book of Hebrews itself. As such, it is fair to observe that although he is here preaching from a single verse on a particular topic (as was his custom), Edwards is careful to consider the text as a cohesive part of a larger passage; he also provides historical background as needed. In this regard, Edwards is not bound by such arbitrary conventions as chapter boundaries, but freely settles on the passage as context would dictate.

A brief digression is warranted, as it amplifies the way in which Edwards examined a biblical passage. While Edwards only very infrequently cites the Greek or Hebrew text, he was familiar with the original languages and used them appropriately: "In explication, he is never pedantic, even on those rare occasions when he introduces Hebrew or Greek words to clarify definitions; he explains carefully, but does not belabor small points."[47]

The Doctrine of "Christian Knowledge"

As he does in the majority of his sermons, Edwards summarizes concisely the doctrine or main teaching of the text, in this case the doctrine of Heb 5:12: "Every Christian should make a business of endeavoring to grow in knowledge in divinity."[48] This particular sermon, perhaps given the nature of this text, expands on doctrinal considerations more so than on application, which is perhaps less common for Edwards, who often spends the greater proportion of a sermon on application.[49] Divinity, he teaches, is

> that science or doctrine which comprehends all those truths and rules which concern the great business of religion. . . . [Divinity] is not learned, as other sciences, merely by the improvement of man's natural reason, but is taught by God himself in a certain book that he hath given for that end, full of instruction. . . . Therefore it cannot be said, that we come to the knowledge of any part of Christian divinity by the light of nature. It is only the Word of God, contained in the Old and New Testament, which teaches us Christian divinity.[50]

---

47. WJE 10:37.

48. WJE 22:86.

49. Wilson Kimnach writes, "The application (or Improvement or Use) is the largest of the three main divisions of the sermon (except in the lecture variant) and in long sermons it may be several times as long as the Text and Doctrine together." WJE 10:38.

50. WJE 22:85–86.

It is God himself who teaches men by Scripture. All Christian knowledge, then, depends on divine revelation and in this way differs from the pursuit of all other forms of knowledge. Lest we conclude that this knowledge is solely cerebral, Edwards explains, "There is nothing in divinity, no one doctrine, no promise, no rule, but what some way or other relates to the Christian and divine life, or our living to God by Christ."[51] True knowledge reverberates in obedient conformity to God's revelation: "Thus there is a difference between having a right speculative notion of the doctrines contained in the word of God, and having a due sense of them in the heart."[52]

For Edwards, the heart, most often spoken of in terms of the "affections," must respond to Scripture with a love demonstrated by faithful obedience.[53] There can be no profitable study of the Bible—we might say no profitable hermeneutical exercise and no worship—without an accompanying inward response of the heart resulting in fruit in one's life. It can be seen in this light how it is that his *Religious Affections* are thereby not indicative of a separate program, one of many topics to be considered in the theological panoply.[54] Rather, the first sentence of this work underscores a theme that rings true in so much of Edwards's preaching: "There is no question whatsoever, that is of greater importance to mankind, and that it more concerns every individual person to be well resolved in, than this, what are the distinguishing qualifications of those that are in favor with God, and entitled to his eternal rewards?"[55]

"Distinguishing qualifications," or distinguishing marks, are those patterns of life that result from a man or woman whose heart has been stirred by the divinely revealed word. There must be an aim for all Christian knowledge, for all right understanding of Scripture. Edwards urgently presses his hearers back upon a consideration of the substance of their relationship with God. He writes, "'Tis no sign that religious affections are truly holy and spiritual, or that they are not, that they come with texts of Scripture,

---

51. WJE 22:86. It is worth noting that Edwards here demonstrates a dependence on the work of Peter van Mastricht, who himself echoes the Puritan William Ames. See Pauw, *Supreme Harmony of All*, 27.

52. WJE 22:87.

53. His sermons on 1 Cor 13 bear this out often. See WJE 8:293–312.

54. WJE vol. 4.

55. WJE 4:84.

remarkably brought to the mind."[56] As such, to understand Scripture is not nearly enough; understanding without a changed heart is worse than a raw ignorance:

> And if [Satan] can bring one comfortable text to the mind, so he may a thousand; and may choose out such Scriptures as tend most to serve his purpose; and may heap up Scripture promises, tending, according to the perverse application he makes of them, wonderfully to remove the rising doubts, and to confirm the false joy of a poor deluded sinner.[57]

It is completely consistent, then, that in "Christian Knowledge" Edwards stresses, "There is no other way by which any means of grace whatsoever can be of any benefit, but by knowledge."[58] Scripture is intelligible, and more, this process of comprehension is the means by which God has ordained to uniquely communicate not only information, but his grace: "God deals with man as with a rational creature. . . . God hath given us the Bible, which is a book of instructions. But this book can be of no manner of profit to us, any otherwise than as it conveys some knowledge to the mind: it can profit us no more than if it were written in the Chinese or Tartarian language, of which we know not one word."[59] A hermeneutical program divorced from an intimate connection to the word of God borne out in Christian obedience—the Bible as a book of *instruction*—would consequently be unintelligible to Edwards.

For all who would thereby accuse Edwards of fanaticism in the revivals that would rise up only a few short years after the preaching of "Christian Knowledge," it must be observed that they fail to discern this clear connection that he consistently teases out between a rational understanding of Scripture and a warm response in the heart. This response can only properly occur when first a clear apprehension of the truths of God's word has taken place: "The faculty of reason and understanding was given for *actual* understanding and knowledge. If a man have no actual knowledge, the faculty or capacity of knowing is of no use to him."[60]

---

56. WJE 4:142.
57. WJE 4:144.
58. WJE 22:87.
59. WJE 22:88.
60. WJE 22:89.

The Application of "Christian Knowledge"

In this particular sermon, the demarcation between doctrine and application is less pronounced than is sometimes employed by Edwards; the two are here especially interwoven. Nevertheless, there is a general movement toward application near the middle of the sermon, and the specific points of application are highly instructive with regard to not only the way in which Edwards understood Scripture, but more, how he pressed for others to understand it. Once again, there is even at this point a close connection between one's knowledge of Scripture and action: "this endeavoring to make progress in such knowledge ought not to be attended to as a thing by the bye, but all Christians should make a business of it. They should look upon it as a part of their daily business, and no small part of it neither."[61] If it is only possible for one to obtain grace by the knowledge of Scripture, then it follows that all Christians should be eagerly and diligently seeking out the truths found therein:

> The doctrines of this nearly concern everyone. They are about those things which relate to every man's eternal salvation and happiness. The common people cannot say, "Let us leave these matters to ministers and divines; let them dispute them out among themselves as they can; they concern not us," for they are of infinite importance to every man.[62]

In this light, it is important to observe that in the section on application in "Christian Knowledge" the greatest preponderance of Scripture used in the sermon is brought to bear. We are to believe and act upon what Edwards is saying not based on his own authority or insight, but because what he is preaching is founded on the clear teachings of Scripture. Given this propensity, one cannot help but marvel how rarely emphasized or considered is this emphasis on Scripture in contemporary studies of Edwards. In 2002 Robert Brown wrote, "Stephen Stein's now decades-old observation concerning the new Edwards scholarship is as true today as when it was first made. It remains puzzling that 'the Bible, one of the shaping forces in the theological development of Jonathan Edwards, has largely been ignored in the assessments of this colonial divine.'"[63] Another point of view may help

---

61. Ibid.
62. WJE 22:92.
63. Brown, *Jonathan Edwards and the Bible*, 2.

resolve this "puzzling" issue. One author, in commenting on Edwards's treatise the *Great Christian Doctrine of Original Sin Defended*, characterizes the Scriptural content of Edwards's writings as the "least interesting" aspect for the "twenty-first century reader," but highlights its centrality to Edwards himself.[64] Patricia Tracy explains, "The urge to enhance Edwards's reputation as a philosopher by finding him to be essentially a modern mind trapped in an antiquated vocabulary has nevertheless distorted his thought. His brilliance has been allowed to obscure a major aspect of his historicity, and the real-life context and impact of his ideas has been neglected."[65]

To further demonstrate how this focus on Scripture dominated Edwards's preaching ministry, and how it bears directly on his understanding of Scripture and its prominence in worship, one need only consider several of his ordination sermons in which direction is given to new ministers for whom Edwards had occasion to recommend a pattern for ministry. If ever there would be a clear indication of what Edwards believed the pattern of understanding for the teaching and preaching of Scripture should be, and the minister's role in worship, it would be here. At the ordination of the Rev. Robert Abercrombie, for example, Edwards urged,

> . . . ministers should be very conversant with the Holy Scriptures; making it very much their business, with the utmost diligence and strictness, to search those holy writings: for they are as it were the beams of the light of the Sun of righteousness; they are the light by which ministers must be enlightened, and the light they are to hold forth to their hearers; and they are the fire whence their hearts and the hearts of their hearers must be enkindled.[66]

In a similar way, Edwards exhorted the Rev. Edward Billing,

> Ministers are not to make those things that seem right to their own reason a rule in their interpreting a revelation, but the revelation is to be the rule of its own interpretation; i.e., the way that they must interpret Scripture is not to compare the dictates of the Spirit of God in his revelation with what their own reason says, and then to force such an interpretation as shall be agreeable to those dictates, but they must interpret the dictates of the Spirit of God by comparing them with other dictates of Scripture.[67]

64. Gura, *Jonathan Edwards: America's Evangelical*.
65. Tracy, *Jonathan Edwards, Pastor*, 6.
66. *Works*[2] 2:959.
67. Minkema and Bailey, eds., "Reason, Revelation and Preaching," 27.

And, Edwards summarizes the doctrine, or principal teaching of 1 Corinthians 2:11–13 thus in another ordination sermon: "Ministers are not to preach those things which their own wisdom or reason suggests, but the things already dictated to them by the superior wisdom and knowledge of God."[68] Thus an evident pattern emerges: the ideas and passions of the minister were to be subjugated to Scripture—what God taught, Christian ministers must preach and teach.

The conclusion of "Christian Knowledge" is consistent with this stream of thought, and is a tremendously succinct distillation of Edwards's emphasis on the need for all believers to assimilate and embrace Scriptural truth. In many ways, it could be considered emblematic of his larger "hermeneutical" program:

1. Be assiduous in reading the holy Scriptures.
2. Content not yourselves with only a cursory reading, without regarding the sense.
3. Procure, and diligently use other books which may help you to grow in this knowledge.
4. Improve conversation with others to this end.
5. Seek not to grow in knowledge chiefly for the sake of applause, and to enable you to dispute with others; but seek it for the benefit of your souls, and in order to practice.
6. Seek to God, that he would direct you, and bless you, in this pursuit after knowledge.
7. Practice according to what knowledge you have.[69]

This list must be something of an embarrassment for those who would construct an image of Edwards as one consumed with purely philosophical notions, or as a great mind regrettably ensconced in an eighteenth-century ideological prison. Perry Miller, representative of many who would strip Edwards of such arcane notions as those expressed in "Christian Knowledge," wrote in commenting on Edwards's *History of Redemption*,

> I agree that if one stops with the surface narrative, *A History of the Work of Redemption* sounds like a story book for fundamentalists,

---

68. Edwards, *Salvation of Souls*, 116.

69. WJE 22:101–2. These seven points are quoted verbatim, but it should be noted that there is further explanatory material in the sermon that has been excluded for the sake of clarity and brevity.

and is hardly to be mentioned with Gibbon, Marx, Spengler, or Toynbee. Measured against modern scholarship, textual criticism, archaeology, and comparative religions, it is an absurd book, where it is not pathetic.[70]

Arguably, Miller should have stopped with the surface narrative. He is at once the progenitor, the real catalyst for the revival in scholarship on Edwards, while at the same time the spokesman for all who would cast him in a more acceptable mold. As a result, *this* Edwards—the Edwards who accepted a straightforward, careful reading of Scripture, informed by appropriate scholarship—is unacceptable. How much more troubling it must be to see his unfashionable but consistent emphasis on how one's "assiduous" study of Scripture is to be intertwined with a spiritual vitality marked by devotion, obedience, prayer, and service. Nevertheless, this is indisputably the true Edwardsean hermeneutical program, which contemporary scholarship has studiously avoided while writing countless books about him. Robert Brown writes, "In spite of 'the quantity of his writings on the Bible, there is an amazing paucity of serious scholarship dealing with it. The contemporary renaissance of interest in Edwards has hardly touched this dimension of his work.'"[71] In another context, Kevin Vanhoozer offers this important perspective, which seems immediately relevant to the manner in which Edwards's works have been studied:

> Ironically enough, many literary critics never raise what I call a "properly interpretive question"; in their haste to analyze and explain the text, they forget to seek understanding of what the text is about. What else can we make of a critic who discusses the way in which a novel reflects the social-historical conditions of its production, the unconscious psychoses of its producer, or the patriarchal ideology of the era, but never that to which the author is primarily attending?[72]

Crosscurrents in "Christian Knowledge"

While numerous other larger themes could be examined relating to Edwards's handling of Scripture, two are most noteworthy, and both are once again observable in "Christian Knowledge." The first of these, which might be more

---

70. Miller, *Jonathan Edwards*, 310.
71. Brown, *Jonathan Edwards and the Bible*, 2.
72. Vanhoozer, *Is There a Meaning?*, 284. See also Steinmetz, "Superiority of Pre-Critical Exegesis," 27–38.

formally labeled his christological emphasis, is perhaps better expressed more simply as a regular focus on recognizing and proclaiming Jesus Christ in and through the text. This focus is regarded as a crosscurrent because it is present in all three major sections of the sermon. Without the larger context of the sermon in view, one could wrongly conclude that these most potent statements Edwards makes are the expression of a program disconnected from the sermon's text. In actual practice, however, these christological statements are very often the culmination of a key point of argumentation, and are often rhapsodic:

> A man cannot see the wonderful excellency and love of Christ in doing such and such things for sinners, unless his understanding be first informed how those things were done. He cannot have a taste of the sweetness and divine excellency of such and such things contained in divinity, unless he first have a notion that there are such and such things.[73]

Further on, he comments that "All Christians are put into the school of Christ, where their business is to learn, or receive knowledge from Christ, their common master and teacher."[74] And, in a statement that is a concise expression of this christological concern, he adds:

> Divinity is commonly defined, *the doctrine of living to God*; and by some who seem to be more accurate, *the doctrine of living to God by Christ*. It comprehends all Christian doctrines as they are in Jesus, and all Christian rules directing us in living to God by Christ. There is nothing in divinity, no one doctrine, no promise, no rule, but what some way or other relates to the Christian and divine life, or our living to God by Christ.[75]

The second crosscurrent worth noting is redemption, both personal and corporate. This fits closely with his concern for spiritual awakening. Redemption is a theme that Edwards returns to with remarkable consistency across the course of his sermons and in many of his larger writings. Edwards's sermon series that has come to be known as *A History of the Work of Redemption* is one obvious and substantial example of this. In the editorial comments introducing the volume, John Wilson remarks, "The application

---

73. WJE 22:88–89.
74. WJ, 22:96.
75. WJE 22:86; emphasis original.

of redemption provided the focus for much of Edwards' mature career."[76] It could be that self-examination, a point of application that Edwards presses as commonly as any other motif in his preaching, might be seen as a fundamental aspect of this concern. Edwards feels the weight of the responsibility of his office keenly; those who are a part of the congregation under his charge must consistently hear from him in the preaching of Scripture an inescapable and clear call to repentance and salvation, and thereby consider their spiritual condition.

Edwards shares with many of the Puritans an unusual fascination with being certain of one's salvation—one might call it an obsession—for there is nothing more important to get right than this. As a result, even when Edwards does not use the word "redemption," this impulse is never far from the surface: "Christians ought not to content themselves with such degrees of knowledge of divinity as they have already obtained. It should not satisfy them, as they know as much as is absolutely necessary to salvation, but should seek to make progress."[77] Christian divinity—and the discipline of studying and interpreting Scripture—has a very practical aim, namely progress toward heaven:

> God himself, the eternal Three in One, is the chief object of this science; in the next place Jesus Christ, as God-man and Mediator, and the glorious work of redemption, the most glorious work that ever was wrought; then the great things of the heavenly world, the glorious and eternal inheritance purchased by Christ, and promised in the gospel; the work of the Holy Spirit of God on the hearts of men; our duty to God, and the way in which we ourselves may become like angels, and like God himself in our measure: all these are objects of this science.[78]

Redemption is thus the very business of God himself: "His works at the same time are wonderful, and cannot be found out to perfection; especially the work of redemption, which is that work of God about which the science of divinity is chiefly conversant, is full of unsearchable wonders."[79]

---

76. WJE 9:30.
77. WJE 22:89.
78. WJE 22:91.
79. WJE 22:95.

Edwards and the Bible

Edwards's approach to interpretation was by no means simplistic. He would have, for example, acknowledged more than one sense in certain biblical passages.[80] Douglas Sweeney draws out some of the textured backdrop for Edwards's views of Scripture: "In response to the early rise of the higher criticism of the Bible, he defends its inspiration, the historicity of its contents, and traditional views of the provenance of its books. He affirms the veracity of the Bible's own account of the miraculous."[81]

It is clearly difficult, if not impossible, to draw conclusions about Jonathan Edwards's handling of the Bible and how one should interpret it based on one sermon, but as can be seen, "Christian Knowledge" has not been chosen at random. Rather, this sermon represents a clear statement of Edwards's view of Scripture in the context of how that knowledge was to be put to use. Robert Brown's *Jonathan Edwards and the Bible* provides one key contribution to understanding how Edwards regarded Scripture: he was indisputably well aware of critical schools of thought, and often responded to them directly.[82] As a result, while Edwards clearly settled on a typically Reformed methodology by which Scripture was to be used and understood, those who would consider Edwards as nothing more than a paradigmatic Puritan cut from an antiquated bolt of cloth must now see how it is that Edwards deftly interacted with the rising critical trends emergent in his day, while nevertheless remaining in line with Reformed hermeneutical approaches.

One historical observation may bring this into clearer focus. It might well be said that a man or woman may best be known by observing who they are when no one is looking. In the case of Edwards, there is an obvious period in which this was most abundantly the situation: his period of ministry at Stockbridge, which included a mission to the Mahican Indians. George Marsden explains, "The Stockbridge experiment centered around a couple of hundred Mahican Indians (also known as Mohican, Muhhakaneok, Stockbridge, Housatonic, or Housatunnuck), the largest part of the remnant of the once-great Mahican confederacy, now struggling for survival

---

80. WJE 20:80–81.
81. WJE 23:29.
82. Brown, *Jonathan Edwards and the Bible*. While Brown's book is ostensibly misnamed, it nevertheless does capably articulate the substantial engagement Edwards exercised with then contemporary critical thinkers such as John Locke and Matthew Tindal.

and willing to be under English protection."[83] While many have observed that, freed from the many responsibilities of pastoring a large congregation, Edwards was able to devote himself to writing four of his major works, less frequently considered is the remarkable nature of his missionary ministry. While Edwards wrote often with an eye toward eventual publication, surely he would never have expected his sermons from this period to see the light of day in print. In point of fact, many of these sermons have only recently been published, more than 250 years after they were first preached.[84]

Notably, then, the same observations that have been made with regard to Edwards's treatment of Scripture in "Christian Knowledge" could be made with little fundamental modification concerning a sermon on a similar subject from this latter period at Stockbridge, a sermon on Luke 11:27–28 that Edwards preached in 1751, roughly twelve years after the preaching of "Christian Knowledge."[85] Once again, the characteristic threefold pattern of Text, Doctrine, and Application is observable. The doctrine drawn from Luke 11 is also the sermon's title: "That Hearing and Keeping the Word of God Renders a Person More Blessed Than Any Other Privilege That Ever God Bestowed on Any of the Children of Men." As noted previously in "Christian Knowledge," we see no illustrations per se in this Stockbridge sermon, no external references or humor, but there is clearly a christological focus, a concern for personal redemption, and a frequent use of Scripture in his argumentation.

It is not simply that Edwards's handling of Scripture in this latter sermon is consistent with that in "Christian Knowledge," although it is, decidedly so. More to the point, Edwards clearly draws from this passage in Luke a wide range of points regarding the majesty of Scripture: "It is a greater blessedness to hear and keep the word of God than to be an apostle or to be endued with any of the miraculous gifts of the Holy Ghost, than to be able to heal the sick, or to speak with tongues, or to remove mountains."[86] One can hear in Edwards's admonitions the fruit of a life not only of study but of personal devotion. His legendary expeditions on horseback to meet with God in the context of his creation are evident in his words: "The hearing and keeping

---

83. Marsden, *Jonathan Edwards: A Life*, 375.

84. The two volumes edited by Michael D. McMullen, BL and *Glory and Honor*, are notable in this regard. See also WJE vol. 25.

85. Edwards, *Glory and Honor*, 190–207.

86. Ibid., 196.

the word of God brings the happiness of a spiritual union and communion with God."[87] His application is by no means solely cerebral:

> Hence we see how precious we ought to esteem the word of God. How precious must that be the receiving and keeping of which renders a person blessed above any other privilege that ever God bestowed on any of the children of men. Doubtless this is an inestimable treasure. Hence we see of how great worth is the written Word, how ought we to prize the Holy Scriptures and how should we value the Word preached. How should we prize therefore the advantage and price that we have in our hands, that precious tablet which Christ has committed to us, in that we do enjoy both the written and preached Word of God.[88]

While numerous similar examples could be brought to bear that would substantiate Edwards's conservative and pietistic treatment of Scripture, one would be hard pressed to find counterexamples. What, then, of Edwards's hermeneutic? And what bearing does this have on his view of worship? It may well be that his view of Scripture and the preaching of the Word might best be understood in light of not only his direct statements about the Bible and its interpretation, but by means of one of his most famous statements regarding God himself. In a sermon entitled "The True Christian's Life a Journey Towards Heaven," based on Hebrews 11:13–14, Edwards sought to draw out for his congregation the meaning of this text, which reads: "And confessed that they were strangers and pilgrims on the earth. For they that say such things, declare plainly that they seek a country." Among other points, Edwards sets forth this instruction, which powerfully illustrates how Edwards's interpretation of a given passage was intended to stir up response in the hearers:

> In heaven alone is attainment of our highest good. God is the highest good of the reasonable creature. The enjoyment of him is our proper happiness, and is the only happiness with which our souls can be satisfied. To go to heaven, fully to enjoy God, is infinitely better than the most pleasant accommodations here: better than fathers and mothers, husbands, wives, or children, or the company of any or all earthly friends. These are but shadows; but God is the substance. These are but scattered beams; but God is the sun. These are but streams; but God is the fountain. These are but drops; but

---

87. Ibid., 202. For Edwards's expeditions on horseback, see *Works* 2 1:xxxviii.
88. Edwards, *Glory and Honor*, 206.

God is the ocean. Therefore it becomes us to spend this life only as a journey towards heaven, as it becomes us to make the seeking of our highest end and proper good, the whole work of our lives; to which we should subordinate all other concerns of life.[89]

Summary Considerations: Edwards's Hermeneutic

Jonathan Edwards's hermeneutic is by no means a dry, wooden, and lifeless regurgitation of the teachings of Scripture. In Edwards's drawing out of the truth of Scripture, we see how a vital, soul-satisfying understanding may rise to view. What makes a contemporary hermeneutical program more satisfying? As we have seen, Edwards believed that actual knowledge was possible, that a deep understanding was required by all believers, that Scripture was to serve as a rule of its own interpretation, but more, that the very moving of God himself was possible and resulted in the transformation of believers. Arguably missing from much of the hermeneutical dialogue—remarkably—is this spiritual dimension.[90] In Edwards's conception, God aided believers in their understanding of Scripture, an understanding that was not only possible, not only real, but satisfying and effectual.

Given the level of ire the likes of Matthew Tindal inspired in Edwards, one wonders what invective Edwards might levy against the likes of Jacques Derrida or Hans Georg Gadamer, not to mention a practitioner such as Bill Hybels.[91] Kevin Vanhoozer is right to underscore how one's worldview, and even one's Christology, greatly shapes and perhaps dictates one's interpretative method.[92] Edwards was no stranger to controversy in responding to contending worldviews in his day; in facing up against the rising threat of Arminianism, a threat he viewed as foundational, he did not apologize for his Calvinistic interpretation. On the contrary, as was customarily the case, he based his pattern for argumentation on Scripture:

> Indeed, it is a glorious argument of the divinity of the holy Scriptures, that they teach such doctrines, which in one age and another,

---

89. WJE 17:437–38.

90. Some examples of this include the significant works by Hirsch, *Validity in Interpretation*; Frei, *Eclipse of Biblical Narrative*; Wittgenstein, *Philosophical Investigations*; and Ricoeur, *Hermeneutics and the Human Sciences*.

91. Consider Gadamer, *Truth and Method*; or Jacques Derrida, *Problem of Genesis*. See also Pritchard, *Willow Creek Seeker Services*, for a perspective on Hybels.

92. Vanhoozer, *Is There a Meaning?*

through the blindness of men's minds, and strong prejudices in their hearts, are rejected, as most absurd and unreasonable, by the wise and great men of the world; which yet, when they are most carefully and strictly examined, appear to be exactly agreeable to the most demonstrable, certain, and natural dictates of reason.[93]

Edwards's own habit of Scriptural study remains instructional to our generation, one too often wearied by skepticism and doubt. He writes, "I seemed often to see so much light exhibited by every sentence, and such a refreshing food communicated, that I could not get along in reading; often dwelling on one sentence to see the wonders contained in it, and yet almost every sentence seemed to be full of wonders."[94]

What Mattered Most in Preaching?

Edwards's manner of preaching might hold a certain fascination, for a number of reasons. He was a towering intellect, but lacked social graces and displayed unique personal habits. How would that odd combination have translated in the pulpit? And, while there are snippets from early biographers that provide insights into how he conducted himself while preaching, we know this one thing beyond all doubt: he was no Whitefield.[95]

But the same could be said for Whitefield—he was no Edwards.[96] Despite the value of their content, for all of his incomparable oratory skill, Whitefield's sermons will likely not be read and studied for long years like those of Edwards.[97] While many other matters could have easily been considered in this section, ultimately only two points have been made: for Edwards, preaching was the key dimension of public worship, and the key feature of that preaching was Edwards's unwavering focus on interpreting Scripture. This is in line with the rest of the Puritans: "This emphasis on the word (broadly defined to include the Bible but much besides) provides the context for understanding why the Puritans made the reading and exposition of Scripture the primary event in the worship service."[98] The portraits

---

93. WJE 1:439.

94. *Works*² 1:xiv.

95. The primary early biographical insights about Edwards are generally obtained from Dwight, *Life of President Edwards*; and Hopkins, *Life and Character*.

96. Chamberlain, "Grand Sower of the Seed," 368–85.

97. Whitefield, *Sermons*.

98. Ryken, *Worldly Saints*, 124–25.

of Edwards, and the caricatures of his preaching, have their place. But if the intent is to understand what public worship was for Edwards, here is the substance: God has revealed himself by his Word, and his ordained servant must preach. Edwards wrote, "if it was plain to all the world of Christians that I was under the infallible guidance of Christ, then I should have power in all the world: I should have power to teach them what they ought to do, and they would be obliged to hear me; I should have power to teach them who were Christians and who not, and in this likewise they would be obliged to hear me."[99]

The Lord's Supper and Baptism

When approaching the sacraments in connection with Jonathan Edwards, it is easy to immediately become engulfed in the communion controversy that led to his eventual expulsion from the Northampton pulpit.[100] As important as this episode is, it is primarily instructive for the work at hand—understanding the place of communion and baptism in worship for Jonathan Edwards—in the sense that so far as communion is concerned, Edwards's beliefs evidently evolved. As a young and inexperienced man called to succeed the titanic Solomon Stoddard, it is easy to understand how Edwards might be submissive to and likely instructed by his grandfather with respect to his views on the proper subjects of communion, which Stoddard conceived of as a "converting ordinance."

Stoddard was larger than life; less a man and more a figurehead or an icon than flesh and blood, so great was his influence in New England near the end of his pastorate at Northampton. Timothy Edwards, Jonathan's father and pastor of a congregation elsewhere in New England, had remained in firm opposition to Stoddard with respect to his understanding of the fit subjects of communion, and believed that only those who had given clear

---

99. WJE 13:222. This is taken from miscellany 40.

100. For a brief summary of Edwards's own take on the communion controversy, consider his letter to the Rev. Peter Clark, written from Northampton on May 7, 1750. See WJE 16:342–47, as well as other correspondence during this period. For the argument against Solomon Stoddard from Edwards's own pen, consider WJE 12:165. Much other material in this volume is devoted to the controversy. See WJE 25:349–440. Useful secondary sources on this topic include Jamieson, "Jonathan Edwards's Change of Position," 79–99; Jamieson, "Jonathan Edwards and the Renewal"; and Stuart, "Mr. Stoddard's Way," 243–53. Finally, Douglas Sweeney offers helpful perspective to this discussion in "Church," 167–68.

evidence of their conversion should be admitted. Timothy Edwards was apparently tremendously rigid about his views, and was at times unyielding in his stance. Claghorn comments that "A couple who had married without their parents' permission wished to baptise [*sic*] their children, but Timothy refused. The argument divided the church, causing Timothy to suspend communion from 1739 to 1741."[101] After the death of Stoddard, and with the passing of time, Edwards's views apparently changed to conform more closely to that of his father's, although he was never in lock step with his father's strict approach to admission. Whatever the timetable, Edwards's views did change, and while initially he held his own ideas privately for a season, a shift took place. In time, his views fundamentally differed from Stoddard's, and also became public. This would have brought him at odds with the majority of his own congregation, dandled as they had been on Stoddard's knee, and the rest is history. With respect to the matter at hand, then, what place did communion and baptism play in the worship of Jonathan Edwards? How were the sacraments conducted? Most importantly, what did they signify? What insights can we glean from his sermons on these matters?

The Lord's Supper

It is a helpful starting point to observe that while the manner of the administration of the sacraments would have been for Edwards important, in the final analysis it was only a secondary consideration.[102] Edwards was never "playful." The solemn occasion of the Lord's Supper, then, brought out in Edwards an even greater soberness and intensity. Far more central than external considerations was the matter of the affections, and a thorough, serious approach to the observance of the Lord's Supper was an urgent requirement:

> How many of you have attended that sacred ordinance of the Lord's Supper, without any manner of serious preparation, and in a careless

---

101. WJE 16:85.

102. Valeri writes that Edwards "addresses the right administration of the sacraments, qualifications for communion, and the prerogatives of the church to excommunicate wayward members. 'Miscellanies' nos. 462, 464, 466 and 485 ... deal with some aspects of these sacramental or disciplinary issues, as do entries [written later], such as nos. 610 and 612." WJE 17:263. The miscellanies referred to appear in WJE vols. 13 and 18. Useful background on the Puritan backdrop for this issue can be found in Kistler, ed., *Puritans on the Lord's Supper*.

> slighty [slight] frame of spirit, and chiefly to comply with custom! Have you not ventured to put the sacred symbols of the body and blood of Christ into your mouth, while at the same time you lived in ways of known sins and intended no other than still to go on in the same wicked practices? And it may be have set at the Lord's table, with rancor in your heart against some of your brethren, that you have sat with there. You have come even to that holy feast of love among God's children, with the leaven of malice and envy in your heart; and so have eat and drank judgment to yourself.[103]

As has been seen, this is very much in line with Edwards's approach to all aspects of public and private devotion: "Nothing is more provoking to God than the hypocritical performance of the parts of divine worship."[104] Very likely, the most important text in the New Testament on the observation of the Lord's Supper is 1 Corinthians 11, and Edwards preached on verses 28 and 29 of this passage on March 21 of 1731 in a sermon entitled "Self-Examination and the Lord's Supper."[105] This sermon is illustrative in two key respects: first, it is instructive with respect to Edwards's attitude and understanding of the Lord's Supper, but also, it underscores the connection between a proper observance of the Lord's Supper and the practice of self-examination, which will be explored more fully later. Edwards's doctrinal summary on this occasion rises directly from the text: "Persons ought to examine themselves of their fitness before they presume to partake of the Lord's Supper, lest by their unworthy partaking, they eat and drink damnation to themselves."[106]

The Lord's Supper is a tangible sign of our connection with God, according to Edwards, and a signification of a spiritual reality that has taken place in the converted. So, "As we are unworthy of these gospel blessings themselves, so we are unworthy of the means, the signs, and the offers of them. As we are unworthy of real communion with God, so we are unworthy of such a visible signification of it."[107] There are consequently a number of ways in which one might approach the Lord's Table in an unworthy manner, and great caution is thereby warranted. Edwards embarks on an in-depth presentation of many

---

103. WJE 19:351.
104. BL 202.
105. WJE 17:262–72.
106. WJE 17:266.
107. Ibid.

of the ways in which believers might examine themselves—the character of their lives, their actual obedience, their intentions, and in numerous other ways—in an effort to ensure that their partaking in the Lord's Supper is done in a manner pleasing to God. "Those that worthily partake," he urges, "they eat and drink eternal life; that is, the eating and drinking will be profitable to their souls and tend to their salvation, and the promise of eternal life is sealed to them."[108]

By contrast, those who fail to examine themselves adequately, "those that eat and drink unworthily, eat and drink their own damnation; that is, by their eating and drinking, they do greatly expose themselves to damnation and seal their own damnation."[109] While some have stayed away from the communion table owing to an overly scrupulous conscience, a larger proportion has been remiss in adequately preparing for it. One can easily picture Edwards reading from 1 Corinthians 11 and employing something similar to this sermon's closing admonition, as a conventional means by which he might have "fenced the table":

> [The] *Use* of this doctrine [is] to warn all persons carefully to examine themselves before they come to the Lord's Supper, that they don't seal their own damnation. If you would [not], as it were, consign yourself over to Satan, be careful {to examine yourself before you come to the Lord's Supper}. And if there be any that belong to this church that have hitherto neglected this duty of self-examination before they come, let them no more neglect it. And if there be any that have not taken up a resolution, any that live in any {wickedness}, let them by no means approach till they have. If upon self-examination, you find yourself unfit in these respects, it won't excuse you from coming. . . . If there be any now about to approach that are in any of these mentioned ways {of wickedness}, I forewarn them in the name of Jesus Christ not to presume to touch till they have taken up a resolution. If you live in any known way of wickedness, don't come here to eat and drink damnation to yourselves.[110]

While it is mildly speculative to consider such a statement as representative, it appears evident that the Lord's Supper was perhaps the most solemn time in Edwardsean church life, with the possible exception of the funeral service.

---

108. WJE 17:270.
109. Ibid.
110. WJE 17:272; emphasis original.

A further point of emphasis bears mention in connection with the practice of the Lord's Supper, and is illustrated well by means of the communion sermon from an earlier period, entitled "The Spiritual Blessings of the Gospel Represented by a Feast."[111] This sermon was preached at some point between August of 1728 and February of 1729, and stands in stark contrast to another sermon from this same timeframe, entitled "The Torments of Hell are Exceeding Great." It appears as if by means of these two sermons Edwards sought to sharpen the contrast between the blessings enjoyed by the converted and the torments endured by the unregenerate, as a means by which to urge their conversion. Here, Edwards focuses his hearers' attention on the manifold blessings of God that are available, as depicted by the Lord's Supper—they represent a spiritual feast: "In this feast, God is the host; 'tis he that makes the provision and invites the guests. And sinners are the invited guests. Believers are those that accept the invitation. And Jesus Christ, with his benefits that he purchased by his obedience and death, and which he communicates by his Spirit, is the entertainment."[112]

God's provisions are in this way lavish, nourishing, excellent, free and abundant, various, and an "inexhaustible fountain of blessings." In this connection, Edwards conveys his understanding of communion: "The word 'communion,' as it is used in Scripture, signifies a common partaking of some good. Thus we read of the communion of the body of Christ and the communion of the blood of Christ, that is, the common partaking of his body and blood."[113]

In this sermon's points of application, Edwards seeks to encourage his hearers to appropriate for themselves the blessings of God signified by the elements of the Lord's Table. "Natural men," the unconverted, are portrayed as "more loathsome than a beggar clothed with rags and full of sores."[114] Despite their poverty, Christ offers "white raiment," and the opportunity to "sit down with him in his feasting and banqueting house."[115] Christ's invitation, while sincere, will not be extended indefinitely, and one's acceptance or rejection of it will result in eternal consequences—for the believer,

---

111. WJE 14:278–96. The latter sermon appears on pages 297–328 of this same volume.
112. WJE 14:281–82.
113. WJE 14:286–87.
114. WJE 14:290.
115. Ibid.

"an eternal feast." Believers, who avail themselves of the signification of communion now, in the bread and wine, will necessarily need to conform themselves to Christ's "spirit and temper" now, and more, will necessarily "bear the cross" as well.

Several years later, Edwards sets before his people the same metaphor as they once again gather to take the Lord's Supper: it is a feast "joyful to us above all things in the world."[116] Clearly, the point Edwards is driving at is not that in the taking of the elements themselves there is joy, but in Christ himself. And what raptures can be found in such an intimate connection with him: "if Christ be among us, we shall [have] reason to sit together and feed at his table with joyful hearts and cheerfully to sing his praises together and may go from the table with a sweet and joyful remembrance of the opportunity and great blessing we have had, and every time we reflect upon it to think of its sweetness."[117]

Finally, with the scars from the communion controversy still fresh in 1751, Edwards preached his last extant sermon on the subject of the Lord's Supper, entitled "Sacramental Union in Christ."[118] The sermon was preached on his winter visit to Stockbridge in 1751, and was based on 1 Corinthians 10:17: "For we being many are one body, and one bread; for we are all partakers of that one bread."

He speaks of three kinds of union—relative, legal, and vital—a union with Christ and with the church that must result in "a sweet harmony among all the members as to temper and as to conversation."[119] So also, communion is seen as a representation and seal, a "representation [of the] union of Christ and his people [in a] union of hearts," and a seal "on Christ's part" and "his people's part" solemnly confirming their union.[120] In Edwards's concluding words, one can hear how he would have administered the sacrament:

---

116. Edwards, *Glory and Honor*, 172. This quote is taken from a sermon preached between April and December of 1737 entitled, "When a Company or Society of Christians Have Christ Present with Them. 'Tis the Greatest Cause of Joy to Them." The text for this sermon was Matthew 9:15, "Can the children of the bride-chamber mourn as long as the bridegroom is with them?"

117. Ibid.

118. WJE 25:582–89.

119. WJE 25:586.

120. WJE 25:586–87.

Let the approaching feast be indeed to us a feast of love. To this end, let us examine ourselves [and] our walk. Let us cast away everything contrary to this holy union of heart. Let us examine our hearts, and suppress every principle contrary [to our unity]; and cry to God to mortify [our sins] and to enflame our hearts more and more, so this ordinance will be a resemblance of the glorious and eternal feast. And our sacraments thus attended will be sure tokens that we shall hereafter drink new wine with Christ in his heavenly Father's kingdom.[121]

Baptism

So far as the external aspects of baptism are concerned, it is fair to categorize Edwards as essentially Presbyterian in his outlook. His early ministry as a supply pastor was to a Presbyterian congregation. Late in life, he was still quoting from the Westminster Confession of Faith.[122] And, to the Rev. John Erskine, he wrote:

> As to my subscribing to the substance of the Westminster Confession, there would be no difficulty; and as to the Presbyterian government, I have long been perfectly out of conceit with our unsettled, independent, confused way of church government in this land. And the Presbyterian way has ever appeared to me most agreeable to the Word of God, and the reason and nature of things.[123]

As such, infant baptism would have been the norm for Edwards, and would have taken place as a part of the afternoon services on Sacrament days.

Once again, however, to consider sprinkling or pouring as the essence of baptism would have grossly missed the heart of baptism in Edwards's view. Baptism was a mark that was inward, real, and lasting. He spoke of it in his resolutions in a manner that was consistent with his handling of the subject throughout the course of his ministry: "Resolved, frequently to renew the dedication of myself to God, which was made at my baptism; which I solemnly renewed, when I was received into the communion of the church;

---

121. WJE 25:589.

122. See for example, Edwards's sermon on Proverbs 28:13, preached in 1752, where he refers to the Westminster Shorter Catechism. BL 134.

123. WJE 16:355. An extended argument for infant baptism also appears in the *Humble Inquiry*. See WJE 11:314.

and which I have solemnly re-made this 12th day of January, 1722–23."[124] Dedication to God was what was typified by the event.

One sermon in particular helps to bring this matter out most fully. In "Born Again" Edwards preached holistically about the change that takes place in regeneration.[125] He states plainly that "baptism [is] useless without the thing signified."[126] He then describes the various aspects of what it is that "the thing signified" should include—indeed, baptism is an almost incidental detail in this account. What matters above all is that the change to the soul of person be initiated by God, that a new nature be implanted, and that the change made infuse the whole of the person, the whole of life. This is the essence of what baptism is intended to signify. Furthermore, in the same way that one can be hypocritical in the manner by which one partakes in the Lord's Supper, so also one can be a hypocrite with respect to baptism: "If they are baptized and go to meeting and seem to show respect to Christ, yet God looks at the heart. He sees that and he sees that their hearts despise Christ, and therefore God doesn't look upon them as belonging to Christ."[127]

In sum, though, the theme of baptism rises to barely a whisper in the corpus of Edwards's sermons. To garner insight into the nuanced thoughts Edwards held on the various aspects of baptism, one needs to delve deeply into his miscellanies.[128] To do so, however, one might well miss the proverbial forest for the trees. Consider one of Edwards's most important treatises, *Original Sin*.[129] The text itself spans over 300 pages in the Yale edition. It is fair to say that Edwards covers the subject of original sin with extraordinary nuance and detail. One might naturally expect that in a work of this breadth—on a topic that could naturally lead into a detailed discussion of

---

124. WJE 16:756. This is resolution 42, and is expanded upon in his diary entry dated January 12th of this same year, which is found on page 762 in the same volume.

125. See WJE 14:186–95.

126. WJE 14:186.

127. BL 244.

128. Miscellanies 577, 595, 694, 816, and 911 are examples. See Gerstner, *Rational Biblical Theology* 3:428–47. In this section, Gerstner also cites a number of unpublished sermons that would bear consideration in a more detailed review. While Gerstner's work is uneven, his command of the Edwards corpus is impressive. The miscellanies cited are found in WJE vols. 18 and 20. See also Edwards's "Blank Bible," where, in commenting on Romans 6, he contends with the mode of baptism practiced by the "Anabaptists." WJE 24:1001.

129. WJE vol. 3.

baptism—at a minimum there would be some interaction with the issue, yet one will be hard pressed to find the subject broached at all.

This is not to say that baptism was not important to Edwards; clearly it was. But even baptism, even though instituted as it was by God himself in Edwards's view, it was peripheral to knowing God himself. George Marsden cites one of the journals of George Whitefield, and his insights serve to round out the outlook that would likely be true of Edwards:

> "The little infants who were brought to baptism, were wrapped up in such fine things, and so much pains taken to dress them, that one would think they were brought thither to be initiated into, rather than to renounce, the pomps and vanities of this wicked world." Whitefield likely made the same remark to the Edwardses, who would have appreciated such sanctified irony.[130]

In this way, both the Lord's Supper and baptism are emblematic of all of the other aspects of worship for Edwards; while they are to be conducted "decently and in order" (1 Cor 14:40), they are not in themselves the end by which one might know God, but the means.

Public Prayer

Scant information exists with respect to public prayer as offered in the worship services conducted by Jonathan Edwards. There is no evidence that any of Edwards's public prayers were captured in any form.[131] Congregants were to arrive at worship having prepared their hearts both the night before and early that same morning with fervent prayer.[132] We do know that prayer bills, or prayer requests, were written down and interceded for in the prayers that took place during worship. One specific example of this is cited by Michael McMullen, as he makes reference to a remark found on Edwards's sermon entitled "Christ Was Worthy of His Exaltation upon the Account of His Being Slain." McMullen comments, "On page 18 of the manuscript there is this written intimation, 'Lyman and his wife pray for their Negro that is dangerously sick. They ask that God would . . . .' The rest of the brief note is

---

130. Marsden, *Jonathan Edwards: A Life*, 207.

131. Charles Hambricke-Stowe writes, "Remnants of public prayer are, of course, exceedingly rare because prayers were delivered orally, without notes." Hambricke-Stowe, *Practice of Piety*, 106.

132. See for example the guidance offered by Bailey, *Practice of Piety*, 193.

uncertain."¹³³ Separately, Edwards commented in his account of the Great Awakening that "it was the most remarkable time of health, that ever I knew since I have been in the town. We ordinarily have several bills put up every Sabbath, for persons that are sick; but now we have not had so much as one for many Sabbaths together."¹³⁴ And it seems reasonable to assume that for Edwards, as was the case for most Puritans, the length of the main prayer was very typically about as long as the sermon.¹³⁵ In addition to this main prayer, an introductory prayer and prayer offered during the Lord's Supper and baptism would have been common features in corporate worship.

In a telling observation, Samuel Hopkins suggests that there was a key difference between Edwards's sermons and his pastoral prayers:

> His prayers were indeed *extempore*. He was the farthest from any appearance of a Form, as to his Words & manner of Expression, of almost any Man. He was quite singular and inimitable in this. . . . He appeared to have much of the Grace and Spirit of Prayer; to pray with the Spirit and with the Understanding: and he perform'd this part of Duty much to the acceptance and edification of those who joined with him.¹³⁶

While Edwards preached periodically on the topic of prayer, one sermon appears particularly representative of his views on how to approach God in prayer, namely, "Hypocrites Deficient in the Duty of Prayer."¹³⁷ While this sermon is focused primarily on what Edwards refers to as the duty of "secret" prayer, he draws out clearly the connection between this duty and prayer as a part of family and public worship. In essence, if one is neglectful of the

---

133. Edwards, *Glory and Honor*, 345.

134. WJE 4:205.

135. Hambricke Stowe, *Practice of Piety*, 104.

136. The citation as it appears in Kimnach's editorial comments in WJE 25:6n5.

137. Other important sermons on prayer include "The Terms of Prayer," in WJE 19: 771–91; "Praying for the Spirit," in WJE 22:213–23; "Importunate Prayer for Millennial Glory," in WJE 22:368–77; "The Suitableness of Union in Extraordinary Prayer for the Advancement of God's," which served as the basis for the *Humble Attempt*, in WJE 25:200–206; "Watch and Pray Always," Edwards's farewell sermon at Stockbridge (it is nothing more than an outline, but is noteworthy in that it is his last dated sermon), in WJE 25:716; and "God's Manner Is First to Prepare Men's Hearts and Then to Answer Their Prayers," in Edwards, *Glory and Honor*, 77–106. Finally, "Hypocrites Deficient in the Duty of Prayer," in *Works*² 2:71–77, is a two-part sermon preached in June of 1740, and is based on Job 27:10—"Will he always call upon God?" For an excellent secondary source on the subject, see Kreider, "Jonathan Edwards's Theology of Prayer."

duty of secret prayer, it is a symptom of a far larger issue. Prayer is the duty of "calling upon God," and to gradually decline in one's habits of prayer is likely evidence that one's conversion was inauthentic.[138] It may well be that such hypocrites were able to "keep up the outside of religion in them for a good while," but ultimately they come to ignore this duty, and since others cannot easily discern whether secret prayer is taking place, the problem can readily go unnoticed.[139]

As a result, despite the fact that their religious exercises are a sham, "They may commonly be present at public prayers in the congregation," even as "vicious persons, who make no pretence to serious religion."[140] Despite being a part of the congregation in worship, "They may be present at these prayers, and yet have no proper prayer of their own."[141] In order for such prayer to be vital, it must be connected to the reality of worship that takes place in private. But for the hypocrite, "Perhaps they attend on Sabbath-days, and sometimes on other days. But they have ceased to make it a constant daily practice daily to retire to worship God alone, and to seek his face in secret places."[142]

As such, while it might be comparatively easy to discern what the external appearance of public prayer may have been like in the worship led by Jonathan Edwards, such matters would have been essentially inconsequential to him. The inner reality of what was to take place in the believer was to be genuine; if the congregation was in prayer to God, it was incumbent on the worshiper, indwelt by the Holy Spirit, to participate by faith. Hypocrites, though present physically, and though ostensibly participating in the external elements of worship, would have failed utterly:

> Hypocrites never had the spirit of prayer. They may have been stirred up to the external performance of this duty, and that with a great deal of earnestness and affection, and yet always have been destitute of the true spirit of prayer. The spirit of prayer is a holy spirit, a gracious spirit. We read of the spirit of grace and supplication; Zech. xii. 10. "I will pour out on the house of David and the inhabitants of Jerusalem, the spirit of grace and supplications." Wherever there is a

---

138. *Works*² 2:71.
139. *Works*² 2:72.
140. Ibid.
141. Ibid.
142. Ibid.

true spirit of supplication, there is the spirit of grace. The true spirit of prayer is no other than God's own spirit dwelling in the hearts of the saints. And as this spirit comes from God, so doth it naturally tend to God in holy breathings with him by prayer.[143]

By contrast, "It is natural to one who is truly born from above to pray to God, and to pour out his soul in holy supplications before his heavenly Father. This is as natural to the new nature and life as breathing is to the nature and life of the body."[144] Ultimately, "True prayer is nothing else but faith expressed."[145] The nature of the prayer is not an act of self-exaltation; on the contrary, true Christian faith will result in self-abasement and profound humility: "He sees himself still to be a poor, empty, helpless creature, and that he still stands in great and continual need of God's help."[146] Prayer, conducted in private, in family, or in public, is commanded as duty, and "A man who knows that he lives in sin against God will not be inclined to come daily into the presence of God; but will rather be inclined to fly from his presence, as Adam, when he had eaten of the forbidden fruit, ran away from God, and hid himself among the trees of the garden."[147]

As a consequence, prayer provides a barometer that determines one's true spiritual condition. If one were in fact a Christian, "if you had indeed such a spirit, would you thus grow weary of the practice of drawing near to him, and become habitually so averse to it, as in a great measure to cast off so plain a duty, which is so much the life of a child of God?"[148] Prayer, then, is an essential aspect of every believer's life, no mere option—"to lead a holy life is to lead a life devoted to God: a life of worshipping and serving God. . . . Prayer is as natural an extension of faith as breathing is of life; and to say a man lives a life of faith, and yet lives a prayerless life, is every whit as inconsistent and incredible, as to say, that a man lives without breathing."[149]

Edwards warns the members of his congregation at Northampton—who, as we have seen, he refers to as "sermon-proof"—in the strongest terms:

---

143. Ibid.
144. *Works*² 2:73.
145. Ibid.
146. Ibid.
147. Ibid.
148. *Works*² 2:74.
149. *Works*² 2:75.

> If you will live in the neglect of secret prayer, you show your good-will to neglect all the worship of God. He that prays only when he prays with others, would not pray at all, were it not that the eyes of others are upon him. He that will not pray where none but God seeth him, manifestly doth not pray at all out of respect to God, or regard to his all-seeing eye, and therefore doth in effect casts off all the worship of God, of which prayer is the principal duty. Now, what a miserable saint is he who is no worshipper of God! He that casts off the worship of God, in effect casts off God himself: he refuses to own him, or to be conversant with him as his God. For the way in which men own God, and are conversant with him as their God, is by worshipping him.[150]

Conversely, Edwards encourages the converted to consider the benefits of prayer afforded by God. He urges, "consider how much you always stand in need of the help of God. . . . We cannot draw a breath without his help. You need his help every day for the supply of your outward wants; and especially you stand in continual need of him to help your souls."[151] Edwards summarizes,

> Consider the great benefit of a constant, diligent, and persevering attendance on this duty. It is one of the greatest and most excellent means of nourishing the new nature, and of causing the soul to flourish and prosper. It is an excellent mean of keeping up an acquaintance with, and of growing in the knowledge of God. It is the way to a life of communion with God. It is an excellent mean of taking off the heart from the vanities of the world, and of causing the mind to be conversant in heaven. It is an excellent preservative from sin and the wiles of the devil, and a powerful antidote against the poison of the old serpent. It is a duty whereby strength is derived from God against the lusts and corruptions of the heart, and the snares of the world.[152]

Fast Days

For Jonathan Edwards, fast days would have been an ordinary part of the religious landscape from the days of his earliest recollections, taken for granted as a necessity when a congregation or the larger community was faced with

---

150. Ibid.
151. *Works*² 2:76.
152. *Works*² 2:77.

a situation that could be interpreted as the judgment of God. They arose to prominence particularly in light of the physical privation of the early Puritans, and even after food supplies were no longer the primary concern, attacks from Indians, threats of war, a particularly gruesome or unexpected death, earthquakes, and all manner of calamity potentially resulted in the declaration of fast days. These were days that were to be marked by nothing short of abject humiliation. They ultimately came to be a less a voluntary public statement of dependence on God, so much as a formal decree in New England: "it became customary for groups of ministers to prepare a proclamation and to present it before the General Court or the governor or council for ratification. . . . Thus the fast day's character of holiness was legally sanctioned and attendance at its services of worship was compulsory throughout New England."[153]

If there was the danger that fast days might become external and formal, there was a corollary effort to ensure that the meaning behind the event remained firmly fixed in the minds of the people: "It was important to know how to prepare for such fast days. *The Westminster Directory for Public Worship* was specific in its recommendations. These included that each family was required to prepare their hearts, to arrive early at the congregation, and to be dressed in simple, unostentatious garments without ornaments."[154] Still, Edwards recognized throughout his life that a certain sterility was often evident in the observation of these fast days, and he addressed it directly, as will be seen.

In many ways, the fast day, and even potentially the funeral service, were two platforms that were likely ideal opportunities for the often austere—and even occasionally severe—Edwards to seek to apply the warnings of Scripture forcibly against the sins of the people or in response to difficulties that were being faced. In a letter to his frequent correspondent, the Rev. Benjamin Colman, Edwards explained matter-of-factly on one such occasion, "We have appointed a day of fasting in the town this week, by reason of this [his uncle's suicide] and other appearances of Satan's rage amongst us against poor souls."[155] For Edwards, a man accustomed to such self-discipline with regard to food that his gauntness was often a point of concern to others, fasting was virtually a way of life. Two of his "resolutions," dating back to his late

---

153. Davies, *Worship of the American Puritans*, 65.
154. Ibid., 66.
155. WJE 16:58.

teen years, deal directly with self-control with respect to food: "20. Resolved, to maintain the strictest temperance in eating and drinking. 40. Resolved, to inquire every night, before I go to bed, whether I have acted in the best way I possibly could, with respect to eating and drinking."[156] Edwards also advocated the practice of individual fasting: "Don't altogether neglect the duty of secret fasting."[157] Sermons marking fast days pepper the vast collection of his sermons from near the beginning of his ministry to its end. In response to an earthquake that took place on October 29, 1727, shortly after Edwards's twenty-fourth birthday, he preached one of his first fast day sermons, entitled "Impending Judgments Averted Only by Reformation."[158] Edwards did not so much seek to bring comfort to the people in light of the recent earthquake so much as to use the event to spur the people to turn toward God. God had brought about destruction on others in the past, and at times through earthquakes. "[T]hough earthquakes and signs in the heavens may have natural causes," he preached, "yet they may nevertheless be ordered to fall out so as to be forerunners of great changes and threatenings of judgments—earthquakes more especially, because they very often are means of great calamities."[159] There is a purpose in view to these warnings, namely "that [the people] may have opportunity of repentance. God warns that they may be awakened and so turn from their evil way."[160]

Even at this early juncture in Edwards's ministry, he is keenly aware of the apparent disconnect between the people's participation in days of prayer and fasting, and their subsequent careless behavior in spiritual matters: "We have kept many days of fasting and humiliation to beg of God the pardon of our sins, and have pretended to humble ourselves for our backslidings, but yet have not grown any better."[161] Edwards takes pains to enumerate many of the more prominent sins he perceives in the community, and concludes, "our land is very much defiled, and no wonder it groans and trembles under us."[162] The earthquake that came at night is a means by which many of the sins that are committed in the dark of night might be recognized as rightly

156. WJE 16:754, 756.
157. See WJE 22:534.
158. WJE 13:213–27.
159. WJE 13:220.
160. WJE 13:221.
161. WJE 13:224.
162. WJE 13:225.

judged and repented of. The sermon closes with the admonition, "Therefore speedily forsake your evil ways; set God before your eyes and consider that he beholds you when other eyes see you not, and that he remembers the sin you commit in secret. Avoid therefore such works of darkness, as you would not feel God's judgments in this world and hereafter suffer the vengeance of eternal fire."[163]

Building on this brief review of this earlier sermon, in another preached a few years later, in April of 1734, Edwards arguably composed his most representative fast day sermon, picking up on some of the themes of this earlier sermon. "Fast Days in Dead Times" is once again aimed very sharply at the too common reality that many were participating in times of fasting without possessing a genuine, heartfelt concern for sin.[164] The following features are easily noted:

> A. Hypocrisy is often practiced on fast days
> B. The sins of the people are set in view, and
> C. Repentance, or reformation, is called for.

Each of these features will be noted in turn. First, in many ways, the whole of the sermon is an extended argument against the hypocrisy of the people in observing fast days, when in fact, they do so only out of habit or for religious show. Edwards laments, "There is a great show of humiliation on fast days, but no reformation."[165] This is not merely a concern for "degenerate" people, but "godly persons may be very hypocritical in keeping fast days, and prevailing degeneracy may have great influence even upon them to cause them to be hypocritical."[166] In sum, "Men will willingly give God the forms of worship, if he will but be at peace with them, and let them enjoy their sins. They can a great deal easier comply with going to meeting, and keeping fasts and thanksgivings, and the like, than they can deny all their fleshly appetites, and cross their ambition and their covetousness."[167]

Edwards is not shy, secondly, to enumerate the sins of the people in various ways. His aim is to set before them the heinousness of their habits in an effort to jar them to a realization of the consequences. "When a people

163. WJE 13:227.
164. WJE 19:60–77.
165. WJE 19:61.
166. WJE 19:66.
167. WJE 19:65.

grow degenerate," he avers, "they grow senseless of their sins, and have no desire to reform.... If we had no sins to confess and humble ourselves for, there would be no occasion for a fast."[168] Sinners fail to observe in the various forms of divine warnings that are offered that they represent a foretaste of the judgment to come: "They pretend to humble themselves before God for their sins; but they ben't sensible of there being a God that has taken notice of their sins, and that has been provoked by them."[169]

Third, in perhaps the most poignant dimension of the sermon, Edwards calls his people to repentance, urging them to emulate the noble character of the godly: "The humble, sensible Christian is most ready to complain of himself. He is ready to cry out of his own badness, is ready to say that he has been the chief of sinners, and has been the most undeserving. His thoughts turn chiefly on what he has done, the hand he has had in provoking God, and bringing down his judgments."[170] Indicting himself among the people, as the prophet Ezra of old, he declares, "We are greatly backslidden, and are become a very degenerate people."[171] The call to change is urgent, but it is a call that has long gone unheeded: "We have a fast every year, and the pretense of every fast is reformation; but yet do we not come to every new fast worse than we were before the last?"[172]

While numerous other fast day sermons are extant, perhaps one more will serve to augment the portrait of the fast day as administered by Edwards. "God's Care for his Servants in Time of Public Commotion" was written on the occasion of a "special colony-wide fast... to call down heaven's blessings on British arms in the latest in a series of imperial conflicts that marked the early eighteenth-century Atlantic world."[173] One might expect an occasion such as this to be marked by a calling on God that he would aid the British against their enemies—it was, after all, the ostensible purpose of the fast. But Edwards believed that he was preaching in the "latter days," and the "commotion" brought about by the impending war was yet another means by which his congregation might be spiritually awakened. He urged self-examination, and declared, "To such as are in a Christless condition... make haste to get

168. WJE 19:67.
169. WJE 19:69.
170. WJE 19:70.
171. WJE 19:73.
172. WJE 19:74.
173. See Stout and Hatch's comments in WJE 22:339.

an interest in Christ, that you may be some of those servants of God that God will take effectual care to preserve in times of public commotion and calamity."[174]

Even as late as April of 1757, less than a year before his death, Edwards included a reference to a fast day spoken of by Aaron Burr, ironically, to take place at Princeton, where he would later die: "I concluded with our pious governor that, as soon as the season would admit of the Trustees meeting, we would keep a day of fasting and prayer, to implore the divine blessing on the College, and humbly to adore him that his providence has so remarkably appeared for it."[175] As such, the practice of fast days was always a good one in Edwards's estimation, throughout the whole course of his life, but there remained the prevailing concern that such fast days be marked by an inward spiritual reality characterized by humiliation and brokenness before God.

Church Discipline

What constitutes a true church? This is a question that has clearly been answered in wide-ranging ways throughout the course of church history. For right or wrong, John Calvin has at times been pointed to as having identified the "Three Marks of the Church," namely, the preaching of the word, the right administration of the sacraments, and church discipline.[176] It is this third head in particular that now commands attention. Whether or not it should be elevated to the status of a true mark of the church or not, church discipline, or community discipline, was clearly a prominent feature in the Puritan worship of which Jonathan Edwards was an inheritor and proponent.[177] Given the sometime severe Puritan excesses in this regard, Edwards

---

174. WJE 22:357.

175. WJE 16:703. This statement by Aaron Burr appears in a letter from Edwards to the Rev. John Erskine, dated April 12, 1757.

176. Did John Calvin hold to these three marks? In the *Institutes* he writes, "Wherever we see the Word of God purely preached and heard, and the sacraments administered according to Christ's instruction, there, it is not to be doubted, a church of God exists." Calvin, *Institutes of the Christian Religion*, 2:1023. In Calvin's divisions, this is bk. 4, ch. 1, ¶9. It is worth noting the editorial footnote at this location: "Important as discipline is for Calvin, he does not distinctly make it one of the *notae*, or marks, by which the church is recognized, as does Bucer." But Calvin does speak of church discipline in virtually these terms. In this light, see Johnson, "Sinews of the Body of Christ."

177. Horton Davies records a variety of the sources of the practice of church discipline in the Puritan tradition, ranging from a more moderate approach to those more apparently

must be recognized as comparatively restrained in the official exercise of church discipline, in that we have extant only one excommunication sermon.[178] This was the first excommunication to take place at Northampton in twenty-eight years, dating back to the ministry of Edwards's grandfather, Solomon Stoddard.

Given the scope of this work, this topic will be considered rather briefly, in view of the fact that in relative terms church discipline was a comparatively minor feature in worship itself for Jonathan Edwards. It must not be missed, however, that two of the most pivotal events in Edwards's life—the so-called "Bad Books" case and the controversy over admission to the Lord's Table—are ultimately matters of church discipline, and were instrumental factors in his ultimate dismissal from the Northampton pulpit. The "Bad Books" case is a classic study in Edwards lore, and is considered a key factor in his ultimate dismissal from the Northampton pulpit. Edwards made the mistake of reading a list of names—some of whom were suspected of a particular offense, others of whom were merely witnesses—without distinguishing between the two groups, and thereby inadvertently casting a shadow of suspicion on the innocent.[179] He refers to this event as the "Young Folks' Bible" case. It is interesting to note that the matter was handled after the worship service, and not in the context of worship. The Lord's Supper controversy was already noted in the section of this book devoted to the sacraments.[180] While these were both extremely complex social matters within the context of that congregation, and while errors were unquestionably made by both Edwards and the congregation, it is decidedly ironic that in an effort to appropriately

---

extreme. See Davies, *Worship of the English Puritans*, 232–42. He writes, "the Puritans were scrupulously rigid in the exercise of Church censures" (232). While the excesses had been tempered to some extent by Edwards's day, the embers of church discipline were by no means extinguished.

178. WJE 22:68–79. The historical context within which this sermon was preached is presented in this volume on pages 64–67, and provides the background for much of the discussion presented in this section as it relates to this sermon. One point of disagreement must be noted. In Stout and Hatch's editorial comments, the claim is made that miscellanies *q* and 485, and the blank Bible entry for 1 Cor 5:11, indicate that Edwards referred to excommunication as an "ordinance," but a close inspection of these three sources by this author does not sustain this assertion. A sermon no longer extant, preached on Hab 1:13a and entitled "God Hates Sin," was also evidently preached as a form of church discipline in the case of Orlando Bridgman, evidently for drunkenness. See WJE 14:545.

179. For an account, see Marsden, *Jonathan Edwards: A Life*, 292–302.

180. See also Johnson, "'Young Folks' Bible," 37–54.

administer church discipline within his own congregation, due to these very efforts Edwards would finally lose his own connection with it.

As such, two matters must be considered with regard to church discipline. First, there is a sense in which with virtually every sermon Edwards preached was about the work of church and community discipline. The editors to the Yale edition in which Edwards's one extant excommunication sermon appears, which is entitled "The Means and Ends of Excommunication," note that the object of that excommunication was a "Mrs. Bridgman," and that there was a sermon Edwards preached about a year earlier in which this same woman was featured.[181] Drunkenness was her besetting sin, and the ultimate cause of her excommunication.

The key doctrinal statement of this early sermon, based on Deuteronomy 29:18–20, while serious, is nevertheless no more severe than many doctrinal statements that can be found in many of Edwards's other sermons: "That those that go on in the sin of drunkenness under the light of God's word are in the way to bring God's fearful wrath and a most amazing destruction upon themselves." It is interesting to note that Edwards preached this sermon virtually in the midst of his sermon series *Charity and Its Fruits*, which was based on 1 Corinthians 13.

Is this not seemingly far less severe than the doctrinal statement in the infamous "Sinners in the Hands of an Angry God," where he declares, "There is nothing that keeps wicked men, at any one moment, out of hell, but the mere pleasure of God"?[182] One could not sit in the pews when Edwards preached, over the course of any sustained period, and avoid "discipline"—not merely on external matters such as Mrs. Bridgeman's drunkenness, but respecting such inward matters as hypocrisy, greed, lust, and supremely, the hardness of an unconverted heart.

Secondly, with the particular matter of excommunication at hand, Edwards did not shrink from setting forth matters pointedly. Excommunication, the most severe form of church discipline, "cut off" the excommunicated from four key privileges: "first, from the charity of the church; second, brotherly society; third, fellowship of the church in worship; fourth, internal privileges of visible Christians."[183] The severity of this fourfold separation is tempered, though, by a desire for the ultimate restoration of the

---

181. WJE 22:64–67.
182. WJE 22:405.
183. WJE 22:71.

one excommunicated: "excommunication is used for that end, that we may thereby obtain their good."[184] Edwards concludes the sermon by drawing attention to the three particular ends, or aims, of excommunication, and is a fit summary for his broader understanding of the place of discipline within the community:

> *First.* That the church may be kept pure and God's ordinances not defiled. This end is mentioned in the context [of the preaching portion, 1 Cor 5:11]: that the other members themselves may not be defiled. 'Tis necessary that they thus bear a testimony against sin.
>
> *Second.* That others may be deterred from wickedness. That others may fear.
>
> *Third.* That they may be reclaimed, [that their] souls may be saved. [After] other, more gentle, means have been used in vain, then we are to use severe means to bring 'em to conviction and shame and humiliation, by being rejected and avoided by the church, treated with disrespect, disowned by God, delivered to Satan, his being made instrument of chastening them.
>
> This is the last means, with concomitant admonitions, that the church is to use for the reclaiming of those members of the church that become visibly wicked; which, if it ben't effectual, what is next to be expected is destruction without remedy.[185]

Collections for the Poor

Collections for the needy, while an irregular aspect of worship, were nevertheless common in Puritan New England; in Northampton, though, Edwards eventually convinced the congregation in 1743 to take up a collection for the poor every Sabbath.[186] The question of how to deal with the poor was a common one in Northampton; during Solomon Stoddard's pastorate, in 1705, the town voted to build a poor house, which was actually never built, and even at that time it appears likely that it was becoming increasingly difficult to "get the successful farmers to take in the indigent."[187] Edwards reported in a letter to Thomas Prince written late in this year, "There has

---

184. WJE 22:74

185. WJE 22:78–79.

186. Hambricke-Stowe, *Practice of Piety*, 130. See also Marsden, *Jonathan Edwards: A Life*, 304.

187. Tracy, *Jonathan Edwards, Pastor*, 42.

also been an evident alteration with respect to a charitable spirit to the poor (though I think with regard to this, we in this town, as the land in general, come far short of gospel rules)."[188] He once chided his congregation with the words that the wicked "think 'tis lost if they feed the poor or relieve the distressed."[189] With respect to almsgiving, it would be easy to acknowledge that Edwards's views on the topic are essentially those of a Biblicist, and move on—the Bible commands Christian giving, and Edwards followed suit. While this is certainly true, Edwards addressed the topic, though, with a particular potency, which bears note. But before considering what Edwards *said* about the topic, it is worth noting what he *did* about it.

While many things could be said about the sprawling Edwards family, despite the comparatively large salary that Edwards drew at Northampton, one would likely never characterize him as wealthy. This despite the fact that he had "as large a salary settled upon me as most have out of Boston"; he added, I "have the largest and most chargeable family of any minister, perhaps within an hundred miles of me."[190] In his letters, Edwards often characterizes his family of eleven children as "large" or "numerous," and it is easy to discern that running the household, which included slaves and frequent guests, was an expensive proposition. His letter to the trustees at Princeton dated October 19, 1757, for example, opens with Edwards's account of their financial situation and the concerns a move would entail; he expresses similar concern with respect to the financial prospects for his family pending his dismissal from Northampton in a letter to the Rev. Thomas Gillespie dated April 2, 1750.[191] An early biographer says of Edwards's wife Sarah that "she was conscientiously careful that nothing should be wasted and lost; and often when she herself took care to save any thing of trifling value, or directed her children or others to do so, or when she saw them waste any thing, she would repeat the words of our Saviour–'that nothing be lost.'"[192] And, if financial matters were a challenge while at Northampton through 1750, the cut in pay that Edwards realized at the missions outpost in Stockbridge was nothing short of dramatic, and money matters were a nearly constant cause of concern. It is no great surprise, then, that after arriving in Princeton to begin

188. WJE 16:115–16.
189. BL 81.
190. WJE 16:284.
191. WJE 6:725 and 16:339.
192. *Works*[2] 1:xlv.

his presidency in January of 1758, and having contracted smallpox, his last letter deals not with the deep theological matters with which he wrestled, but is addressed to the college treasurer, a reminder about his salary.[193]

With these personal financial trials in view, Edwards's own personal practice of liberality provides a profound insight into not only his beliefs about giving, but of the intensity of these beliefs:

> Samuel Hopkins maintained that Edwards had "uncommon regard" for "liberality, and charity to the poor and distressed." Edwards spoke often of the need for every congregation to keep up "a public stock" for its poor and, said Hopkins, he backed up his public advice with private action. Much of his almsgiving was in secret. Hopkins knew of one case firsthand. Edwards had heard of a man, neither acquaintance nor kin, who was in great distress due to an illness and asked Hopkins to deliver "a considerable sum" to him, but to tell no one. Hopkins was sure there were many such instances that would be "unknown till the resurrection."[194]

Certainly, Edwards preached about the practice. In the midst of his famous series of sermons on 1 Corinthians 13, *Charity and Its Fruits*, Edwards takes time while preaching on verse 4—"Charity suffereth long and is kind"—to present the Christian motivation for generosity:

> Let us consider how kind God and Christ have been to us, and how much good we have received from them. How much outward kindness have we received, and what great things hath God bestowed for our spiritual and eternal good! God hath given more than if he had bestowed on us all the kingdoms of the world; he hath given his own Son. God hath not been short-handed, but exceedingly liberal. Christ has done great things; he hath gone through great labors. . . .[195]

Edwards then cites no fewer than fifteen texts of Scripture in an effort to stimulate and entice giving in his hearers, in order that they might "freely do good to others."[196] This sermon is noteworthy in that it demonstrates that Edwards's emphasis on giving to the poor was not merely an ethical or social

---

193. *Works*[2] 1:738. It is perhaps also worth noting that in the home Jonathan grew up in, financial struggles, and even constant wrangling with the congregation over salary, were also evident in Timothy Edwards's situation, to an even greater degree. See Tracy, *Jonathan Edwards, Pastor*, 56.

194. Marsden, *Jonathan Edwards: A Life*, 304.

195. WJE 8:215.

196. Ibid.

concern, but a theological one: such giving to one's fellow man was a necessary response to the generosity that each Christian had experienced in God's provision of his only son.

Arguably Edwards's most important sermon on the topic was preached some years earlier, "The Duty of Charity to the Poor."[197] In a clear departure from other sermons, in his common threefold sermon division of text, doctrine and application, Edwards spends the vast majority of the time spent in this sermon on application. The sermon's doctrine is particularly trenchant: "'Tis the most absolute and indispensable duty of a people of God to give bountifully and willingly for the supply of the wants of the needy."[198] There are limits to be established for giving, so for example, if "persons are idle, or spendthrifts," but his emphasis is elsewhere: "'Tis mentioned in Scripture not only as a duty, but as a great duty. . . . I know of scarce any particular duty that is so much insisted upon us, both in the Old Testament and New, as this duty of charity to the poor."[199] Once again, Edwards accentuates the theological as opposed to the ethical basis for giving: "considering how much God hath done for us, how greatly he hath loved us, and what he hath given us when we were so unworthy. . . . How unsuitable will it be for us that live wholly by kindness to be unkind!"[200]

Edwards begins the sermon's application with a call to self-examination, and then sets out, by means of exhortation, seven motivations for obedience to this duty of giving, contrasted with eleven objections that might be raised. The proportion of objections raised here is not incidental: Edwards forcefully presents the contention that since this duty is a hard one, all manner of opposition will potentially arise. It is the Bible that sets forth the pattern for Christian obedience in this matter: "We are professors of Christianity, pretend to be the followers of Jesus, pretend to make the gospel our rule. We have the Bible in our houses; let us not behave ourselves in this particular as if we had never seen the Bible, and were ignorant of Christianity, and did not know what kind of religion it was."[201] The motivations and objections introduced in this sermon frame well Edwards's attitude regarding giving to the poor:

197. WJE 17:371–404.
198. WJE 17:373.
199. WJE 17:374–75.
200. WJE 17:376–77.
201 200 WJE 17:379.

Motivations:
1. Consider that what you have is not your own, i.e., you have no absolute right to it, have only a subordinate right.
2. Consider that God tells us that he shall look upon what is done in charity to our neighbor that is in want as done unto Him, and what is denied unto them as denied unto Him. . . .
3. Consider that there is an absolute necessity of our complying with the difficult duties of religion.
4. The Scripture teaches us that this very particular duty is necessary.
5. [W]hat abundant encouragement the Word of God gives you, that you shall be no loser by your charity and bounty to them that are in want.
6. God has threatened to follow them with his curse that are uncharitable to the poor. . . .
7. You know not what calamitous and necessitous circumstances you yourself or your children may be in.[202]

Objections:
1. I am in a natural condition, and if I should give considerable to the poor, I should not do it in a right spirit, and so should get nothing by it.
2. If I am liberal and bountiful, I shall only make a righteousness of it, and so it will do me more hurt than good.
3. I have given to the poor in times past and never found myself the better for it.
4. [S]ome may object against charity to such or such particular persons, that they are not obliged to give 'em [charity], for though they are [in] need yet they ben't in extremity.
5. Some may object against charity to a particular object, that he is an ill sort of person and has been injurious to them.
6. Some may object from their own circumstances, that they have nothing to spare; they han't more than enough for themselves.
7. Some may object, concerning a particular person, that they don't certainly know whether he be an object of charity or no.
8. Some may say they ben't obliged to give to the poor till they ask. . . .
9. He has brought himself to want by his own fault.
10. Some may object and say others don't do their duty.

202. WJE 17:379–87.

11. The law makes provision for the poor and obliges the town to provide for them.[203]

In sum, then, while the "wicked" will fail to give—or if he should give, will give with the wrong motivations—the sincere believer will give in a manner that exalts God.[204] To the degree possible, giving is to be a highly private, normative aspect of the Christian experience. As Edwards says elsewhere, "Let godly persons be hence exhorted to abound in deeds of charity. They who are the subject of so much of the free mercy and kindness of God are above all persons obliged to this duty and, if they neglect it, will in a peculiar manner act beside their character. For in Scripture language the merciful man and the good man are the same thing."[205]

Special Days of Prayer and Thanksgiving

Occasions were set aside to mark the blessings of God in the life of the community, analogous to the days of fasting wherein his favor was sought in the midst of perceived judgments. These days of prayer and thanksgiving also included the preaching of the Word, and several of the sermons Edwards preached on such occasions are available to us. Two such examples will prove representative.[206]

The first, "God Amongst His People," in keeping with the tradition established by his Puritan forebears, was preached to mark Thanksgiving in 1735.[207] We hear hopes for seasons of spiritual awakening as, in opening

---

203. WJE 17:390–403. In addition to bearing relevance to the matter at hand, this sermon is illustrative of the manner in which Edwards often deals with objections, presenting not only the rationale for adopting a particular viewpoint, but anticipating many of the immediate concerns that would be in the minds of the congregation. This is clearly not a sermon that was written in haste.

204. See also BL 76 and 81.

205. Kimnach et al., *Sermons of Jonathan Edwards*, 209.

206. The two sermons chosen as representative of this motif are Thanksgiving sermons. For what may be the most illustrative sermon written for the occasion of a formal day of prayer, see "Undeserved Mercy," in WJE 19:628–55. This sermon was preached shortly after the congregation at Northampton had avoided serious injury or loss of life "on the occasion of the front gallery's falling," an incident described by Edwards in WJE 16:65–67.

207. WJE 19:453–72. The text for this sermon is Isa 12:6: "Cry out and shout, thou inhabitant of Zion: for great is the Holy One of Israel in the midst of thee." For additional perspective on the development of Puritan fast days and days of thanksgiving, see Love, *Fast and Thanksgiving Days*.

his text from Isaiah, Edwards declares, "They are very glorious times of the church that are there prophesied of, by reason of an extraordinary flourishing of religion, and the glorious kingdom of Jesus Christ."[208] Edwards's summary doctrinal statement is in many ways a statement of how it is that a community might observe Thanksgiving: "When God is in the midst of a people, 'tis just cause of exceeding joy and praise in them that so great and holy an one is amongst them."[209] God himself is the cause for thanksgiving among the people, more so than the community's immediate circumstances.

There would be no cause for thanksgiving if God was not present, but where he has shown himself, and even more, where he has brought about the refreshing, reviving work of his Spirit, thanksgiving will flow naturally from his people, and will be marked by singing, praise and even shouting unto God: "'Tis the greatest cause that a people can have to rejoice and to praise."[210] Ironically, according to Edwards, Northampton was blessed by God's visitation not because there was a greater spirit of prayer; on the contrary, God's mercy toward them was all the more unexpected because of their dullness and hardness of heart.

By virtue of this unexpected blessing, and in light of the particularly great mercy of God that led to the beginnings of revival, Edwards urges renewed attention to worship. He urges that individuals, families, all private societies, and supremely the congregation gathered for worship be marked by praise and thanksgiving to God: "Let us with the greatest joy and exaltation of soul, praise God in our public solemn assemblies. We never had so much cause to rejoice and praise God in public; for when we meet together, God is now more remarkably amongst [us], and great is the Holy One of Israel in the midst of us."[211] Because God has put this "new song into their mouths," Edwards exults, "How beautiful and becoming it is for a congregation, a multitude, to join together in sincerely praising and magnifying the Most High God.... Ps. 149:1, 'Praise ye the Lord. Sing unto the Lord a new song, and his praise in the congregation of saints.'"[212]

Several years later, when the longed-for flames of revival had been kindled at Northampton—at the peak of the Great Awakening, in November

208. WJE 19:453.
209. WJE 19:455.
210. WJE 19:456.
211. WJE 19:469.
212. WJE 19:470.

of 1740—Edwards picked up a similar theme on the occasion of another Thanksgiving sermon. Only a month earlier, George Whitefield had preached in Edwards's own church on four separate occasions. Conversions were frequent within the congregation during this season. If there was ever an occasion for thanksgiving, this was it. With such an atmosphere, on November 13, 1740, Edwards rose to preach "They Sing a New Song."[213]

One might expect to find Edwards here emphasizing the beauty of singing praises to God, and there is such an emphasis. It is essential to grasp, however, the kind of singing Edwards has in view: "true saints and redeemed from the earth, do sing a new song in the sincere praises they offer to God."[214] The focus is emphatically set not on the external auditory splendor of the voice, so much as on the inner reality of the heart. It is a *new* song, one that far surpasses any that might have sounded forth in their "natural state" when unconverted: "So their song is far more excellent than anything that was before their conversion, as much more excellent than all their external formal praises that they offered to God before conversion as light is more excellent than darkness, or as gold is more precious than the dirt."[215]

On these special days, then, Edwards, as had many other Puritan pastors, leveraged positive circumstances within the community to draw his congregation's attention to the source of their "undeserved" blessings—God himself.[216] If fast days would allow the congregation to mourn for their sins in the midst of adversities, so also days of prayer and thanksgiving helped to galvanize the community's perspective that obedience would be blessed by God. Even in the midst of giving thanks, Edwards was studious to emphasize how "so many remarkable frowns of divine providence on a town are not for nothing. God's meaning in his external providence towards a people, is much more easily discerned than towards a particular person. . . . They are rewarded or punished according to their deeds in this world."[217]

---

213. WJE 22:227–44.

214. WJE 22:229.

215. WJE 22:235.

216. A method describing how one might rightly practice "holy feasting" can be traced back, for example, to Bayly, *Practice of Piety*, 219–62.

217. WJE 19:647. This quote is taken from the sermon "Undeserved Mercy," cited previously.

three

The Practice of Self-Examination

While each aspect of public and private worship could be considered in far greater depth, only a few have been chosen for review in more detail, largely because of the uniqueness of Edwards's perspective on that topic—or because of the stark contrast to currently prevailing notions of worship. By far the fullest review included in this study is on the topic of self-examination. Although this is the worship practice here considered to the greatest extent, representative as it is of a key facet of worship for Edwards, it must be stressed that even this review must be seen as comparatively brief, given the frequency with which Edwards discusses the subject. Moreover, this review of Edwards's approach to the practice of self-examination explores essential background information, namely, the roots of this doctrine as presented by his Puritan forefathers, information that would similarly provide valuable background to each of the other aspects of public and private worship under consideration.

In short, Edwards emphasizes the practice of self-examination to an astounding degree, and although he does modify to some extent the manner in which it is communicated by some of his ancestors, his approach seemingly grows organically from that of the Puritans. Self-examination was frequently the key point of emphasis, not only in Edwards's preaching, but similarly, in the observation of the Lord's Supper, on fast days, and even on days of celebration.[1] In addition, the prominent place of self-examination in public worship was similarly emphasized as a key dimension of private devotion, as will be shown. The practice of self-examination, which Edwards learned from the Puritans and developed to a near art form, was the bridge between public and private acts of worship.

---

1. For a helpful perspective on self-examination and the Lord's Supper, see Church, "Self-Examination as Preparation."

Puritan Perspectives on Self-Examination

In many contemporary Christian churches, it may be more difficult to know where to set down one's Starbucks coffee than to find a ringing assurance of one's salvation. Contrast the availability of hot coffee or other comforts with the Puritan experience of worship: "In colonial days in New England the long and tedious services must have been hard to endure in the unheated churches in bitter winter weather, so bitter that, as Judge Sewall pathetically recorded, 'The communion bread was frozen pretty hard and rattled sadly into the plates.'"[2] Such assurance may too often be found even by means of a near mechanical recitation of a formulaic prayer or by mere mental assent to certain basic objective truths. As just one example, Joel Osteen sets forth a gospel offer that is by no means atypical at present:

> You might have never accepted Jesus. Maybe you have never asked Him to come into your heart. Today can be your day for a new beginning in God. I invite you to pray a simple prayer with me. Maybe you do not know how to pray. All you have to do is say this prayer and mean it with your heart. . . . Jesus, come into my heart. Save me. Be my Lord. Be my Savior. I repent of my old way of living. Jesus, I want to serve You all the days of my life. I'm not everything I want to be Jesus, but I know You'll make me into what You want me to be. Jesus, I'll serve You all the days.[3]

To contrast such presentations with Puritan invitations to conversion would make it appear as if two completely different religions were in view. One author lamented in this vein, now nearly fifty years ago, that "Many in our churches have been encouraged to profess Christ after little, if any, preparatory law-work. Of these, some have come to know their sinfulness later; others, however, continue in danger of falling away when a crisis tests their faith and exposes its shallow character. But most of these people have no doubt about their salvation."[4] As such, the kind of Puritan anguish regarding one's spiritual condition that resulted in an often desperate search for assurance would be for many modern churchgoers as foreign a notion as that of chickens at the opera: both would be equally incomprehensible and equally undesirable.

2. Earle, *Sabbath in Puritan New England*, 85.
3. Osteen, "Find Your New Beginning." It should be noted that Osteen's Web site, as of October 3, 2009, evidently no longer presents such an offer.
4. Mingard, "William Guthrie."

Consider Matthew Mead's treatise *The Almost Christian Discovered*, merely one of many possible counterexamples to the contemporary situation, and representative of the Puritan concern about assurance and how to obtain it. With each characteristic of one who is "almost a Christian" dwelt on at considerable length, Mead traverses no fewer than twenty such traits a man may have, and yet be but almost a Christian:

1. He may have much knowledge.
2. He may have great gifts.
3. He may have a high profession [of religion].
4. He may do much against sin.
5. He may desire grace.
6. He may tremble at the word.
7. He may delight in the word.
8. He may be a member of the church of Christ.
9. He may have great hopes of heaven.
10. He may be under great and visible changes.
11. He may be very zealous in the matters of religion.
12. He may be much in prayer.
13. He may suffer for Christ.
14. He may be called of God.
15. He may, in some sense, have the Spirit of God.
16. He may have some kind of faith.
17. He may love the people of God.
18. He may go far in obeying the commands of God.
19. He may be, in some sense, sanctified.
20. He may do all, as to external duties, that a true Christian can, and yet be no better than almost a Christian.[5]

As Karl Barth observed, "It is a bad theology which has no assurance of salvation."[6] In this light, then, some might pointedly charge the Puritans with bad theology. While the Puritans themselves would vigorously affirm the reality of a present assurance for the believer, with examples such as that

---

5. Ibid., 86–87. Mead's treatise is founded on a portion of Acts 26:28: "Almost thou persuadest me to be a Christian."

6. Barth, *Church Dogmatics*, 4/1:773.

of Mead in view, it cannot be disputed that often, agonizing years-long self-examination probing for evidence of the genuineness of one's conversion was the effect of much Puritan preaching. This was the case to such a degree that numerous treatises were necessarily produced in order to bolster the confidence of the poor, doubting believer. As just two examples, consider Thomas Hooker's *The Poor Doubting Christian Drawn to Christ* or Obadiah Sedgwick's *The Doubting Believer*. Members of congregations were urged to be sure—to be *certain*—that in fact they were genuine believers, not mere "false professors." There was no question of working out one's salvation with "fear and trembling," or of testing oneself to "see whether you are in the faith"; there was no other way proposed (cf. Phil 2:12, 2 Cor 13:5). Anathema would be the assertion that "All you have to do is say this prayer and mean it with your heart." One writer warns, in effect accusing the Puritans of the kind of bad theology Barth decried,

> It was by no means the least serious aspect of the grievous error of the Puritans regarding assurance, as it is not the least serious aspect of the teaching of their modern disciples, that, as the rule, they reserved, and reserve, assurance for old people. Assurance comes only with age, usually old age. The children and young people of the church are taught to live in doubt of their salvation. As a result they do live in doubt, terrifying doubt.[7]

On the other hand, while this kind of extreme uncertainty did at times occur, it may well represent the far end of a spectrum in which congregants were rightly encouraged to be certain of their eternal destiny. In particular, self-examination was the method by which a man or woman could be encouraged to soberly consider their spiritual estate. To be rightly understood, this concept of self-examination cannot be effectively considered in isolation, as an independent concept, inasmuch as it is a natural outgrowth of the Puritans' exacting emphasis on the nature of sin and on the preaching of the law. Sin was presented as man's great concern, the evil of evils, and Puritan writings on sin are available in abundance. Further, sin's great potential for self-deception necessarily suggests that one must scrupulously consider whether or not one's conversion is genuine or not; there is no arguing that this is the most important issue that must be decisively resolved for every Christian. As such for the Puritans, characterizations of true and false conversion, of true and false professions of faith (or "professors"), are also

---

7. Engelsma, "Assurance for All the Children."

common whenever the topic of self-examination is broached.[8] As a result, this serves as the soil in which the frequent point of application, or the "use" of a given text, often presses the hearer toward such self-examination.

What is more, once believers have thoroughly searched themselves, and have discerned more completely their infirmity and their profound need, ultimately they must cast themselves on Christ alone, trusting only in his merit. Self-examination, then, must not end in morose self-absorption, but rather must break forth in an exaltation of Jesus Christ. Four noteworthy features in Puritan instruction thereby are recognizable with respect to the practice of self-examination:

1. An understanding of the true nature of sin is set forth,
2. The hearer is urged to consider true and false conversion,
3. Sober reflection is pressed, and
4. The absolute necessity of turning to Christ in faith is emphasized.

These four heads, presented in various forms and with differing degrees of emphasis, convey a typical dynamic in Puritan though.[9] They should not be conceived of as a formula or as a straightjacket, a product of the Puritan fondness for Ramian logic within which assurance would be the inevitable end result. On the contrary, these are notable features common in Puritan preaching, a kind of resounding drumbeat within Puritan thought. Over the course of years of sitting under such preaching, all of these elements would be set forth at different seasons and with varying degrees of emphasis, and self-examination would be the duty of the hearer in response.

One point of clarification is in order. Self-examination as such is a practice that was to be undertaken by both believers and unbelievers alike. While the emphasis here will be primarily on self-examination with a particular focus on searching out the genuineness of one's conversion, bear in mind that the Puritan preacher often indiscriminately cast the seed of God's word, or to use a common Puritan metaphor, watered both the flowers and the weeds at the same time. So also, self-examination was a regular point of emphasis in discussions centered around the Lord's Supper.[10]

---

8. See, for example, Burgess, *Spiritual Refining*; Crook et al., *Ta diapheronta*; Firmin, *Real Christian*; and Shepard, *Parable of the Ten Virgins*.

9. See for example, Brooks, *Heaven on Earth*.

10. As one example, see Durham, *Unsearchable Riches of Christ*.

As the Westminster Directory explains, the preeminent concern is that the preacher's "auditors feel the word of God to be quick and powerful, and a discerner of the thoughts and intents of the heart; and that, if any unbeliever or ignorant persons be present, he may have the secrets of his heart made manifest, and give glory to God."[11] This was not an optional activity for the preacher to occasionally engage in, no mere trifle; instead it veritably defined Puritan preaching:

> the Puritans were *very thorough* in their probing of a man's state, and they realised the great seriousness of allowing any man to rest in a false sense of security when in point of fact he is not truly a child of God. Bolton refers to those who too readily administer the comfort of the gospel as "dawbing ministers, a generation of vilest men, excellent idiots in the mystery of Christ, and merciful cut-throats of many miserable, deluded souls, to whom they promise life and peace; when there is no peace towards, but terrible things at hand, tumblings of garments in blood, noise of damned souls and tormenting in hell for ever."[12]

Contrary to much contemporary practice, then, and in opposition to the potentially liberal dispensing of comfort without cure, "It is evident that 'assurance' to the Puritans was something quite other than the 'assurance' commonly given to the convert of five minutes' standing in the enquiry room ('You believe that John 1:12 is true and you have 'received him'? Then you are a son of God.')."[13] The Puritans would have generally been looking for assurance of their *election*, as distinguished from contemporary congregants—at least those few who might be concerned—who are normally looking for assurance regarding the genuineness of their conversion.

Were the Puritans guilty of bad theology? In particular, why was the call to self-examination such a regular feature of their preaching? What did it entail? What were its effects? To such questions we now turn, in particular by exploring the four primary features of Puritan preaching revolving around self-examination, as already noted.

---

11. Packer, "Puritan Conscience," 2:251.
12. Hemming, "Puritans' Dealings," 1:34; emphasis added.
13. Packer, *Quest for Godliness*, 182.

Sin: Man's Great Concern

Spend any time with the Puritans and you will quickly observe that they took sin seriously. Several works by different authors remain extant bearing titles *The Sinfulness of Sin* or *Sin, the Evil of Evils*, or in countless similar themes (such as Thomas Watson's *The Mischief of Sin* and *Hell's Furnace Heated Hotter*, or Thomas Vincent's *Fire and Brimstone* and *God's Terrible Voice in the City*). Considered as such, without a larger purpose in view, such works might appear odd, or worse, misguided. Perhaps Robert Murray M'Cheyne, speaking in a later age, expressed the intent of such works best when he suggested, "For every look at self take ten looks at Christ. But when you look, take a good look."[14] While this ratio was at times ignored, or perhaps forgotten, no one would ever accuse the Puritans as a whole of failing to take a good look at sin in its effect and nature. The goal was no mere morose reflection, but rather, the preaching of the law was intended to peel back one's pride and compel a more accurate and penetrating assessment of one's real condition in light of the truths of Scripture.

Given that the practice of self-examination has perhaps fallen out of vogue, a practice wherein one was entreated to consider wherever sin was present in the heart, the shrillness of the alarm sounded with regard to indwelling sin might be unexpected for many. It was sin that self-examination would reveal, not one's inner child or a cause for self-esteem. Sin was not simply a weakness, or a mistake, or a minor indiscretion to be dealt with. It was instead a mortal wound, and even one's motivations were suspect: "If you compare the evil of sin with other evils, you shall see how short all other kinds of evils are to this evil of sin. . . . Poverty, sickness, disgrace, all these are great evils, but these, and all others, have an end. Death puts a conclusion to them all. But this evil of sin is of an eternal nature that shall never have an end."[15] In *God's Terrible Voice in the City*, Thomas Vincent, an eyewitness of both the plague of 1665 and the great fire of London in 1666, portrayed these horrific events as judgments against the sins of the people.[16] After compiling a list of no fewer than twenty-five sins for which London was guilty, he writes, "By this time, it may be, the reader may be wearied with reading, as I am with thinking and writing of London's sins. But how hath the Lord

---

14. M'Cheyne, *Memoir and Remain*.
15. Bolton, "Sin: The Greatest Evil," 6.
16. Vincent, *God's Terrible Voice*.

been wearied with the bearing of them!"[17] In this way, Puritan preaching regularly connected adversities small and great in their congregations with individual and corporate sin, and was frequently calling for days of fasting and repentance as a consequence. The pilgrim was meant to mindfully consider, "Have I brought this calamity upon myself, upon my family, or upon my community?"

From the seed of original sin springs all actual sin, and as Adam was rightly judged for his sin, sinners in Puritan pews were rightly deserving of the hot displeasure of a God described as a "consuming fire" (Heb 12:31). Samuel Bolton explained, "Sin is the cause, the meriting, the procuring cause of all. All evils are but the births of sin. Sin is a big-bellied evil and all other evils are but the births of sin. Those upon your bodies: sickness, aches, pains, weaknesses. Those upon your souls: fears, heart-breakings, terrors, horrors."[18] To the sinner listening in the Puritan pew, the true, loathsome nature of sin was exposed for what it was, and its temptations were never glossed over or minimized. Instead, they were instructed, "Pleasures are the baits which cover sin and make it swallowed down with eagerness."[19] More than anything, the discussion of sin was intended to pierce the sinner's heart and reveal man's overwhelming need and desperate plight. First, though, the ground must be thoroughly plowed up in order to bring in the harvest.

For all of the stereotypical talk of Puritans as cold and emotionless, the reality of the Puritan pulpit was the very opposite: the preaching of the word of God was intended to convey both heat and light.[20] Nathaniel Vincent, the brother of Thomas Vincent and another witness to the calamities of London, passionately implored, "The Lord pleads with the ungodly by the ministry of the Word after this manner: 'What! Though you are told of sin's deceitful, defiling, and damnable nature, will you still embrace and hold it fast to My dishonor and your own destruction?'"[21] And Joseph Alleine, whose *A Sure Guide to Heaven* set generations to trembling, wrote with equal fire and directness,

> Hear then, O sinners, hear as you would live. Why should you wilfully [sic] deceive yourselves, or build your hopes upon the sand? I

17. Ibid., 157.
18. Bolton, "Sin: The Greatest Evil," 14.
19. Vincent, "Conversion of a Sinner," 88.
20. Bickel, *Light and Heat*.
21. Vincent, "Conversion of a Sinner," 103.

know that he will find hard work that goes to pluck away your hopes. It cannot but be unpleasant to you, and truly it is not pleasing to me. I set about it as a surgeon when about to cut off a mortified limb from his beloved friend, which of necessity he must do, though with an aching heart.[22]

Albert Martin, in the preface to *The Puritans on Conversion*, writes, "While Joseph Alleine's book *Alarm to the Unconverted*, and Richard Baxter's *Call to the Unconverted* have gone through numerous reprints in the last few decades, [they] have become a model of Puritan preaching on the doctrine of conversion...."[23] In this way, Vincent and Alleine do not so much represent exceptions, but the rule.

As such, the sight of sin, for all of its horrors, is only preparatory. The Scottish Puritan William Guthrie serves as a further illustration of this viewpoint; his work *The Christian's Great Interest* was influential, to the degree that John Owen averred, "That author I take to have been one of the greatest divines that ever wrote; it is my *Vade-mecum*, and I carry it and the Sedan New Testament, still about with me."[24] Guthrie wrote, in explaining why one would preach forcefully about sin, that

> The most ordinary way by which many are brought to Christ, is by a clear and discernable work of the law, and humiliation; which we generally call *the spirit of bondage*.... We do not mean that every one, whose conscience is awakened with sin and fear of wrath, does really close with Christ.... But there is a conviction of sin, an awakening of conscience, and work of humiliation, which, as we shall point out, rarely miscarries.[25]

Once again, we are here confronted with a concept largely foreign to our age. As G. A. Hemming comments, "The Puritans seldom concerned themselves with the moment, real or imagined, of a man's turning to God; they were much more concerned with a man's present state.... they resolutely refused to offer any comfort unless they were convinced that a real sense of sin was present."[26] He goes on:

---

22. Alleine, *Sure Guide to Heaven*, 23.
23. Martin, *Puritans on Conversion*, iv.
24. Guthrie, *Christian's Great Interest*, 18.
25. Ibid., 43.
26. Hemming, "Puritans' Dealings," 1:32.

> Thus "the conscience is not to be healed if it be not wounded. Thou preachest and pressest the law, comminations, the judgment to come, and that with much earnestness and importunity. He which hears, if he be not terrified, if he be not troubled, is not to be comforted. Another hears, is stirred, is stung, takes on extremely; cure his contritions, because he is cast down and confounded in himself." Or again, says Perkins, "First of all a man must have knowledge of four things, of the law of God, of sin against the law, of the guilt of sin, and of the judgment of God against sin, which is eternal wrath."[27]

In this way, "All the Puritans agreed that the way by which God brings sinners to faith is through a 'preparatory work,' longer or shorter, of contrition and humbling for sin."[28] As has been suggested, this is the backdrop against which the impetus for self-examination is discovered, and importantly, it must be understood that this was not a process to be rushed; better to be thorough than wrong.

It would be difficult to overstate the frequency or forcefulness with which Puritan pastors spoke about sin from their pulpits. Obadiah Sedgwick, who preached often on fast days before Parliament and before the assembly at Westminster, proclaimed:

> Brethren, how many are there who apparel themselves in the secret thoughts of abhorred wickedness, but even in the secret actings of the same, as if there were not God to look on them, nor conscience to spy on them, nor judgment day to arraign them! Oh, how infinitely odious you must be in the eyes of that holy God, who dare to court him in public, and yet dare to provoke Him to His face thus in private.[29]

True and False Conversion

Having seen the heinous nature of sin, the Puritans would urge their auditors to correspondingly consider carefully its potential to deceive. Judas was one of Christ's twelve disciples. He ate with Jesus every day, sat under his teaching for three years, and carried the disciples' bankroll. For all intents and purposes, he looked like a genuine and perhaps exemplary believer. He had left his home, as had the other disciples, and followed Jesus. Ostensibly,

---

27. Ibid.

28. Packer, "Puritan View of Preaching," 1:267.

29. Sedgwick, *Anatomy of Secret Sins*, 25. This work was last reprinted in 1818. For a brief life of Sedgwick, who lived from 1600–1658, see Barker, *Puritan Profiles*, 130–32.

he had sacrificed, and labored, and served. In the end, though, for all of the apparent genuineness of his conversion, he proved himself to be a traitor. The Puritans would assert that if Judas could fall into condemnation, a man with so many evident privileges and so many outward signs of faith—likely more privileges and outward signs than we enjoy—should we not then make very certain of our eternal state? Are we like that good soil in which the seed of the gospel might spring up and grow? Or will instead the sun burn up the seed of the gospel that springs up on hard soil, or will it be choked out as on thorny soil? Using a similar example, "If this parable [the parable of the wise and foolish virgins] proves one thing for Thomas Shephard, it is the reality and importance of one problem—the existence of the gospel hypocrite. . . . We must recognize how real, constant, and universal is the danger of self deception as to one's spiritual state."[30]

This was thereby a theme requiring the most sober and thoughtful reflection possible, given that a "false professor" might not even recognize his soul's jeopardy. "Many" would say on that great day of judgment to come, "Lord, Lord," as Jesus explained in the sermon on the mount, to whom he would respond, *"I never knew you*: depart from me, ye that work iniquity" (see Matt 7:21–23; emphasis added). The Puritans therefore implored their hearers to exert all possible effort in order to determine with certainty their eternal state and be reconciled to God. Thomas Watson, one of the most well known of the English Puritans and among the so-called ejected ministers of 1662,[31] pressed his hearers, in the words of the Apostle Paul, to "work out their own salvation." He urged,

> Salvation is a beautiful thing. It is far above our thoughts as it is above our desserts. Oh, how should this add wings to our endeavors! The merchant will run through the intemperate zones of heat and cold for a little prize. The soldier, for a rich booty, will endure the bullet and the sword. He will gladly undergo a bloody spring for a golden harvest. Oh, then, how much more should we spend our holy sweat for this blessed prize of salvation![32]

---

30. Johnston, "Thomas Shepard's 'Parable,'" 1:122, 127.

31. On August 24th of 1662, St. Bartholemew's Day, the Act of Uniformity was set in force, which required the use of the Book of Common Prayers in all Christian services, and "unfeigned" subscription to it by all ministers. In the wake of this, nearly 2,000 ministers resigned for conscience sake rather than comply, representing roughly one-fifth of all ordained clergy in England.

32. Watson, "One Thing Necessary," 202.

This required all diligence, indeed, holy *violence*, in the language of the King James of Matthew 11:12, whereby the kingdom of heaven is taken by force.[33]

It would be easy to conclude given the strenuous labor to which the Puritans called the church, that salvation was to be found in such effort, but Watson provided the appropriate balance: "Though we are not saved without working, yet we are not saved for our working."[34] He added, "If we could pray as angels, shed rivers of tears, build churches, erect hospitals, and should have a conceit that we merited anything by this, it would be as a dead fly in the box of perfume."[35] Self-examination's purpose for the earnest seeker is not then aimed at looking for the *means* of salvation, but for *evidence* of salvation, and in particular, seeking to determine that one's conversion was genuine against all who would be found imposters. The foundational element for the quivering listener in the Puritan pew who was called to practice self-examination was obedience—only pure, unfeigned, heart obedience would produce peace: "we trust that we have a good conscience, desiring to conduct ourselves well in all things. Our glorifying is the testimony of our conscience. . . . By which we shall assure our hearts."[36]

This was therefore the ultimate goal of self-examination, to scrutinize one's life in an effort to find the fruits of faith, because with genuine conversion "There always follows from this confirmation of soul a zeal for holiness."[37] Correspondingly, then, the "assurance of salvation is not, properly speaking, justifying faith but a fruit of such faith."[38] The Reformation's emphasis on justification by faith was maintained, but obedience to the commandments of God was the primary means by which the sincerity of one's faith was demonstrated. In sum, for the Puritans, true Christian faith "only becomes well-grounded when it evidences fruits, such as love to God and for His kingdom, filial obedience, godly repentance, hatred for sin, brotherly love, and humble adoration."[39]

Self-examination, with the result of godly living, was thereby a common and longstanding emphasis in Puritan preaching and writing. It was a

---

33. Consider, for example, Watson, *Heaven Taken by Storm*. Watson died in 1686.
34. Watson, "One Thing Necessary," 192.
35. Ibid., 209.
36. Ames, *Marrow of Theology*, 224.
37. Ibid., 248.
38. Ibid., 167.
39. Beeke, *Puritan Reformed Spirituality*, 297.

practice that became a way of life, as pastors oversaw the souls of their congregations. Such teachings were passed down from generation to generation. As one such source, consider how "For a century and a half, William Ames's *Marrow of Theology* held sway as a clear, persuasive expression of Puritan belief and practice."[40] Ames had warned that "Repentance is not true and sound when it does not turn a man from all known sin to all known good, or when it does not continue in strength and actually renew itself continually from the time of conversion to the end of life."[41] Ames's *Marrow of Theology* went through numerous editions, and many of the Puritans echoed his convictions on this point, warning that "If you are a professor but not a practicer of religion, consider, 'tis not a feigned conversion, but a turning with the whole heart upon which life is promised and assured."[42] So many pitfalls endangered the trembling soul. Ames sets forth the predicament:

> First, the feeling of persuasion is not always present. It may and often does happen, either through weakness of judgment or various temptations and troubles of mind, that a person who truly believes and is by faith justified before God may for a time think that he neither believes nor is reconciled to God. Second, there are many degrees in this persuasion. Believers obviously do not have the same assurance of grace and favor of God, nor do the same ones have it at all times.[43]

At this point, Ames anticipates themes that found their way into the Westminster Confession, as well as the Larger and Shorter Catechism.[44] Arguably, the most concise distillation of the Puritan understanding of assurance and self-examination may be discovered in the Westminster Confession. In chapter 18, we read:

> 1. Although hypocrites and other unregenerate men may vainly deceive themselves with false hopes, and carnal presumptions of being in the favour of God, and estate of salvation; which hope of theirs

---

40. Ames, *Marrow of Theology*, 1. See also Brook, *Lives of the Puritans*, 2:405–8.
41. Ames, *Marrow of Theology*, 160.
42. Vincent, "Conversion of a Sinner," 76.
43. Ames, *Marrow of Theology*, 163.
44. The Shorter Catechism touches only incidentally on assurance, principally in question and answer 36: "What are the benefits which in this life do accompany or flow from justification, adoption, and sanctification? A The benefits which in this life do accompany or flow from justification, adoption, and sanctification, are, assurance of God's love, peace of conscience, joy in the Holy Ghost, increase of grace, and perseverance therein to the end."

> shall perish: yet such as truly believe in the Lord Jesus, and love Him in sincerity, endeavouring to walk in all good conscience before Him, may, in this life, be certainly assured that they are in the state of grace, and may rejoice in the hope of the glory of God, which hope shall never make them ashamed.
>
> 2. This certainty is not a bare conjectural and probable persuasion grounded upon a fallible hope; but an infallible assurance of faith, founded upon the divine truth of the promises of salvation, the inward evidence of those graces unto which these promises are made, the testimony of the Spirit of adoption witnessing with our spirits that we are the children of God: which Spirit is the earnest of our inheritance, whereby we are sealed to the day of redemption.[45]

Assurance does not rise, then, from "bare conjectural and probable persuasion"; rather, "inward evidence" is required. And, the Larger Catechism states:

> Q. 80. Can true believers be infallibly assured that they are in the estate of grace, and that they shall persevere therein unto salvation?
>
> A. Such as truly believe in Christ, and endeavour to walk in all good conscience before him, may, without extraordinary revelation, by faith grounded upon the truth of God's promises, and by the Spirit enabling them to discern in themselves those graces to which the promises of life are made, and bearing witness with their spirits that they are the children of God, be infallibly assured that they are in the estate of grace, and shall persevere therein unto salvation.
>
> Q. 81. Are all true believers at all times assured of their present being in the estate of grace, and that they shall be saved?
>
> A. Assurance of grace and salvation not being of the essence of faith, true believers *may wait long before they obtain it; and, after the enjoyment thereof, may have it weakened and intermitted*, through manifold distempers, sins, temptations, and desertions; yet they are never left without such a presence and support of the Spirit of God as keeps them from sinking into utter despair.[46]

The influence of the Confession and the Larger and Shorter Catechism should not be underestimated. Given that the aim of these documents was to teach Scriptural doctrine, their guidance was authoritative.

In this context, it is appropriate to avoid the exhaustingly detailed lists of internal evidences and steps that various Puritan authors suggested were

---

45. See *Westminster Confession*, 75–77.
46. Ibid., 171–72; emphasis added.

needed in order to make certain of one's salvation. But tests of assurance, it must be stated, were produced, and a consideration of a more manageable and arguably more balanced view would be worthwhile. Nathaniel Vincent (1639–97) was one of the so-called ejected ministers of 1662, "but returned to London after the fire of 1666 and preached to large multitudes in the ruins of the city. He spent many years in prison and under persecution for his nonconformity."[47] His description of conversion and its fruits appear comparatively more clear and concise than those of other Puritan authors. Vincent explained, "we gather that conversion lies in four things:

1. In being turned from darkness;
2. In being turned unto light;
3. In being turned from the power of Satan;
4. In being turned unto God."[48]

Correspondingly, there are five signs whereby individuals may rightly gauge the veracity of their conversion:

1. In true conversion the heart is turned from the love of every known iniquity.
2. In true conversion, there is a renewing of the whole man.
3. In true conversion, there is a desire to be turned more and more.
4. In true conversion, there is a pure and fervent love to converts.
5. In true conversion, there is a pity toward the unconverted.[49]

Similarly, Robert Bolton suggests that every human being will need to "know what shall betide them after this life; if any be desirous to know even the secrets of God, I mean his determination as touching themselves, their wives, their children, friends, or foes after death. . . ."[50] And he adds, as a further point of caution, "every Christian ought to endeavor after holiness, that thereby he may prove himself to be truly engrafted into Christ."[51]

---

47. See Kistler, *Puritans on Conversion*. Information on Vincent is taken from the scant information on the book's jacket—there is little biographical information available on Vincent's life.

48. Vincent, "Conversion of a Sinner," 116–17.

49. Ibid., 136–38. Note that these characteristics each have explanatory text that has been omitted here.

50. Bolton, *Carnal Professor*, 11.

51. Ibid., 10.

The Necessity of Self-Examination

The effects of sin, and its potential for deceit, are thereby profound:

> "Good Lord, deliver me from myself," said Augustine. You had better be given up to the lusts of men, to the malice and cruelties of bloodthirsty men; better to be given up to the utmost rage and malice of our bloody Irish rebels than to be delivered up to yourselves, to the lusts of your own hearts. Nay, you had better to be given up to Satan than to be given up to yourselves, your sins.[52]

One could be wrong about a great many doctrinal issues, and the consequences would range from nearly inconsequential to severe. But the Puritans rightly recognized that a right or wrong determination about salvation was a matter—indeed, it was *the* matter—wherein error would have the most profound consequences imaginable. If heaven and hell are real, and they represent the only possible *eternal* states, all other determinations pale by comparison. An immediate, pressing response was warranted: "Behold, now is the favorable time; behold now is the day of salvation" (2 Cor 6:2, ESV).

Salvation is thereby of necessity the touchstone of all Christian life, and no small preoccupation. And the concern for the Puritans, of course, was less with the potential consequences—indeed, rewards—of heaven, than around the potential consequences of hell. The believer was in no jeopardy. It is no surprise, then, that self-examination was a theme often pressed forcefully upon Puritan congregations, over whom those who preached viewed themselves to be responsible as the shepherds of their people's souls. Puritan ministers spoke often of the parable of the lost sheep, and of how it was that the shepherd would seek out that lost sheep. The Puritan pastor was in this way, week by week, probing his congregation: "where possible, able and experienced ministers were to help their congregations in the work of self-examination by giving what are called 'notes of trial,' that is, tests based on the teaching of Scripture, by means of which the people could try themselves, and judge their spiritual state and Christian progress."[53]

Given the reality of the terrors of hell, they pulled no punches: "Be ashamed, you who spend so much time in reading of romances, in adorning your persons, in hawking and hunting, in consulting the law concerning your outward state in the world, and it may be in worse things than these

---

52. Bolton, "Sin: The Greatest Evil," 20–21.
53. Caiger, "Preaching—Puritan and Reformed," 2:170.

... Be ashamed, you that spend so little time in search of this, whether ye be an heir of glory or not?"[54] John Owen, considered by some to be the father of the Puritans, asks,

> What do men come to hear the Word of God for? What do they pray for? What do they expect to receive from him? Do they come unto God as the eternal fountain of living waters? As the God of all grace, peace and consolation? Or do they come unto his worship without any design as unto a dry and empty show? ... Or do they think they bring something unto God, but receive nothing from him? ... To receive anything from him they expect not, nor do ever examine themselves whether they have done so or no? ... It is not for persons who walk in such ways, ever to attain a due delight in the ordinances of divine worship.[55]

How could one fail to feel the weight of such concerns, especially given the frequency with which the subject of self-examination was pressed? "The most characteristic feature," J. I. Packer writes, "in the Puritan ideal of preaching was the great stress laid on the need for searching applications of truth to the hearers' consciences. One mark of a 'spiritual,' 'powerful' preacher, in the Puritan estimation, was the closeness and faithfulness of application whereby he would 'rip up' men's consciences and make them face themselves as God saw them."[56]

As such, as has been observed, self-examination serves two fundamental purposes. On the one hand, for the believer, self-examination is a means of Christian sanctification, whereby one grows increasingly sensitive to sin in all its forms, and seeks out new occasions for obedience. With regular frequency, in many sermons, however, attention is given to the unbeliever, or to the individual unsure of their eternal destiny: "Hast thou not a God and a Christ to think of? And is not salvation by him, and everlasting glory, worthy of your choicest thoughts? You have thoughts enough and to spare for other things—for base things, for very toys—and why not for God and the word of God."[57] Vincent urged, "Since God calls upon sinners again and again to turn, it highly concerns all to examine whether this call has been obeyed!"[58] A response is demanded: "If sin is the greatest evil, then it calls out:

---

54. Guthrie, as cited by Mingard, "William Guthrie on the Trial," 1:204.
55. Packer, *Puritan Papers*, 3:13–14.
56. Packer, "Puritan Conscience," 2:250.
57. Manton, *Works of Thomas Manton*, 7:480.
58. Vincent, "Conversion of a Sinner," 133.

1. for the greatest sorrow
2. for the greatest hatred
3. for the greatest care to avoid it
4. for the greatest care to get rid of it."[59]

A trial marked by intense, soul-searing reflection is often thereby spoken of as a common experience. The effect of the word preached was to prepare the soil, to break up and plant, that growth might follow. Pain sometimes comes so that healing might begin. Goodwin asserts, "triumphing assurance, Rom 8:37, 39 . . . comes after a trial, as none are crowned till they have striven."[60] The clouds may well nigh be broken through, and at long last God himself might be known. As William Guthrie explains,

> A man may clearly know, if from known distress in himself, upon the report and fame of Christ's fulness, his heart is pleased with God's device in the new covenant; if it goeth after Christ in that discovery and approacheth Him as Lord of the life of men, terminating and resting there, and nowhere else, acquiescing in that contrivance with desire and complacency. This is a discernible thing; therefore I call upon men impartially to examine themselves, and if they find that their heart has closed so with that device of salvation, and is gone out after Him as precious, that thereupon they conclude a sure and true interest in Jesus Christ, and a good claim and title to the crown, since "he that believeth shall never perish, but have everlasting life."[61]

What Guthrie calls here "a sure and true interest in Jesus Christ" must be the preoccupation of the unbeliever until new birth has at last come. In order to be confident about this transformation, a clear, honest, and genuine view of one's self was warranted. Bolton agreed: "If therefore thou are desirous to know in particular, whosoever art in this present assembly, whether thou be carnal or not, enquire of the word of God, what thou art by nature in all the parts of soul and body, how unapt and incapable of all holiness, how prone and disposed unto all manner of wickedness. . . ."[62]

By this point, it should be clear how high the pressure could be in Puritan congregations, as they were urged to repent, and to match up their lives and experiences with others who were true believers. Horton Davies

59. Bolton, "Sin: The Greatest Evil," 35.
60. Goodwin, *Works*, 8:346.
61. Guthrie, *Christian's Great Interest*, 72.
62. Bolton, *Carnal Professor*, 57.

details how this process of discerning genuine faith in one's life often unfolded.[63] Davies points out how much of the doctrinal material that was written (and which was usually based on sermons) was sometimes supplemented by conversion narratives detailing the experiences of believing congregants. In this way, the inquirer was able to weigh his life, and potentially pattern his or her experience, after that of others who had wrestled with spiritual matters themselves. In describing these most revealing conversion experiences, Davies writes,

> Unlike Saul's dramatic conversion on the road to Damascus, these conversions were the result of an extensive period of agonizing introspection, and of considerable doubts and fears that any sense of assurance was prompted only by hypocrisy. Recurring temptations followed by renewed repentance and debilitating uncertainty marked the preparatory path to salvation, always leaving the soul afraid of unworthiness and frequently seesawing between fear and hope. Brother Crackbone's wife, for example, reported: "and so [I] thought of seeking after the ordinances, but I knew not whether I was fit. Yet heard I was under the wings of Christ, one of them, yet not under both."[64]

It seems important to observe in this light how difficult a concept this notion of rigorous self-examination must be for many in our own congregations to grasp in our day, at a time when the more typical pulpit will not emphasize sinfulness, but rather encourage abounding self-esteem. But a thoroughgoing consideration of sin, an honest assessment of whether or not one was a true or false professor of Christ, had one objective: to lay bare the soul, and prepare it to see Christ as man's only hope.

The Only Cure: Casting One's Self on Christ

Puritan speech in preaching was consciously intended to be plain. No fine oratory or scholarly erudition was to be on display. Rather, clarity and ease of access to all hearers was held in far greater esteem. When it came to thoughts of Christ, though, here the Puritans grew most nearly rhapsodic. Having let the law do its work, then and only then, grace as found only in Christ might be known: "If sin is the greatest evil, then see the utter impossibility

---

63. Davies, *Worship of the American Puritans*, 28–36.
64. Ibid., 30. Davies is here citing Selement and Woolley eds., *Thomas Shepard's Confessions*, 7:140.

of anything under heaven to relieve and help us from under the guilt of sin save Jesus Christ alone. Have you committed but one sin? You have done that which all the treasures of righteousness in heaven and earth are not able to relieve or help you in save JESUS CHRIST."[65] Thomas Doolittle, who taught much about the dangers of sin, after allowing his hearers much travail, set forth Christ:

> Clearly understand, and be thoroughly convinced of thy lost estate, and miserable condition, for conviction, sight, and sense of sin, and of our lost estate thereby, usually go before the setting of the heart and love upon Jesus Christ; though God doth not deal with all sinners, in all circumstances, alike, in working and begetting in them consent and love unto his Son.[66]

Goodwin added in a similar vein,

> Now, of all miseries, sin is the greatest; and whilst you yourselves look at it as such, Christ will look upon it as such only also in you. And he loving your persons, and hating only the sin, his hatred shall all fall, and that only upon the sin, to free you of it by its ruin and destruction; but his compassion shall be the more drawn out to you, and this as much when you lie under sin, as under any other affliction. Therefore, fear not: "What shall separate us from Christ's love?"[67]

To the Puritans, this was no ancillary doctrine. Setting forth Christ was the aim of every sermon, the only means by which sin could be overcome and paradise restored. In the same way that a jeweler sets a diamond against a black velvet backdrop so that it might be best seen and appreciated, a thorough consideration of sin was not to end there, but instead served to present Christ, the sinner's friend, with greater luster. Fenner observed,

> We must use the assurance of faith in applying the blood of Christ; we must labour to purge and cleanse our consciences with it. If we find that we have sinned, we must runne presently (i.e., at once) to the blood of Christ to wash away our sinne. We must not let the wound fester or exulcerate, but presently get it healed.... As we sinne dayly, so he justifieth dayly, and we must dayly go to him for it.... We must every day eye the brazen serpent.... Let us not sleep one night without a new pardon. Better sleep in a house full of adders and venemous

---

65. Bolton, "Sin: The Greatest Evil," 26; emphasis original.

66. Doolittle, *Love to Christ*, 184.

67. Goodwin, *Christ Set Forth*, 323. Goodwin's work is bound with Bolton's *Carnal Professor* in this edition.

beasts than sleep in one sinne. O then be sure with the day to clear the sinnes of the day: Then shall our consciences have true peace.[68]

Thomas Vincent, who, as we have seen, wrote with true vitriol about and against sin, was also one of the great Puritan spokesmen for the glories of Christ. In *The True Christian's Love to the Unseen Christ*, a treatise produced for those who were genuinely converted and should be warmly comforted in the assurance of the Spirit of God, Vincent wrote,

> Whatever beauty and loveliness there is to be found in any, or in all visible creatures, there is infinitely more beauty and loveliness in Jesus Christ. All visible beauty is but a shadow; in Christ there is substantial beauty. All visible beauty is like the flower that soon withers, like the leaf that soon fades, but in Christ there is permanent beauty. All visible beauty is inferior and mean, yea, deformity, compared with Christ's transcendent loveliness. There is no discovery to the eye of the mind comparable unto the eye of faith.[69]

In this way, having seen the terrors of the law, and having been shaken by the reality of one's true condition, Christ would be better understood and more highly prized. The aim of extensive preaching about sin, judgment, hell, and the call to self-examination was not to end there. Rather, when one has come to an end of all self-regard, Christ alone might be esteemed: "Lord Jesus Christ! O blessed Lord! O sweetest Jesus! O loving lovely Christ! Lord Jesus Christ! Methinks the sound of his name is melody to mine ears, is honey to my taste, is light unto mine eyes, a sweet perfume of precious ointment; it is balm to my sinking spirit, to my fainting soul."[70]

If it can be said of the Puritans that they both understood and described in lurid detail the reality of sin, it must also be affirmed that they understood Christ, and sought with all their energies to esteem him aright, bounded by the capacities of human language. John Owen's *The Glory of Christ* is in this way representative of the Puritans in their finest hour.[71] Owen writes, "if we desire strong faith and powerful love, which give us rest, peace and satisfaction, we must seek them by diligently beholding the glory of Christ by faith."[72] The Scriptures are fully brimming over with his glory:

68. Packer, *Puritan Papers*, 2:248.
69. Vincent, *True Christian's Love*, 126–27.
70. Doolittle, *Love to Christ*, 184.
71. Owen, *Glory of Christ*. Note that this edition is an abridgement by R. J. K. Law.
72. Ibid., 7.

> The glory of Christ under the Old Testament is revealed under many metaphorical expressions. So Christ is called the rose, for the sweet perfume of his love, grace and obedience. He is called the lily for the beauty of his grace and love. In the New Testament he is called the pearl of great price because he is precious to believers. He is called the vine for his fruitfulness. He is called the lamb for his meekness and fitness for his sacrifice.[73]

In this way, Christ was set before the believer as all-satisfying. Samuel Rutherford, who like Owen, was representative of Puritanism at its best, remarked,

> I am in as sweet communion with Christ as a poor sinner can be; and I am only pained that He hath much beauty and fairness and I little love; He great power and mercy, and I little faith; He much light, and I bleared eyes. O that I saw Him in the sweetness of his love, and in His marriage clothes, and were over head and ears in love with that princely one, Christ Jesus my Lord![74]

Summary of the Puritan Approach to Self-Examination

For the Puritans, human language was incapable of adequately conveying either the judgment of God against sin or the glory of God in Christ. But it is evident why some have been concerned that these two truths were not always set in adequate tension. Thomas Vincent writes,

> Oh, what a vast number of all kindreds, nations, and languages will there be tormented in hell forever! What a vast number of professing Christians, yea, of professors of the gospel!... Most men and women who live this day upon the face of the earth are in danger of being thrown into the flames of hell. The whole world may be divided into two parts: they are either those who are in a state of nature or those who are in a state of grace. The former are *many thousands of times greater in number*....[75]

One can appreciate the impulse to protect the Puritans from being maligned any further, given that so many misconceptions about their beliefs and practices have been propounded that their legacy is forever distorted.

But perhaps Joel Beeke is wrong when he asserts, "People who accuse the Puritans and Second Reformation divines of morbid introspection and

---

73. Ibid., 73.
74. Rutherford, *Letters of Samuel Rutherford*, 258.
75. Vincent, *Fire and Brimstone*, 122–23; emphasis added.

anthropocentrism have simply missed the mark."[76] On occasion, at least, the real effect of the constant call to self-examination in many Puritan congregations was a lack of assurance that often persisted to the grave. The evidence of the Spirit's sure work, rather than a consistent source of peace and confidence, was instead often discerned by means of tediously enumerated points, and in some quarters, missing one of these fine points of detail was tantamount to establishing the likelihood of perdition. This was no minor failing; one must hear with great sympathy this account:

> They gave the impression (despite parenthetical disclaimers) that God's work of humbling men for sin invariably followed the same course, in every detail of the process, and if you had not experienced it all you must be a stranger to true grace. In his teens, Richard Baxter went through much fear and distress, because, examine himself as he might, "I could not distinctly trace the Workings of the Spirit upon my heart in that method which . . . *Mr. Hooker, Mr. Rogers*, and other Divines describe."[77]

J. I. Packer has in this way observed, "by concentrating attention on this preliminary work of grace, and harping on the need for it to be done thoroughly, these writers effectively discouraged seeking souls from going straight to Christ in their despair."[78]

Perhaps Robert Bolton is illustrative of this seemingly morbid emphasis: "Brethren, think of this, the more vile any man is in his own eyes, the more precious he is in God's. And the best way to bring a man to a base esteem of himself, is to turn his thoughts seriously upon his own estate, to view himself in his natural condition. . . ."[79] But Bolton was greatly esteemed among the Puritans, and it was said of him, "Mr. Bolton has been a notorious sinner, and having been reclaimed by great terrors, his writings are excellent both for conviction and consolation."[80] Under a steady stream of such preaching, then, one might nearly despair: "'If you that are now converted had lived in our younger days,' wrote Goodwin in later life, 'you would have seen that we were held long under John Baptist's water, of being humbled for sin.' This

---

76. Beeke, *Puritan Reformed Spirituality*, 295.

77. Packer, "Puritan View of Preaching," 1:267; emphasis original.

78. Packer, *Quest for Godliness*, 172. It must be noted here that Packer is not characterizing all Puritans as teaching doctrine that produced this effect. He here has in view specifically John Rogers, Thomas Hooker, and Thomas Shepard.

79. Bolton, *Carnal Professor*, 48.

80. Brook, *Lives of the Puritans*, 2:394.

naturally led to much morbidity."[81] Thomas Brooks, notably warm-hearted among the Puritans, suggests,

> Again, God delays the giving in of assurance, not because he delights to keep his children in fears and doubts, nor because he thinks that assurance is too rare, too great, too choice a jewel to bestow upon them; but it is either because he thinks their souls do not stand at a sufficient distance from sin, or because their souls are so taken up and filled with creature enjoyments as that Christ is put to lodge in an out-house, or else it is because they pursue not after assurance with all their might; they give not all diligence to make their calling and election sure; or else it is because their hearts are not prepared, are not low enough, for so high a favour.[82]

Indeed, one cannot help but wonder how anyone obtained assurance, how anyone concluded they were true professors, how anyone found at the end of their self-examination cause for celebration, were it not for the fact that, as has been observed, all of this was intended to convey to the soul one's absolute need for Christ.

Given this, it would be easy to conclude that such Puritan preaching, with its relentless return to the practice of self-examination, is best left with the moth-tattered pages of their exanimate manuscripts. If the end result is a faith void of any assurance, of what value is it? It would appear in this light that the Puritans were in fact guilty of the bad theology that produced faith lacking assurance. Such consideration is only partial, though. It should be observed that it is far worse to allow a congregation to have *false* assurance than to have *little* assurance. But this was by no means the ultimate Puritan aim either. William Gurnall averred, "It is not the least of a minister's care and skill in dividing the word, so to press the Christian's duty, as not to oppress his spirit with the weight of it, by laying it on the creature's shoulders, and not on the Lord's strength."[83] If all of the consideration of sin, and of the nature of true and false conversion, and all of the conviction regarding the necessity of self-examination does not result in casting oneself on Christ, it is all for naught. But if Christ is better seen by such labor, if his work is more rightly prized, if his sacrifice is more highly regarded, then and only then, genuine, soul-satisfying assurance may rise to view.

81. Packer, *Quest for Godliness*, 172.
82. Brooks, *Heaven on Earth*, 48.
83. Gurnall as quoted by Caiger, "Preaching—Puritan and Reformed," 2:180.

Too often undervalued, perhaps, was a corollary responsibility for the minister; in addition to urging one's congregants toward self-examination was the responsibility to bring comfort: "In consolation, indications are profitably given to a man's conscience to assure him that he shares the benefits with which the minister comforts the conscience of believers. Thoughts to the contrary, which may arise in a pious and troubled mind, are dispelled and refuted."[84] O. R. Johnston suggests, "We must preserve the balance of scriptural truth in teaching on this subject. Too much emphasis on self-scrutiny reflects a morbid depression in ourselves (as it did in Shepard, who was notoriously melancholic) and induces a similar depression in those we instruct. Morbid introspection is sin, and has nothing to do with scriptural self-examination."[85] A balance must be sought out, given the importance of this issue now, and surely then—"In one sense, assurance was the most crucial issue of the post-Reformation."[86]

Humans are prone to error. Even still, the Puritan emphasis on self-examination is now a notion that has virtually completely fallen out of view in Christendom. It could well be argued that few contemporary Christians would even understand the concept. Packer explains:

> It may be asked, Does not this stress on the searching of conscience produce a morbid and introspective type of piety? Does not this emphasis on constant self-suspicion and self-examination actually weaken faith, by diverting our gaze from Christ in His fullness to ourselves in our emptiness, so leading us to spiritual despondency and depression? No doubt it would if it were made an end in itself; but of course, it never was. The Puritans ripped up consciences in the pulpit and urged self-trial in the closet only in order to drive sinners to Christ and to teach them to live by faith in Him. . . . Morbidity and introspectiveness, the gloomy self-absorption of the man who can never look away from himself, is bad Puritanism; the Puritans themselves condemned it repeatedly.[87]

Thomas Goodwin, the independent Congregational Puritan, noted among "five dissenting brethren" against the Presbyterian majority in the Westminster Assembly,[88] describes assurance as effecting nothing less than a metamor-

---

84. Ames, *Marrow of Theology*, 194.
85. Johnston, "Thomas Shepard's 'Parable,'" 1:127.
86. Beeke, *Puritan Reformed Spirituality*, 295.
87. Packer, "Puritan Conscience," 2:252.
88. Barker, *Puritan Profiles*, 70.

phosis in the believer: "'It is a new conversion,' says Goodwin; 'it will make a man differ from himself in what he was before in that manner almost as conversion doth before he was converted. There is a new edition of all a man's graces.'"[89] True Christians inarguably struggle at times to find this assurance. Jeremiah Burroughs remarked, "I remember . . . that Luther had a speech concerning trouble of conscience for sin in his commentary upon Genesis. 'It is a harder matter to comfort an afflicted conscience for sin than to raise one from the dead.'"[90] And Obadiah Sedgwick observed, "There is none had faith, but has found his doubtings. Did you ever see a fire without smoke? Smoke is no part of the fire, yet it streams from that fuel to which fire is put; so it is with faith and doubtings."[91]

One might contend that the Puritans were too extreme in their characterizations of the heinous nature of sin, or in their advocacy of self-examination. On the other hand, and at the other extreme, Zane Hodges now teaches that one can enjoy a conversion that entails "no spiritual commitment whatsoever."[92] To the Puritan mind, in light of the consequences at stake—one's eternal destiny in heaven or hell set in the balance—such a notion might have seemed tantamount to eternal murder. They would have asked, what might the Apostle Paul have meant when he said, "work out your own salvation with fear and trembling" (Phil 2:12)?

Consider that much of the information presented in this review of the Puritans and self-examination derives from individual sermons and collections of sermons, and it is easy to discern how pivotal such admonitions were to worship itself. In the immediacy of the preaching moment, self-examination was routinely expounded from the pulpit upon the congregation, but more, it was intended to produce a life of ongoing reflection in the individual's private devotional life.

Edwards on Self-Examination

As will be seen, while Edwards avoids some of the excesses of the more extreme practices employed by the Puritans, he was decidedly cut from the same bolt of cloth, and in some ways elevated the practice of self-examination to an art

89. Goodwin as quoted by Packer, *Quest for Godliness*, 75.
90. Burroughs, *Evil of Evils*, 228.
91. Sedgwick, *Doubting Believer*, 9.
92. Hodges, *Gospel under Siege*, 14.

form.[93] The practice would have been embedded from his earliest recollections, a part of his DNA, in his bloodstream, a part of the way things were done, as unquestioned as breathing. In 1687, years before Edwards's birth, his grandfather Solomon Stoddard taught at length about the necessity of self-examination: "To put you upon the examination whether you put your trust in the righteousness of Christ."[94] He urged his readers "strictly to examine" their belief by various means: "There is a preparatory work necessary before a sinner's closing with Christ. This is a work that comes between the rest of the soul in sin and the sinner's accepting of Christ."[95] For more than fifty pages, Stoddard explores true and false professions of faith, as expressed by genuine converts and "hypocrites," warns the unbelieving, and dispels the doubts of true believers.

When Edwards was twelve years old, in a letter to his sister Mary he spoke of "the wonderful mercy and goodness of God," which had produced a "very remarkable stirring and pouring out of the spirit of God."[96] By virtue of this work of God, he noted that "About thirteen have been joined to the church in an estate of full communion." Interestingly, Edwards adds, "I think there comes commonly a-Mondays above thirty persons to speak with father about the condition of their souls." Thirteen were recently counted as genuine converts—but thirty came to his father Timothy Edwards for counsel on a weekly basis respecting the "condition of their souls." Concern for one's spiritual well-being and self-examination, then, is a part of Edwards's earliest recollections and immediate heritage, and conversion did not result in an end to spiritual introspection.

It would be difficult to overstate how fervently Edwards himself practiced the discipline of self-examination. Consider, as an obvious starting point, a few of his celebrated resolutions, penned largely during his late teen years. In resolution 9 Edwards writes, "Resolved, to think much on all occasions of my own dying, and of the common circumstances which attend death."[97] In resolution 25, Edwards similarly calls himself to deep introspection: "Resolved, to examine carefully, and constantly, what that one

93. Many often varying estimations of the connection between Edwards and the Puritans exist. For a review of these issues, see Stout, "Puritans and Edwards," 274–91.

94. Stoddard, *Safety of Appearing*, 204.

95. Ibid., 205.

96. This is the oldest letter now extant from Edwards's pen. See WJE 16:29. The two subsequent quotes that follow are also taken from this letter.

97. WJE 16:753.

thing in me is, which causes me in the least to doubt of the love of God; and to direct all my forces against it."[98] And in resolution 37, Edwards adds, "Resolved, to inquire every night, as I am going to bed, wherein I have been negligent, what sin I have committed, and wherein I have denied myself: also at the end of every week, month and year."[99] In truth, though, each of his seventy resolutions are a form of self-examination to one degree or another, as Edwards determines to scrutinize his thoughts, motivations, attitudes, and behaviors from every conceivable vantage point. George Claghorn remarks, "The 'Resolutions' were Edwards' guidelines for self-examination. Puritans set great store by biblical injunctions to submit themselves to divine searching and to monitor their motives and actions. On a community level, congregations were exhorted to practice introspection as a duty of great consequence."[100] Edwards added in resolution 60, "Resolved, whenever my feelings begin to appear in the least out of order, when I am conscious of the least uneasiness within, or the least irregularity without, I will then subject myself to the strictest examination."[101]

It is natural to turn next to Edwards's so-called diary in order to understand how he actually practiced self-examination. While the document has the general appearance of a diary, its character is rather different; the majority of the document is comprised of self-analysis pertaining to the various aspects of Edwards's efforts to live out the Christian life. Consider this entry, recorded matter-of-factly: "The last night, in bed, when thinking of death, I thought, if I was then to die, that, which would make me die, in the least degree fearfully, would be, the want of a trusting and relying on Jesus Christ, so distinctly and plainly, as has been described by divines."[102] And the aim of this introspection? "Supposing there was never but one complete Christian, in all respects of a right stamp, having Christianity shining in its true luster, at a time in the world; resolved to act just as I would do, if I strove with all my might to be that one, that should be in my time."[103]

---

98. WJE 16:755.
99. WJE 16:756.
100. From Claghorn's editorial remarks in WJE 16:741.
101. WJE 16:758.
102. WJE 16:773. This entry is dated July 4, 1723.
103. WJE 16:764. This is from the entry dated January 14, 1722/23 (the more modern form for this date would be January 14, 1723).

Edwards's diary, though, offers a very incomplete portrait of his inner life. Of the 148 of its entries, only a handful are dated after his twenty-first birthday. Given Edwards's many other writings, certainly his thoughts can be easily discerned, but this dimension of inner personal spirituality Edwards kept largely hidden from posterity. Compare this notion with Edwards's comments on the diaries of David Brainerd, which form the majority of the biography Edwards later produced:

> 'Tis fit, the reader should be aware, that what Mr. Brainerd wrote in his diary, out of which the following account of his life is chiefly taken, was written only for his own private use, and not to get honor and applause in the world, nor with any design that the world should ever see it, either while he lived or after his death. . . . He showed himself almost invincibly averse to the publishing any part of his diary after his death . . . but being by some of his friends there prevailed upon to withdraw so strict and absolute a prohibition, he was pleased finally to yield so far as that his papers should be left in my hands.[104]

There is a striking similarity between the entries in Edwards's own diary and those of David Brainerd, and Edwards published Brainerd's diary as an evidence of "true religion and virtue."[105] It is fair to characterize Brainerd's diary as evidence of a life full of such self-examination as Edwards aimed at in his own life.

One of Edwards's most famous letters was written to Deborah Hatheway, and has been reprinted frequently as "Advice to Young Converts."[106] It is illustrative of how comfortably the notion of self-examination is interwoven into his most straightforward forms of communication. He writes, "Don't leave off seeking, striving, and praying for the very same things that we exhort unconverted persons to strive for, and a degree of which you have had in conversion. Thus pray that your eyes may be opened, that you may receive your sight, that you may know your self, and be brought to God's foot."[107] When hearing sermons, even those aimed at the unconverted, Edwards counseled that Hatheway ask herself, "in what respects is this that I hear spoken applicable to me, and what improvements ought I to make for my

---

104. WJE 7:96.
105. WJE 7:89.
106. WJE16:90–95. This letter is dated June 3, 1741.
107. WJE 16:91.

own soul's good?"[108] And, he adds, "Though God has forgiven and forgotten your past sins, yet don't forget 'em yourself: often remember what a wretched bond slave you was in the land of Egypt. Often bring to mind your particular acts of sin before conversion."[109] Also, take note of the extended discussion of the letters of Edwards to his own children in the section of chapter 4 entitled "Morning and Evening Family Devotions." In many ways, each such letter offers a direct or indirect call to self-examination.

While it would be difficult to make the case that self-examination is a frequent topic in Edwards's treatises, there is one point in his writings where the theme recurs consistently—in his accounts of the revivals of religion at Northampton. If, however, the notion of self-examination is broadened to include the religious affections, and one's discernment of true and false motions toward God, the frequency of this theme would be substantial. He writes,

> When awakenings first begin, their consciences are commonly most exercised about their outward vicious course, or other acts of sin; but afterwards, are much more burdened with a sense of heart sins, the dreadful corruption of their nature, their enmity against God, the pride of their hearts, their unbelief, their rejection of Christ, the stubbornness and obstinacy of their wills, and the like. In many, God makes much use of their own experience, in the course of their awakenings after saving good, to convince them of their own vile emptiness and universal depravity.[110]

Edwards saw it as his duty as a minister to ensure that he did not too quickly ease the tension that the members of his congregation might be experiencing. In fact, he emphasized thoughts that would heighten their terror, counseling that "God is under no manner of obligation to show mercy to any natural man, whose heart is not turned to God."[111] Conversion necessitated the sinner's recognition of their true state before God, and one could only apprehend this reality at God's initiative. A genuine recognition of sin—the fruit of honest self-examination—would compel his hearers to cast themselves upon the mercy of God in Christ. Edwards would have endorsed the Shorter Catechism's definition of repentance unto life: "Repentance unto life is a saving grace, whereby a sinner out of a true sense

---

108. WJE 16:92.
109. Ibid.
110. From the *Faithful Narrative* in WJE 4:164.
111. WJE 4:167.

of his sin, and apprehension of the mercy of God in Christ, doth, with grief and hatred of his sin, turn from it unto God, with full purpose of and endeavor after new obedience."[112]

Edwards observed that, once converted, the members of his congregation were often surprised to find that sin still held a deep appeal: "They never realized it, that persons were wont to meet with such difficulties. . . . When they are thus exercised with doubts about their state, through the deadness of their frames of spirit, as long as these frames last, they are commonly unable to satisfy themselves of the truth of their grace, by all their self-examination."[113] Such a condition necessitated that the same Spirit of God that converted the soul initially "revive the lively actings of grace, the light breaks through the cloud, and doubting and darkness soon vanish away."[114] As such, self-examination was by no means an end in itself, but a preparatory work, breaking up the fallow ground so as to see spiritual life blossom and grow.

Edwards viewed self-examination to be a necessary and ongoing dimension of the congregation's spiritual vitality. In an incredibly far reaching covenant that Edwards drew up for his congregation, taking advantage of the revivals of religion, he wrote, "wherein any of us, upon strict examination of our past behavior, may be conscious to ourselves that we have by any means wronged any of our neighbors in their outward estate; we will not rest till we have made the restitution, or given that satisfaction, which the rules of moral equity require."[115] In this way, self-examination was to become a part of the congregation's rule of self-government, a part of the ideal pact of love toward one another.

Edwards's Preaching and Self-Examination

While self-examination is not an especially pronounced theme in Edwards's theological and philosophical treatises, it is *everywhere* in his preaching. It can be found in his earliest sermons, and over thirty years later, in his "last

---

112. See "Shorter Catechism," 27.
113. WJE 4:187.
114. Ibid.
115. This covenant is included in a letter to the Rev. Thomas Prince. See WJE 4:551, or WJE 16:122. The sermon "Renewing our Covenant with God" also rises from this occasion. See WJE 22:509–18.

major homiletical effort," one finds a vigorous call to self-examination.[116] It is in this light that self-examination is recognized as uniquely a part of Edwards's understanding of divine worship: one was to encounter God in worship, and supremely in the preaching of the Word, and then, to meet with God in secret prayer wherein one would carefully examine one's heart and conscience, applying the impressions of the Spirit of God received in the preaching of the Word. There are dozens, perhaps hundreds, of brief admonitions to self-examination in his sermons, as well as numerous whole sermons devoted to the topic.[117]

Self-Examination on Fast Days and at the Occasion of the Lord's Supper

It is fair to characterize Edwards as uniquely serious and sober. While just past seventeen years of age and still a student at Yale, Edwards once wrote to his uncle, the Rev. Stephen Mix, "To my great surprisal I find my cousin Elisha [Mix] to be discontented with his dwelling with me. I have inquired of him strictly what is the reason of it. It cannot be because I hinder him from his studies, but as far as I can judge from his own words, it's because I hinder him from a superabundance of that which he loves much better."[118] Edwards's seriousness only increased over time, and fast day sermons as well as the observation of the Lord's Supper provided particularly fit occasions for an emphasis on the practice of self-examination.

In preaching on Ezekiel 7:16, a grave text—"But they that escape of them shall escape, and shall be on the mountains like doves of the valleys, all of them mourning, every one for his iniquity"—Edwards identified this

---

116. WJE 25:698.

117. A few representative examples of sermons on self-examination include "Duty of Self-Examination," based on Hag 1:5 and preached during the summer of 1722 and the spring of 1723, in WJE 10:482–92; "Self-Examination and the Lord's Supper," based on 1 Cor 11:28–29 and preached most likely on Mar 21, 1731, in WJE 17:264–72; "Persons should be much concerned to know, whether they do not live in some way of sin," based on Ps 139:23–24 and preached in September 1733 (it is also known as "Christian Cautions: The Necessity of Self-Examination"), in *Works*² 173–85; and "Application" (as yet unpublished; Edwards discusses the importance of self-examination among the godly and ungodly), based on Mt 25:1–2 and preached in February or March 1738, see WJE 19:809. Numerous other sermons do not have "self-examination" explicitly included as part of the title, but are in fact almost wholly devoted to the topic.

118. WJE 16: 35. The letter to the Rev Stephen Mix dates to approximately November 1720.

doctrine on a day of "public humiliation": "So it becomes everyone in a time of humiliation to mourn each man for his own iniquity."[119] Edwards considers this doctrine from a wide range of different perspectives, and concludes, "But most of all doth it become us at such times to look into our hearts and examine our ways and to mourn for our own iniquity. These are the sins that we have most especial reason to lament because 'tis we ourselves who have been the author of them."[120] He warns, "When we see God coming forth against us and manifesting his displeasure, certainly we ought to meet him, prostrating ourselves in the dust with tears of repentance, the deepest humiliation, and most humble confessions of those sins of our own which have partly incensed him."[121]

In the second sermon on this same occasion, employing the same text and doctrine, Edwards gathers together several points of application, offering direction with respect to the kind of self-examination appropriate to the gravity of the subject at hand:

1. Let us particularly recollect our sins. . . . Let us go back as far as our memories will lead us and trace our own footsteps over again and follow ourselves in our thoughts in all the way that we have gone. . . . Our misimprovements of sabbaths, our slight and disobedience to his Word, our abuse of God's ordinances and our opportunities.

2. Let us recollect the aggravations of our sins. Let us behold our own sin in its own proper hue and not paint and mask it over as we have done. . . .

3. Let our reflections be accompanied with the humblest confessions while we are viewing our works and their aggravations. Let us spread them before God and acknowledge the ill desert of them.

4. Let our sins be accompanied with thorough reformation. This is what God chiefly looks at and is the better half of repentance without which God will not accept our confessions and our fasting and external humiliation nor will he hear our supplication.[122]

On the occasion of another fast, Edwards similarly emphasized the need for self-examination. "We in this land pretend every year to keep a solemn day

---

119. BL 183.
120. BL 188.
121. BL 189.
122. BL 208–9. In the sermon, each of these points is expanded upon beyond what is quoted.

of public fasting, humiliation, and prayer, to humble ourselves for our sins, deprecate judgment, implore mercy. We herein do more than other lands. We make a show and pretense, as though we were extraordinary [in] religion and carefulness to keep at good terms with God." And coming to the heart of the matter, Edwards continued, "But let it be inquired whether or no we are not exceeding hypocritical in these our pretenses."[123] Hypocrisy, and the reality of pride, were twin dangers that were often featured as sins to be rooted out by this practice.

Two examples from Edwards's communion sermons also help to illustrate how he would use the seriousness of a given occasion to call forth a corresponding seriousness of practice in the lives of his hearers:

> If you would be strong in grace and abundant fruitfulness, you must often be comparing your heart and life with the rule. There must be a continual watching over your own heart every now and then, examining and searching to see if you can't find some wicked way in you. Try your heart: see if you can't find some instances wherein it is unchristian and contrary to the rule of God's Word; this must be done especially before a sacrament: there should be a set and solemn examination of this nature at such a time, according to that rule, I Cor. 11:28, "Let a man examine himself, and so let him eat." This he must do lest he eat and drink judgment to himself. But this should not be the only time. It should be done frequently. If it be done every day, it is not too often. We should be continually doing as David, "thinking on our ways, and turning our feet into God's testimonies" [Ps. 119:59].[124]

And so even daily, probing self-examination would not be too frequent. The intent was to bring the congregation to an end of all self-sufficiency. Edwards urged in another communion sermon,

> Have you been as it were cut down by a despair in your own sufficiency and worthiness; that whereas formerly you was wont to think you could do a great deal for yourself, you have had all hope in your own strength cut off, so that you have been brought to be sensible of your being in the hands of God, that unless he helped you by his power, you was undone forever.[125]

---

123. WJE 19:74. This quote is taken from the sermon entitled "Fast Days in Dead Times," which was preached in April 1734, and was based on Isa 58:3–5.

124. WJE 14:276–77.

125. WJE 22:313.

Self-Examination for the Converted and Unconverted

As has been seen, the Puritans employed the practice of self-examination in order to compel men to consider that most important question regarding the state of their eternal soul. In this, Edwards was no different. The wicked were frequently urged to consider their ways. And, to those "under convictions," the firstfruits of the working of the Holy Spirit, Edwards directed, "Labor to see your own wickedness. And to that end be very much in self-reflections and confessions. As you have power in measure over your own thought, turn your thoughts often upon your own sins." The auditor was to be unsparing in this pursuit: "And be very particular in setting your own sins in order before your own eyes. And be very particular and frequent in confessing them to God. Keep a catalogue of your sins in your mind and be often reading of it and often spreading of it before God, for 'tis the greatness of your guilt that you want to be sensible of."[126]

Self-examination was to be characterized by a kind of pointed, withering self-questioning. In the context of an exhortation to practice self-reflection, Edwards illustrates the practice with respect to contemplation on one's use of time:

> How much may be done in a year? How much good is there opportunity for doing in such a space of time? How much service may persons do for God, and how much for their own souls, if persons do their utmost to improve it? How much may be done in a day? But what have you done in so many days and years that you have lived? What have you done with the whole time of your youth, you that are past your youth? What is become of all that precious season of life? What have you to show for it all? Has not all that precious season of life, even the time of youth, been in vain to you? Would it not have been as well or better for you, if you had been all that time asleep or in a state of nonexistence?[127]

It is difficult to overstate the value of self-examination to Edwards. Ultimately, the genuineness of one's conversion can be tested by its use, given that its effects were to be far-reaching:

> If it be so that in a true conversion men's bodies are changed as well as their souls, this should put such as hope they are converted in examining themselves, whether their bodies have passed under such

---

126. WJE 17:171.
127. WJE 19:252.

a change as has been spoken of.... Inquire wherein your body was corrupt before your supposed conversion. What appetites of body chiefly prevailed and inquire whether there be any considerable alteration in that respect since your body was brought under.... And consider after what manner you used to employ the members of your body—your eyes, ears, tongues, and hands—in the service of sin before what you call your conversion.[128]

All members of the congregation were called upon frequently to ensure that their conversion was genuine. While Edwards did not call upon his congregation to labor through the various steps toward conversion laid out by many of his predecessors, the frequency with which he put the question as to whether or not one is genuinely saved may well have left comparatively greater numbers of tender consciences lacking certainty about their eternal state, perhaps for the whole of their lives. And, while his example of the conversion of the child Phebe Bartlett in his *Faithful Narrative* may have offered hope to some, his later use of his wife Sarah as a model—a spiritual titan in her own right—likely did nothing to help the common Christian identify with such spiritual "transport."[129]

Consider a few of the manifold ways in which Edwards pressed the point. "This doctrine," that "there is such a thing, as a spiritual and divine light," "may well put us upon examining ourselves, whether we have ever had this divine light, that has been described, let into our souls."[130] One another occasion, he preached, "Examine yourself therefore by this: is not your heart chiefly {in this world}? Is it not more your concern, and care, and endeavor to further your outward interest than to {have eternal life}? And is not this the very reason, because you never have seen the reality of eternal things?"[131] Certain texts necessitated that the doctrine "put all upon strictly examining whether they be saints or not."[132] Similarly, the sermon entitled "Saints Dwell Alone" presses the same point through a series of six questions.[133] Christians are to be suspicious of their motivations; they are to "examine all

---

128. BL 307.

129. See WJE 4:199, 331. While Sarah is not mentioned specifically by name, her account appears in *Some Thoughts Concerning the Present Revival of Religion in New England*.

130. WJE 17:423.

131. WJE 19:103.

132. WJE 19:487.

133. See WJE 25:55–56 C.

[their] supposed spiritual affections,"¹³⁴ and are to look for "better evidences of saving grace."¹³⁵

As such, while in practice some may have experienced concern about their eternal state—and joined long lines in seeking counsel from Edwards, just as others had previously sought out Timothy Edwards—a certainty with respect to one's spiritual state was ultimately possible. For those who labor earnestly,

> assurance is a prize that God has set up for all Christians to run for. ... To use self-examination alone without any other means is not the way for persons to attain to this privilege. There be fair rules of trial given in the Word of God and the way in which God has made of the qualifications of those who have an interest in Christ be very full and clear. Self-examination ought by no means to be left undone. Yet, says Christ, one can use no other means to obtain otherwise, but only to examine themselves, however good rules may be given for them to examine themselves by and however strict and frequent they only be an examination of themselves. ... All the self-examinations in the world won't satisfy the soul of all its good efforts 'til the Achan is destroyed, and when that is slain, another must not be admitted.¹³⁶

Edwards concludes this same sermon with the following admonition, listing self-examination as one of the prerequisites to this longed-for assurance: "Christians should be often examining themselves. They ought to deal truthfully, looking to God to help, by the influence of his Spirit. He would help them oppose the wickedness and deceitfulness of their hearts. He would search them and try them and lead them in the way everlasting."¹³⁷

Practicing Self-Examination Appropriately

A number of pitfalls were possible as one practiced the examination of conscience, an act that was to comprise a substantial and ongoing dimension of private devotion. First and foremost, there is a peculiar temptation with the discipline of self-examination, namely, that one might become prideful—believing, for example, that only the truly spiritual would practice it—but for Edwards, this is not a practice one could ever outgrow the need for as a means of identifying and rooting out sin. So also, hypocrisy was a real

---

134. WJE 22:309.
135. WJE 22:630.
136. BL 64–65.
137. BL 69.

concern: "If it be so that perseverance be absolutely necessary to salvation, then inquire whether or no your religion be of a persevering sort. The religion of the hypocrites is not so; and therefore we read of the foolish virgins that their lamps went out."[138] And still worse, if practiced wrongly or superficially, it might be easier to recognize sin in others first. In speaking of the danger that people are in who, having found an interest in Christ, retreat once again to the enticements of the world, Edwards asks, "Let everyone look to himself, and consider whether he is not guilty. . . . We can observe the error in others, but can we observe nothing in ourselves?"[139] Were one to avoid these various pitfalls and maintain a right sense of one's position before God, as a sinner desperately in need of a savior, one would always see how far short one falls of the requirements of God's Word: "'Tis experience of ourselves, and finding what we are, that God commonly makes use of as the means of bringing us off from all dependence on ourselves."[140]

Self-examination is sometimes referred to as "testing," and one could use it as a barometer for where one stood with respect to what is valued most in life—the things of earth, or the things of heaven. One could so easily become self-deceived:

> Let all examine themselves, and know whether they use this world just as if they would carry their earthly enjoyments into the other world with them, or whether they set their hearts chiefly on things which are not seen; and let all be exhorted to apply themselves immediately to the preparations for eternity. Set about it with the greatest seriousness and diligence, with the utmost vigor and most fixed resolution, for such things as concern eternal happiness or eternal misery are not to be trifled with, nor to be trusted to a mere peradventure; for what shall it profit you, if you gain the whole world, and lose your own soul?[141]

As has been suggested, self-examination, an unseen act that one might assume to be comparatively simple, would in fact require the greatest diligence and exertion, were it to be accomplished with the requisite thoroughness. It was to be hard, gut-wrenching work. Effective self-examination would never bring about the dreaded possibilities of pride, hypocrisy, or judgmentalism

---

138. WJE 19:603.
139. BL 261.
140. WJE 19:285.
141. WJE 10:412.

in the believer, but would rather produce humiliation, self-forgetfulness, and absolute self-abnegation:

> The best, if they examine themselves, will find deficiencies enough to make them blush, and it would be greatly to their advantage if they would often compare their lives with the life of Christ and see how far their humility, meekness, and charity falls short of his; if they would compare their lives to the gospel rule and see wherein they fall short; if they would let their consciences frequently whisper to them this question: how much the better is the honor of Christ in the world for my living in it? Wherefore, let all be exhorted and persuaded to do so.[142]

While humility was greatly prized by Edwards, he did not go as far as some of the Puritans in discussing what one's attitude should be with respect to the judgment of God. Some taught that unless one was willing to be ultimately condemned, because it would be just and righteous, and would glorify God, one's assurance would be in question.[143] Yet, while he avoided this particular excess, he did look over the edge of the same cliff:

> If God hath appointed a day {to judge the world}, let us judge and condemn ourselves for our sins. This we must do if we would not be judged and condemned for them at that day. If we are to escape condemnation, we must see that we justly might be condemned. We must be so sensible of our vileness and guilt as to see that we have deserved all that condemnation and punishment that is threatened; that we are in God's hands and that he is sovereign disposer of us. Let us therefore be often reflecting on our sins, and be truly humbled before God for them, and confess them to God."[144]

And so, while Edwards does not teach that a believer must be *willing* to be condemned, a thoroughgoing self-examination would result in a recognition of the fact that one's condemnation would ultimately be just; in this way, one would in this way be compelled to more clearly discern the mercy of God in Christ. A failure to recognize these realities was tantamount to revealing that one was in fact unconverted.

142. WJE 10:575.
143. Consider, for example, Baxter, *Practical Works*, 156. Samuel Hopkins, who lived for a time in Edwards's home, is also noted for holding this doctrine. See Rubin, *Religious Melancholy*, 185. Conversely, Solomon Stoddard was vigorously opposed to this view. See Stoddard and Mather, *Guide to Christ*, 76. Finally, Stephen Munzer offers valuable perspective on this point in "Self-Abandonment and Self-Denial."
144. WJE 14:540.

At the outset of this review of Edwards's teachings on self-examination, it was noted that the subject appears virtually everywhere in his sermons throughout the whole course of his ministry. As a means of summarizing his teachings on this subject, consider the following excerpt, in which he explains the practice concisely. Imagine the time and effort that would be required to heed Edwards's counsel on this one occasion, and then consider further that he routinely pressed this same point on countless others. To be a part of one of Edwards's congregations would mean that one would routinely be confronted with such lessons:

> Be much in thinking on your own sins. This is a duty directly required by the words of the text: "See thy way in the valley." Think of your sins in order. Sit down and make a business of recollecting your sins and revolving of them in your mind, viewing of 'em in all their circumstances. Set them in order before you.
>
> Begin with your childhood, and go through your whole life. Follow your own track. View the path that you have gone in through all its mazes, through all its windings and turnings. Bring to mind as many of your sins as you can, and let there be distinct conviction of them. Be as particular as you can.
>
> And that you may be more thorough in the work, it may be profitable for you to observe some method and order in your self-reflections. Think of your sins according to the order of time, or according to their several natures: your sins against the light of nature, or sins against the [Holy Ghost], or according to the commandments that have been broken by them, or according to the lusts that you have exercised in them. Think wherein you have gratified your sensuality, {your} pride, {your} covetousness, {your} hatred, {your} envy and revenge.
>
> Think distinctly of your sins of your thoughts and imaginations: {sins of your} words, {and sins of your} deeds.
>
> {Think of your sins according to their} time: sins on sabbath days, and sins on ordinary days.
>
> [Think of your sins] according to their circumstances: sins committed alone, [and] sins in company.
>
> [Think of your sins] according to the objects: sins committed more directly against God, {and} sins against your neighbor.
>
> [Think] also of the aggravations of your sins in order. {Think of the} aggravations of your sins in general: [what] light you have lived under, how favored beyond the heathen; {what} outward mercies enjoyed; {what} means [have] been used with [you]. [Think of] aggravations of particular sins.
>
> It may be profitable to dwell on one sort at one time, and another at another. At one time set yourself to think over the sins of

> your childhood, at another time {set yourself to think over the sins of your youth}.
> And let these self-reflections be often repeated....[145]

As such, self-examination of this type represents a frequent point of application in Edwards's sermons, counseling the use of the practice in private, as one is called upon to probe every facet of one's life in an effort to see sin for what it is. Often, Edwards will assist in the exercise by posing questions to his congregation rising from the passage in question that were to be asked by the believer in private:

> If none are in the way to heaven but those that are holy, let us try and examine ourselves by this doctrine to see whereabouts we are, and see whether or no we are in the way to heaven.... let us try ourselves by these five following things:
>
> 1. Meditate on the holiness of God, and see if you can not see a conformity, a *likeness* in your mind.
> 2. See if you can see any resemblance in your life to the life of Christ.
> 3. Is there an agreeableness between your souls and the Word of God?
> 4. Do you find by a comparison of likeness and agreeableness between your hearts and lives, and the hearts and lives of those holy men that we [are] assured were such by the Word of God?
> 5. Do you in a measure imitate the saints and angels in heaven?[146]

For each of these five points, Edwards offers further explanatory information. In this way, the preaching of the Word was intimately connected to private practice, as one sought to take to heart such probing questions. The value of the practice, for Edwards, was evident:

> Therefore you that are complaining of darkness and difficulties, and are longing that you might have more light and more sweet experience, as some others have, seek it in this way: strive earnestly to break your heart more off from worldly and carnal objects, and to wean yourself more entirely from 'em, and that it may be more humbled and broken with a sense of your unworthiness.... There is nothing in the world that does so much prepare the heart of a saint for sweet communion with Christ as these two things....[147]

---

145. WJE 19:267–68.
146. WJE 10:477–78.
147. WJE 22:395.

In conclusion, for Jonathan Edwards self-examination was an indispensable aspect of private devotion to be exercised not only to mortify one's self owing to one's sinful heart, but to discern what is required to delight God, which should be the ultimate aim of the Christian life. This practice was to produce seriousness, earnestness, diligence, humility, assurance, and usefulness. "You have heard what temper the truly godly are of," he preached, "That it is their spirit and disposition to exalt God and to abase themselves before him. Wherefore, let all examine themselves by this, whither they are truly godly or not. Let all examine and see what temper they themselves are of lest they should deserve that rebuke which Christ gives in Luke 9:55, 'Ye know not what manner of spirit ye are of.'"[148] And, like strong medicine, self-examination was to be taken consistently: "be more frequent in examining yourself, in searching and trying your hearts and your ways, to see when you have turned aside from the path of duty, and wherein your life needs amendment."[149] In sum, the Christian is to "Be much therefore in heart work, in self-examination, {in} self-reflection, {in} watching and striving against heart sins. *Let this be your daily and continual work.*"[150] In this way, as the Puritans before him, it was from the pulpit, in the context of public worship, that Edwards stressed this daily "heart work," the private devotional life that will now be considered in further detail.

---

148. BL 80.
149. WJE 10:576.
150. WJE 19:271; emphasis added.

four

Private Devotion

In sports or in politics, as in any other field of endeavor, those who excel stand out clearly among their peers. But then there are some who so far and away surpass their colleagues and competitors as to not merely stand out, but rather stand alone. Even when charming, they can be intimidating. Their names and faces rise easily to mind; and to be in their presence can be awe-inspiring. Others may naturally claim how watching them prepare or practice offers a profound form of education, and more, reveals something of the chasm between them and their rivals.

This notion is complicated greatly within the bounds of the Christian church, and Edwards would have been well familiar with the various Scriptural commands that would need to be brought to bear. On the one hand, that one should strive to excel in the Christian faith is not an option so much as a command: "Do you not know that in a race all the runners compete, but only one receives the prize? So run that you may obtain it" (1 Cor 9:24, ESV). On the other hand, humility, and even self-effacement, is also commanded: "But Jesus called them to him and said, 'You know that the rulers of the Gentiles lord it over them, and their great ones exercise authority over them. It shall not be so among you. But whoever would be great among you must be your servant, and whoever would be first among you must be your slave, even as the Son of Man came not to be served but to serve, and to give his life as a ransom for many'" (Matt 20:25–28, ESV). Even more, the Christian who takes the Bible seriously recognizes that success is ultimately derived in large measure from his earnestness in helping *others* succeed: "Each of you should look not only to your own interests, but also to the interests of others" (Phil 2:4, ESV).

Holding these ideals in tension represents no small challenge. But it is in the intensity of his personal devotional life that Jonathan Edwards might be seen as most thoroughly intimidating. Most of his resolutions were written while still a teenager, and if any one resolution is considered in isolation it might seem to violate the spirit of the verses cited above. But if his resolutions are considered instead as one larger whole, they reflect these varying biblical ideals concisely. Edwards unmistakably sought to excel in the Christian faith:

> On the supposition, that there never was to be but one individual in the world, at any one time, who was properly a complete Christian, in all respects of a right stamp, having Christianity always shining in its true luster, and appearing excellent and lovely, from whatever part and under whatever character viewed: resolved, to act just as I would do, if I strove with all my might to be that one, who should live in my time.[1]

So also, Edwards esteemed humility: "Resolved, to act, in all respects, both speaking and doing, as if nobody had been so vile as I, and as if I had committed the same sins, or had the same infirmities or failings as others; and that I will let the knowledge of their feelings promote nothing but shame in myself, and prove only an occasion of my confessing my own sins and misery to God."[2] And similarly, Edwards gauged his success in line with his ability to promote religion in others: "Resolved to do whatever I think to be my duty, and most for the good and advantage of mankind in general."[3]

It is one thing to consider some of the many points of application that Edwards made in his sermons with respect to the pursuit of the Christian life. It is another matter entirely to understand that his resolutions were merely the early distillations of a young man's preternatural reflections, the firstfruits of what was to follow. The pattern for his private devotional life, as well as that of his family, bore the marks of such rigor. George Marsden summarizes the observations of Samuel Hopkins in this way:

> He began the day with private prayers followed by family prayers, by candlelight in winter. Each meal was accompanied by household devotions, and at the end of each day Sarah joined him in his study for prayers. Jonathan kept secret the rest of his daily devotional routine, following Jesus' command to pray in secret. Throughout the day, his goal was to remain constantly with a sense of living in the presence of God, as difficult as that might be. Often he added secret days of fasting and additional prayers.[4]

1. Resolution 63, in WJE 16:758
2. Resolution 8, in WJE 16:753.
3. This is the latter portion of Edwards's first resolution, found in ibid.
4. Marsden, *Jonathan Edwards: A Life*, 133.

This might seem to lead to a dead end—if Edwards "kept secret the rest of his daily devotional routine," what more might there be to say? While it is true that the details about Edwards's private devotional habits are unknown, what he admired respecting prayer is not. David Brainerd earned Edwards's respect and admiration for his approach to prayer:

> His manner of prayer was very agreeable: most becoming a worm of the dust, and a disciple of Christ, addressing to an infinitely great and holy God, and Father of mercies; not with florid expressions, or a studied eloquence; not with any intemperate vehemence, or indecent boldness; at the greatest distance from any appearance of ostentation, and from everything that might look as though he meant to recommend himself to those that were about him, or set himself off to their acceptance; free too from vain repetitions, without impertinent excursions, or needless multiplying of words. He expressed himself with the strictest propriety, with weight, and pungency; and yet what his lips uttered seemed to flow from the fullness of his heart, as deeply impressed with a great and solemn sense of our necessities, unworthiness, and dependence, and of God's infinite greatness, excellence and sufficiency, rather than from merely a warm and fruitful brain, pouring out good expressions. . . . In his prayers, he insisted much on the prosperity of Zion, the advancement of Christ's kingdom in the world, and the flourishing and propagation of religion among the Indians. And he generally made it one petition in his prayer, that we might not outlive our usefulness.[5]

Similarly, Edwards describes the case of the young girl Phebe Bartlett in his *Faithful Narrative*: "she was observed very constantly to retire several times in a day, as was concluded, for secret prayer; and grew more and more engaged in religion, and was more frequent in her closet; till at last she was wont to visit it five or six times in a day, and was so engaged in it, that nothing would at any time divert her from her stated closet exercises."[6] And, his extended consideration of Sarah Edwards's devotional experiences reflect one that was "swallowed up with light and love and a sweet solace, rest and joy of soul, that was altogether unspeakable; and more than once continuing for five or six hours together . . ."[7] While conventions for punctuation were different in Edwards's day, it is possible to make the case that Edwards's

---

5. WJE 7:446. A portion of this reference is cited by Marsden, *Jonathan Edwards: A Life*, 325.

6. From Edwards's *A Faithful Narrative*, in WJE 4:199.

7. WJE 4:332.

account of Sarah's piety is different from others of his writings in the unusual length of its sentences. In Goen's editorial footnote in this account, it is stated that a particular sentence ran for three pages in the original printing.[8] The importance of this observation rests in the probability that Edwards is here demonstrating unusual emotion, and indeed admiration, as he considers his wife's deep devotion.

His own sense of responsibility in prayer was likely intense, given the counsel he frequently offered to his congregation with respect to prayer, and indeed, offered even to other ministers: "Ministers, in order to their being burning and shining lights, should walk closely with God, and keep near to Christ; that they may ever be enlightened and enkindled by him. And they should be much in seeking God, and conversing with him by prayer, who is the fountain of light and love."[9] For Edwards, hypocrisy was a most sinister evil; with such admonitions frequently on his lips, it seems likely that his "secret" prayer would genuinely be often preoccupied with the concerns he proclaimed publicly.[10]

In one of his few diary entries, written when still nineteen, it is possible to obtain a rare glimpse into Edwards's personal devotional life:

> I have been before God; and have given myself, all that I am and have to God, so that I am not in any respect my own. . . . I have given myself clear away, and have not retained anything as my own. I have been to God this morning, and told him that I gave myself *wholly* to him. I have given every power to him; so that for the future I will challenge no right in myself, in any respect. I have expressly promised him, and do now promise almighty God, that by his grace I will not. I have this morning told him, that I did take him for my whole portion and felicity, looking on nothing else as any part of my happiness, nor acting as if it were; and his law for the constant rule of my obedience; and would fight with all my might against the world, the flesh, and the devil, to the end of my life.[11]

---

8. WJE 4:336.

9. WJE 25:100.

10. For example, he warned, "Nothing is more provoking to God than the hypocritical performance of the parts of divine worship." See the sermon Edwards preached on an unknown date entitled "That at a Time When a People Are Called for a General Humiliation, It Becomes Each One to Mourn for His Own Iniquity," which is based on Ezek 7:16 ("But they that escape of them shall escape, and shall be on the mountains like doves of the valleys, all of them mourning, every one for his iniquity"), in BL 202.

11. From Edwards's diary entry dated January 12, 1723, in WJE 16:762.

Later in life, we see that this same fervor appears unmitigated. It appears that for Edwards religious devotion was by no means restricted to the study, and, perhaps surprising to some, it was at times filled with deep emotion. He writes,

> Once, as I rid out into the woods for my health . . . and having lit from my horse in a retired place, as my manner commonly has been, to walk for divine contemplation and prayer; I had a view, that for me was extraordinary, of the glory of the Son of God; as mediator between God and man; and his wonderful, great, full, pure and sweet grace and love, and meek and gentle condescension. This grace, that appeared to me so calm and sweet, appeared great above the heavens. The person of Christ appeared ineffably excellent, with an excellency great enough to swallow up all thought and conception. Which continued, as near as I can judge, about an hour; which kept me, the bigger part of the time, in a flood of tears, and weeping aloud. I felt withal an ardency of soul to be, what I know not otherwise how to express, than to be emptied and annihilated; to lie in the dust, and to be full of Christ alone; to love him with a holy and pure love; to trust in him; to live upon him; to serve and follow him, and to be totally wrapt up in the fullness of Christ; and to be perfectly sanctified and made pure, with a divine and heavenly purity. I have several other times, had views very much of the same nature, and that have had the same effects.[12]

Even if one were to spend all of this life in such "ecstasy," it would be a life well spent, in that it would be a fitting preparation for the worship to follow in heaven.[13] And conversely, Edwards taught, a lack of sufficient interest in such devotion points to a deep-seated problem: "All the difficulty there is in any of God's commands, arises from the sinfulness of men's own hearts. From thence it is that there is any difficulty in prayer, or meditation, or reading the holy Scriptures, or keeping the Sabbath, or attending to the Word preached, or in a suitable attendance on ordinances."[14]

It is true that Edwards largely kept hidden from the world his most intimate habits of personal devotion. Despite this, Sereno Dwight has captured his impressions of what that devotional life was like. He writes,

---

12. From Edwards's *Personal Narrative*, in WJE 16:801.
13. WJE 13:191.
14. WJE 14:184.

his whole life was a continued course of self-examination; and in the duty of secret fasting, and humiliation, which he very frequently observed,—a duty enjoined by Christ, on his followers, as explicitly, and in the same terms, as the duty of secret prayer; enjoined too, for the very purpose of discovery, confession, and purification,—he was accustomed, with the greatest unreservedness of which he was capable, to declare his ways to God, and to lay open his soul before him, all his sins, temptations, difficulties, sorrows, and fears, as well as his desires and hopes; that the light of God's countenance might shine upon him without obstruction.[15]

This chapter will consider his outlook on the main elements of private devotion beyond that of self-examination. These include the practices of keeping spiritual journals, morning and evening family worship, private reading of Scripture, and conference with other Christians, and also a consideration of what would be entailed in a comprehensive observance of the Sabbath.

Keeping Spiritual Journals

The question at hand is not so much whether or not Edwards *kept* a spiritual journal, so much as whether or not he *advocated* the practice.[16] Neither is the issue whether or not the Puritans themselves advocated the practice; that they did is unquestioned: "It may be unreasonable to believe that 'most' New Englanders kept a diary. But from the large volume of personal writing—diaries and journals, spiritual autobiographies, notes on self-examination exercises, and religious and meditative poetry—that has survived, we may conclude that many of the devout did write extensively."[17] In short, what evidence might be considered to demonstrate that Edwards would promote a spiritual journal as a useful dimension of personal Christian piety?

Given that the scope of this work is largely restricted to a consideration of Edwards's published sermons, one might potentially conclude that keeping a spiritual journal was not something Edwards actively promoted in any substantial way. It is certainly no small challenge to identify points of application in Edwards's sermons where the practice is explicitly called for. It

---

15. *Works*² 1:clxxxiv.
16. For a description of some of Edwards's personal habits with respect to journaling, see Piper and Taylor, *God Entranced Vision*, 119–23.
17. Hambrick-Stowe, *Practice of Piety*, 187.

might appear easy to conclude, then, that if Edwards advocated keeping a spiritual journal, he only did so as a very minor emphasis.

Such a conclusion would be utterly unwarranted, and three considerations will be brought to bear to sustain the conclusion that Edwards was in fact a strong advocate for this spiritual discipline. First and foremost, the evidence to be considered may well begin, ironically, with his preaching—despite the fact that in it the practice is not explicitly advocated in any measure. As has been shown, the practice of self-examination was for Edwards far and away the most important spiritual exercise to be undertaken—taught from the pulpit, to be practiced in one's secret exercises. And how was self-examination to be undertaken? Soberly, seriously, and thoroughly. As has been seen, the very fact that a "large volume of personal writing" has survived from the period, and since the practice of keeping a spiritual journal in some form was closely associated with the practice of self-examination, it seems natural to conclude that if self-examination was the key point of application in so many of Edwards's sermons, putting pen to paper as a part of the practice would be at times a necessary element. In some ways, keeping a spiritual journal represented the very way in which self-examination was to be practiced.

Second, Edwards does offer at great length, as an example of piety to be followed—and arguably the most important such example Edwards ever set forth—a man whose chief legacy was in fact his spiritual journal. What would we know about David Brainerd were it not for his spiritual journal, and for the spiritual biography that Edwards published? In many ways, *The Life of David Brainerd* is a statement, an endorsement by Edwards, that, in effect, this is ideally how the Christian life is to be lived. Brainerd was a "bright example," and by the publication of his journals one could discern through a consideration of them the spiritual transformation that took place within him in "his inward frames, thoughts, affections and secret exercises."[18]

A review of Edwards's "reflections and observations" on Brainerd's memoirs reveals, very likely, the best manner in which to understand the place of a spiritual journal in the life of the believer. In this summary statement, Edwards repeatedly points to different aspects of Brainerd's Christian experience: "His first love and other holy affections, even at the beginning, were very great; but after months and years became much greater and more remarkable; and the spiritual exercises of his mind continued exceeding great

18. WJE 7:91.

... without indulged remissness and without habitual dwindling and dying away, even till his decease."[19] The spiritual exercises to which Edwards here refers would have included his private writings, but these would have been nothing more than one expression of the substance of the reality that these exercises represented. Edwards does not see journal-keeping as Brainerd's chief accomplishment. On the contrary, he writes, "But particularly, his example and success with regard to one duty in special may be of great use to both ministers and private Christians; I mean, the duty of secret fasting."[20] The value of Brainerd's journals, however, is immeasurable:

> The Providence of God is also worthy of remark, in so overruling and ordering the matter that he did not finally leave absolute orders for the entire suppressing of his private papers; as he had intended and fully resolved, in so much that all the importunity of his friends could scarce restrain him from doing it when sick at Boston. . . . after this, he the more readily yielded to the desires of his friends, and was willing to leave them in their hands to be disposed of as they thought might be most for God's glory: By which means, "he being dead yet speaketh" [Heb 11:4] in these memoirs of his life taken from those private writings: Whereby it is to be hoped he may still be as it were the instrument of much promoting the interest of religion in this world; the advancement of which he so much desired, and hoped would be accomplished after his death.[21]

One final topic bears discussion with respect to Edwards's attitude toward the keeping of a spiritual journal. It might seem possible to conclude, given the fact that there are only 148 entries in Edwards's own journal, which are concentrated over a short period of time early in his life, that journaling was a relatively minor experiment with respect to his own practice. It should be noted, however, that we know of at least one diary of Edwards that has been lost: "Sometime in 1722, probably after his appointment in August as supply minister to the small English Presbyterian church near Wall Street in New York, Edwards began a diary, now lost, of almost daily confessions of self-doubt and spiritual decay."[22] George Claghorn clarifies: "Diaries were kept by many colonial New Englanders, clergy and laity alike. Sometimes they recorded the weather or passing events; at other times they contained sermons;

19. WJE 7:501.
20. WJE 7:531.
21. WJE 7:540.
22. See Lesser's editorial comments in WJE 19:243.

but in their fullest development, they logged their authors' spiritual progress. In the case of Edwards, this enterprise took on Pauline proportions."[23]

If Edwards's diary was all that was available of his inward spiritual reflections, the practice of writing down spiritual impressions might be seen as one easily dismissed. But beyond the connection already proposed between journal-keeping and self-examination, one need only consider the vast corpus of writings Edwards left as evidence of his inner spiritual life. As just a representative sampling, consider his miscellanies (hundreds of carefully organized spiritual notations, often lengthy), his personal narrative, his notes on Scripture, and his blank Bible—not to mention his diary! The volume of these writings suggests that writing down spiritual impressions was for Edwards an inevitable, almost necessary element of meeting with God. Sereno Dwight records one of Edwards's methods of "journaling":

> In solitary rides of considerable length, he adopted a kind of artificial memory. Having pursued a given subject of thought to its proper results, he would pin a small piece of paper on a given spot in his coat, and charge his mind to associate the subject and the piece of paper. He would then repeat the same process with a second subject of thought, fastening the token in a different place, and then a third, and a fourth, as the time might permit. From a ride of several days, he would usually bring home a considerable number of these remembrancers; and, on going to his study, would take them off, one by one, in regular order, and write down the train of thought of which each was intended to remind him.[24]

Edwards's diary, while brief, does offer insight into his own spiritual habits, about which he was especially guarded throughout the whole course of his life. In it he considers various elements typically conceived of as standard parts of a vibrant inward spiritual life, such as the reading of the Scriptures and prayer. But such tools are only means to an end—the end being God himself. As such, there is a clear intensity in these journal entries, written as they were primarily during Edwards's days at Yale and during his early New York pastorate. Fasting and singing as practices of personal devotion are also featured. Still more, however, self-examination appears on almost every line, as Edwards seeks to consider his own actions for a day, week, month, or season—to wrestle with overcoming temptation, to ferret

23. WJE 16:743.
24. *Works*[2] 1:xxxviii.

out the reasons why particular sins were committed, to soberly reflect on his actions and thoughts, his sins of omission and commission. In all, the aim was constant: "I have been before God; and have given myself, all that I am and have to God, so that I am not in any respect my own."[25]

Later that same year, Edwards resolved, "When I want books to read; yea, when I have not very good books, not to spend time in reading them, but in reading the Scriptures, in perusing Resolutions, Reflections [i.e., his miscellanies], etc., in writing on types of the Scriptures, and other things, in studying the languages, and in spending more time in private duties."[26] These "private duties," then, in Edwards's estimation, would clearly have included all manner of recording spiritual impressions.

Morning and Evening Family Devotions

The practice of morning and evening family devotion is one worth expanding on within the context Edwards's marriage and home life. It must be stated bluntly, though, that in relative terms, marriage and family life, as topics in themselves, held virtually no interest for Jonathan Edwards. As a consequence, there is a real danger that by considering these topics as extracted from his corpus one might conclude it was a major theme. It was decidedly not. Were it not for the vastness of Edwards's writings, such a study would not even be possible. This is not reflective of a lack of love for wife, or child, or home, but rather of how, in Edwards's eyes, God utterly dominated the landscape. Christ was the soul's one true lover. The cross was paramount. One's home, and personal relations, and all manner of personal life were ultimately subservient to and subsumed by the resplendence of God. His lifelong obsession was elsewhere: "it appears that all that is ever spoken of in the Scripture as an ultimate end of God's works is included in that one phrase, 'the glory of God . . .'"[27] The value of an involved discussion at this point, then, is in seeing how Edwards believed a home should operate in order to grasp the ways in which worship would not merely be considered a public or private moment, but an extension of the whole of life.

If one wants to catch a glimpse of Edwards in a comparatively rare moment, so far as revealing his key interests or concerns regarding his marriage

---

25. From Edwards's diary entry dated January 12, 1723, in WJE 16:762.
26. From Edwards's diary entry dated August 28, 1723, in WJE 16:780.
27. WJE 8:526.

and family, or with respect to his family's pattern for devotion in this light, one would expect to find it in his personal letters—generally never prepared for publication—moments that likely divulge his particular accentuation on these facets of life. As such, what does Edwards's personal correspondence reveal about his views on marriage, and the manner in which the family is to be governed? What advice and counsel does he offer to others that has a bearing on how one's spiritual life is to be conducted? Moreover, by considering these letters, what might be discerned about how Edwards dealt with his own wife and family, and how it is he may have conducted worship within the home? Most importantly, is there a different emphasis in Edwards's personal correspondence than in his sermons and theological treatises? Does the glory of God remain the preeminent concern even here? By a consideration of such questions, we will discern how devotions would take place within the family, but even more, what is the real essence of such practices.

Edwards's Personal Correspondence: Overview and Early Letters

Only 236 letters remain extant from Edwards's personal correspondence, despite a "search that spanned many years and several countries."[28] While not inconsequential, one might have expected many more, given Edwards's self-declaration noted previously: "So far as I am able to judge of what talents I have, for benefiting my fellow creatures by word, I think I can write better than I can speak."[29] There is no disputing that his written legacy is voluminous. But since his earliest available autograph letter is dated May 10, 1716, while he died on March 22, 1758, only an average of five or six letters a year are known to us.[30] Claghorn concludes, "the extant record represents only a fraction of the letters he wrote."[31]

As a consequence, this survey should not on the whole be considered as final or definitive, since based on such partial data. Still more, consider that only a small proportion of Edwards's extant letters are addressed to members of his own immediate family, even though separation from them was not uncommon. The vast preponderance of available correspondence is instead addressed to other ministers or to leaders and officials in the New England

---

28. From Claghorn's editorial introduction in WJE 16:3.
29. WJE 16:729.
30. It is Edwards's letter to his sister Mary that is dated May 10, 1716, in WJE 16:29.
31. From Claghorn's editorial introduction in WJE 16:5.

community. This is, in its own right, an important observation. Based on the correspondence we do have available, it would be an order of magnitude easier to draw from it insights into Edwards's ecclesiology than to discern decisively his views on family worship.

From two of Edwards's earliest extant letters written while at Yale, one detects a potential degree of loneliness, and even immaturity, as he pines for his sister to correspond. To Mary he writes, "Of all the many sisters I have, I think I never had one so long out of my hearing as yourself. . . . I thought it was a pity that there should not be the least correspondence between us, or communication from one to another, [when] no farther distant."[32] Nearly two years later, he plucks at this same string: "I at length obtained the wished for opportunity of sending a letter to you, though disappointed of the much more desired one of receiving one from you."[33] Such personal moments, even in the young Edwards, are rare. Instead, one discerns an uncommon seriousness, and even isolation, in Edwards's time at Yale. Simply put, he did not fit in; he wanted to study, while others wanted to play. To accept Edwards's assessment, his precocious roommate and cousin Elisha, for example, did not know his place, was unwilling to draw cider like the other freshmen, and was unwilling to study as he should.[34] It was a source of great consternation to Edwards, especially in light of the fact that Elisha was a near family relation: "I had rather have my cousin to be my chambermate than anybody, if he would but demean 'im becomingly and be contented."[35]

Only 9 of the 236 letters that have been found in Edwards's hand are dated earlier than the end of 1723, when he was barely 20 years old. Significantly, a large gap of nearly 12 years exists, from the period between October of 1723 and May of 1735, during which time no letters from him are available. As a consequence, so far as his extant correspondence is concerned, the themes found in his letters move quickly from those of youth and school to concerns about family and ministry. Tantalizingly, his New York pastorate, his courtship and marriage to Sarah Pierpont, and his arrival at Northampton under the watchful eye of Solomon Stoddard are events that all unfold during this interlude in which no correspondence remains.

---

32. WJE 16:31.
33. WJE 16:39.
34. WJE 16:35–36.
35. WJE 16:36.

Letters to Edwards's Children

We have a number of letters Edwards sent to his children, spanning roughly twenty years and concerning wide range of circumstances. What pleases Edwards so far as his children were concerned? Are his thoughts often settled upon their financial well-being, their prospects for marriage, or their personal enjoyment? Does Edwards wonder about how his children feel, or express interest in their self-esteem? In a letter to the Rev. Benjamin Colman, Edwards provides a window into what he regards most highly in his own home, and a first real glimpse into what happened in it:

> This winter has been a time of the most remarkable and visible blessing of heaven upon my family that ever was; all our children that are capable of religious reflections have been under remarkable impressions, and I can't but think that salvation is come into my house, in several instances. I hope that my four eldest children (the youngest of them between six and seven years of age) have been savingly wrought upon, the eldest some years ago.[36]

Yet he writes with comparable passion, and even similar language and seemingly equal relish, about the spreading revival among the youth of his congregation: "In the summer and fall the children in various parts of the town had religious meetings by themselves for prayer, sometimes joined with fasting; wherein many of them seemed to be greatly and properly affected, and I hope some of them were savingly wrought upon."[37]

Two themes consistently rise to view in the letters he sent to his children: that they should utterly devote themselves to God, and that they soberly consider the nearness of death. Even in the briefest of notes to his children, both themes are typically evident. The youthfulness of his children presents no boundary to a vigorous expression of either motif. To the twelve-year-old Sarah he writes, "I hope you will well improve the great advantage God is thereby putting into your hands for the good of your own soul. You have a very weak and infirm body, and I am afraid are always like to have it; and it may be are not to be long-lived. . . . But if your soul prospers you will be an happy blessed person, whatever becomes of your body."[38] As George Claghorn observes, Sarah, despite any infirmities Edwards might have been

---

36. WJE 16:88.
37. WJE 16:118.
38. WJE 16:95–96.

concerned with on this occasion, nevertheless lived on to the age of seventy-six. Here Edwards expresses his heart's desire for this daughter, in an expression emblematic of his hopes for all of his children: "I wish you much of the presence of Christ and communion with him, and that you might live so as to give him honor in the place where you are by an amiable behavior towards all."[39] This one sentence could well serve as the banner for Edwards's "program" for youth—for his own, and for all. We can be certain that in his home "Christ's presence and communion" were often sought.

Similarly, he writes to fourteen-year-old Timothy, "whether you are sick or well, like to die or like to live, I hope you are earnestly seeking your salvation. . . . Make haste and delay not in the great business of religion."[40] He adds soon thereafter, "I hope you will improve life and health while God continues them to prepare [Timothy's brothers and sisters] for sickness and death, which you must expect: death will certainly come at the time which God has appointed, whether you are prepared or unprepared."[41] As such, two subjects some consider beyond the grasp of youth—religion and death—are routinely pressed by Edwards to his children for their mature and serious reflection. Moreover, concerns regarding the genuineness of their conversion—in effect, calls to self-examination—consistently rise to view. We can thus surmise that in the same way that Edwards privately practiced self-examination, this discipline would have been routinely featured in family devotional moments as well.

During periods of separation from his family, Edwards frequently contrasts the impulse that his children may have had for the comfort and familiarity of family life, with the far more urgent concern that his children draw near to the almighty God. His letter to his daughter Esther is in this way typical: "I would not have you be discouraged and melancholy, though you are far from home; God is everywhere, and I hope you will walk closely with him, and will have much of his presence."[42] And to Mary he writes, "I had rather you should remain hundreds of miles distant from us and have God nigh to you by his Spirit, than to have you always with us, and live at a distance from God."[43] God's omnipresence is in this way no mere formal

39. WJE 16:96.
40. WJE 16:579.
41. WJE 16:598–99.
42. WJE 16:215.
43. WJE 16:289.

dogma, but a comfort to all God's people, and in particular a source of comfort, a balm applied by Edwards, from father to child. To Esther he writes, "If you lived near us, yet our breath and yours would soon go forth, and we should return to our dust, whither we all are hastening. 'Tis of infinitely more importance to have the presence of an heavenly Father, and to make progress toward an heavenly home. Let us take care that we may meet there at last."[44] And to Timothy he adds,

> Young persons are very apt to trust in parents and friends, when they are sick, or when they think of being on a deathbed. But this providence [the possibility of Timothy's contraction of smallpox] remarkably teaches you the need of a better friend, and a better parent, than earthly parents are; one who is everywhere present, and all-sufficient ... who is able to save from death or make happy in death; to save from eternal misery and to bestow eternal life.[45]

Finally, to Jonathan he writes, "Though you are at so great a distance from us, and from all your relations, yet this is a comfort to us, that the same God that is here, is also at Onohquaga; and that though you are out of our sight and out of our reach, you are always in God's hands, who is infinitely gracious; and we can go to him, and commit you to his care and mercy."[46]

It may well appear that Edwards lacked originality given the frequency with which he brought forth this motif—that although his child might be far removed, and far from the blessings of home and family, it was far more essential that they draw near to God, their true source of hope and comfort under all circumstances. This feature, though, far from a lack of imagination, instead demonstrates an expression of his lifelong concern for his own children. Their salvation, and their lives demonstrating the fruit of genuine conversion, remained paramount; surely if pressed this vigorously during periods of separation, it would also have been pressed similarly while they were at home. George Claghorn observes, in an editorial comment concerning a letter written by Edwards to his daughter Mary, "No matter how pressing the demands or cares of the moment, Edwards always put his paternal and pastoral responsibilities first."[47] We rarely see Edwards speak of temporal concerns. At times he will correspond with Timothy about matters relat-

44. WJE 16:577.
45. WJE 16:579.
46. WJE 16:666.
47. Claghorn in WJE 16:288.

ing to his needs while at Princeton, for example, but even in these instances spiritual concerns predominate.[48] To Mary he writes,

> [M]y greatest concern is for your soul's good.... My desire and *daily prayer* is that you may, if it consist with the holy will of God, meet with God where you be, and have much of his divine influences on your heart wherever you may be, and that in God's due time you may be returned to us again in all respects under the smiles of heaven, and especially in prosperous circumstances of your soul; and that you may find us all alive.[49]

He adds, in words that perhaps summarize well his view of what a private devotional life should look like,

> I hope you will maintain a strict and constant watch over yourself and against all temptations: that you don't forget and forsake God; and particularly that you don't grow slack in secret religion. Retire often from this vain world, and all its bubbles, empty shadows, and vain amusements, and converse with God alone; and seek that divine grace and comfort, the least drop of which is worth more than all the riches, gaiety, pleasures and entertainments of the whole world.[50]

Letters to Edwards's Wife

Two letters that Edwards wrote to his wife Sarah are extant, both of which are noteworthy in different ways. In the first, Jonathan conveys to his wife that his "business trip" will be longer than expected; a neighboring congregation needs his counsel in the midst of immediate difficulties arising from what George Claghorn refers to as "revival excesses."[51] Edwards speaks as a husband to a wife, who will care about and understand his physical makeup better than others: "I have been considerably amiss since I came from home; riding in such tempestuous weather increased my cold, and almost overcame me. But am now a little better."[52] His conclusion is ostensibly tender:

---

48. See, for example, WJE 16:599.
49. WJE 16:289; emphasis added.
50. WJE 16:289–90.
51. WJE 16:103.
52. WJE 16:104.

"Remember me in your prayers. I am, my dearest companion, your affectionate consort, Jonathan Edwards."[53]

The second letter is written not while Jonathan is away, but while Sarah is in Boston tending to family business. He addresses her as his "dear companion," and signs it as "your most affectionate companion."[54] The same letter contains a poignant statement that is perhaps the most revealing of Edwards's dependence on his wife: "We have been without you almost as long as we know how to be."[55] As has been suggested, some devotional writers have made a great deal of this statement, and have forged a view of Jonathan and Sarah's marriage that ostensibly goes beyond the evidence.[56] While a tender declaration, two observations must be added. First, despite this avowal of his and the family's need for Sarah, Edwards adds in this letter that his wife should "obey the calls of providence" in dispatching any necessary business in Boston—if God needed Sarah more than Edwards, he was only too pleased to acquiesce. Further, in the very next sentence he suggests that she "buy us some cheese" if she has enough money. He is by no means caught up in a solely wistful, romantic remembrance. It is important, then, not to make too much of Edwards's poignant declaration of his need for Sarah—this is a warm marriage, but also very definitely a functional one.

The Edwards Home

The size of Edwards's family—eleven children, and also servants—was a frequent cause of strain and concern. More than that, there was seemingly a revolving door of visitors, particularly during their time at Northampton:

> I have a growing family; and if God preserves our lives, as he, by distinguishing mercy, has done hitherto, the charge of my family is likely to grow, not only by the increase of it, but by the increase of my family's acquaintance, whereby my house will probably become still more a place of resort, as it has been more and more so for many years past. There may also perhaps be extraordinary charge hereafter

---

53. WJE 16:105. It is worth commenting, as an aside, that Edwards frequently requested prayer from those with whom he corresponded.

54. WJE 16:247.

55. Ibid.

56. Piper, *Faithful Women*, 23.

arising, by bringing up a son to learning, or by settling of my children in the world.[57]

That prayer was a part of the Edwards home is no mystery. To Esther he writes, "We daily remember you in our prayers to God, who I hope will be with you continually and will in every respect be gracious to you."[58] Over six years later, he reminds her, "we daily remember you in our prayers."[59] He also repeatedly asks for prayer for himself and for the family frequently in his correspondence.

Edwards makes reference to a church contract, a vow made by the congregation in March of 1741, in a letter to Rev. Thomas Prince. While this contract is noteworthy for a number of historical reasons, there are two statements that perhaps articulate Edwards's understanding of how children should live and, taken together, how families should function. It may in this way reflect an idyllic picture of the Edwards home, and his ideal for the family's pattern of devotion. Regarding children, he writes,

> [a]nd those of us that are in youth do promise never to allow ourselves in any youthful diversions and pastimes, in meetings or companies of young people, that we in our consciences, upon sober consideration, judge not well to consist with, or would sinfully tend to hinder the devoutest, and most engaged spirit in religion; or indispose the mind for that devout and profitable attendance on the duties of the closet, which is most agreeable to God's will, or that we in our most impartial judgment, can think tends to rob God of that honor which he expects, by our orderly, serious attendance on family worship.[60]

The contract adds this second statement pertaining to the governance of families: "We also promise, with great watchfulness, to perform relative duties, required by Christian rules, in the families we belong to; as we stand related respectively, towards parents and children, husbands and wives, brothers and sisters, masters or mistresses and servants."[61] One expects that Edwards would have sought to model this behavior in his own home.

---

57. WJE 16:150.
58. WJE 16:215.
59. WJE 16:578.
60. WJE 16:123–24.
61. WJE 16:124. Servants, and anyone else in the home, would be included in the family's devotional activities.

Edwards speaks routinely about the large size of his family. In 1749, with the possibility of being cast out of his pulpit looming large, he wrote to the Rev. Thomas Foxcroft, "I am now comfortably settled, have as large a salary settled upon me as most have out of Boston, and have the largest and most chargeable family of any minister, perhaps within an hundred miles of me."[62] Just a year later, to the Rev. William McCulloch, while expressing confidence in God, he nevertheless lamented, "I have now nothing visible to depend upon for my future usefulness, or the subsistence of my numerous family."[63] And years later, to the trustees at Princeton, he expressed concern regarding the challenge of moving his "numerous family."[64]

Financial concerns seemed to have been a comparatively constant concern in the Edwards home, whether wrangling with the congregation at Northampton over his salary concerns, or more keenly, at the mission outpost that was Stockbridge. In 1752, Edwards included this significant assertion in a letter to Thomas Foxcroft: "if the bookseller can be agreed to let me have a number for the copy [of his forthcoming book, *Misrepresentations Corrected*], it would be pleasing. If not, I must go without."[65] That Edwards could not afford a single copy of his own book is especially noteworthy. Hand-me-downs are discussed in a letter to his son Timothy.[66] Even in his role as president at Princeton financial concerns remained pressing, so much so that his last extant letter, written while dying of smallpox, states simply, "This is to desire that when you come next to this place, you would come prepared to pay me an £100, for so much will be due to me from the College Treasury, in the month of March approaching. I also desire to borrow an £100 of the college the next May, which the Trustees have consented to."[67] Still, the Edwards home, while at times struggling financially, was generally not impoverished: Edwards helped his son Timothy pay for college,[68] and, while the family often faced financial difficulties, they did have servants:

---

62. WJE 16:284.
63. WJE 16:358.
64. WJE 16:725.
65. WJE 16:486.
66. WJE 16:599.
67. WJE 16:731.
68. WJE 16:692–93.

"God has lately frowned on my family in taking away a faithful servant, who was a great help to us."[69]

In the conclusions of many of Edwards's letters, we are often given a brief glimpse into the matter of the particular season of life unfolding in the Edwards home. Sickness and health are commonly reported on, and these issues, coupled with ongoing financial matters, would have been routine matters for prayer and petition. In the midst of the Northampton controversy, to the Rev. Thomas Foxcroft he writes, "My youngest child [Elizabeth], about three years old, is in a very languishing, dangerous state, and my wife is pretty near her time. I desire your prayers for them; and for me under all my trials."[70] To the Rev. John Erskine he writes, "My youngest child but one [one year old, that is, Jonathan, Jr.] has long been in a very infirm, afflicted, and decaying state with the rickets and some other disorders. I desire your prayers for it."[71] And in a later letter to Erskine, he comments, "My family were in their usual state of health when I left 'em, excepting my youngest child [Pierpont] who had something like an intermitting fever."[72]

Was there strife in the Edwards home? Little conflict is easily discerned. In an admittedly minor moment of disagreement, in writing to a fellow minister Edwards declares Sarah's possible mild impertinence: "My wife seems to be very unwilling that our sheep should be sold."[73] Clearly, such a report is a tepid source for gossip. It seems reasonable to assume, given the overall tenor of genuine affection expressed in letters among the family, the mention of prayers in the home and for one another, and the abundance of visitors, that the Edwards home was most likely governed by a prevailing concern for efficient function, as well as by mutual respect and love.

Prevailing Concerns: Religion, Correction and Instruction

Edwards's letter to George Whitefield dated December 14, 1740, reflects his consistent heart's concern, as well as the result of Whitefield's impact even in Edwards's own family:

69. WJE 16:681.
70. WJE 16:323.
71. WJE 16:356.
72. WJE 16:380.
73. WJE 16:362.

> I have joyful tidings to send you concerning the state of religion in this place.... I have reason to believe that a considerable number of our young people, some of them children, have already been savingly brought home to Christ. I hope salvation has come to this house [Edwards's own home] since you was in it, with respect to one, if not more, of my children. The Spirit of God seems to be at work with others of the family.... as God seems to have succeeded in your labors amongst us, and prayers for us, I desire your fervent prayers for us may yet be continued, that God would not be to us as a wayfaring man, that turns aside to tarry but for a night, but that he would more and more pour out his Spirit upon us, and no more depart from us; and for me in particular, that I may be filled with his Spirit, and may become fervent, as a flame of fire in my work, and may be abundantly succeeded, and that it would please God, however unworthy I am, to improve me as an instrument of his glory, and advancing the kingdom of Christ.[74]

What inflames his interests and passions? We are here reminded that Edwards is concerned primarily about the working of God above all things, and by extension, any discernible growth of interest in the business of religion, of which progress in his own home was a vital facet. He was ever the consummately theocentric revivalist, and this concern as well would have been a feature of the family's devotional life. With his characteristic excitement he reports to the Rev. Thomas Prince, "the minds of the people in general appeared more engaged in religion, showing a greater forwardness to make religion the subject of their conversation, and to meet frequently together for religious purposes, and to embrace all opportunities to hear the Word preached."[75] Such notions were no passing interest, but a fundamental, prevailing exigency; his reason for writing, and as a result, the interests of home and family, were integral, but seemingly always secondary to this more dominant preoccupation.

To his good friend John Erskine, to whom he wrote frequently, Edwards expressed matters of essential import to this larger program. What kinds of topics concerned him? Consider the books he requested from Erskine: those "tending either to the illustration, or defense of the truth, or the promoting the power of godliness, or in any respect peculiarly tending to advance true religion."[76]

74. WJE 16:87.
75. WJE 16:116.
76. WJE 16:260.

To detect how this primary thrust at times intersected with Edwards's home life, consider how he responded in the midst of his greatest personal travail, the occasion of the death of his especially beloved daughter Jerusha, "the flower of the family," likely from tuberculosis, as she had cared for David Brainerd as he died from the disease.[77] Even here his concerns, so far as his letters reveal, remain entirely God-directed and spiritual. In three separate letters Edwards relates the death of Jerusha. For example, to the Rev. Ebenezer Parkman he expressed the weight of that moment in the Edwards home: "[It has] pleased a holy God of late sorely to [try our] family, by taking away by death [our] daughter, Jerusha.... This is [to ask your] prayers for us under our great [affliction], that it may be sanctified to us and [that God] would fill up the melancholy vacancy [made] by death in this family, with his [gracious] and comfortable presence."[78] In these statements, we see both how dearly Edwards prized this daughter (Brainerd had referred to her as "not only a saint, but as a very eminent saint"[79]) and also how he sought to set even this most heavy blow to the family in the larger context of the loving sovereignty of God.

This intersection between programmatic concerns and personal sensibilities extended to the work of the church as well. Families were to be instructed in order that they might strengthen the church. This is well illustrated by an instance in which Edwards conveys with positive affirmation the statement of an association of ministers aimed at "promoting religion," written in response to the question, "What things shall be done by us for preventing the awful threatening degeneracy and backsliding in religion, in the present day?"[80] This statement includes a number of directives for families. Three are most prominent:

> We must consider what evils there are to be found among them [the congregation in relation to their ministers], which do especially need reforming; as the profanation of the Lord's day, which is enough to destroy all religion; tavern-haunting, company-keeping, chambering, uncleanness, profaneness, etc. And we ought loudly to testify against 'em. And that what we do may be effectual, let us endeavor to convince their consciences of the evil of sin, and of these sins. We are not to fail to warn people solemnly against the dreadful guilt of

---

77. WJE 16:249.
78. WJE 16:245.
79. WJE 16:246.
80. WJE 16:276.

unthankfulness under God's single mercies, and of incorrigibleness under heavy and sore judgments. Could we in wisdom do it, we should also warn 'em against their oppressing the Lord's ministers in their maintenance.

Let us endeavor to revive good customs and practices among 'em; particularly, the ancient good practice of catechizing, family order, worship and government, religious societies under good regulation, godly conference and conversation among Christians; and in brief, whatever is laudable and of good tendency.

Church discipline should be revived; brotherly watchfulness and admonition. Nor are we to forget to take special care of the children and youth of the flock.[81]

In this light, it was unthinkable that children should live without deep respect for their parents, much less their minister. Edwards reflects back on his removal from the pulpit at Northampton in a revealing moment: "It has often been observed what a curse persons have lived under, and been pursued by, for their ill-treatment of their natural parents; but especially may this be expected to follow such abuses offered by a people to one which in their own esteem is their spiritual father."[82] There is no question that Edwards was the undisputed head of his home, and that he would have sought to put into practice each of the principles enumerated in this letter, "catechizing, family order, worship and government," and the like.

A Letter to Sir William Pepperell and the Period at Stockbridge

At a later period of his life and ministry, much of Edwards's philosophy of education in the home can be observed in an instructive letter to Sir William Pepperell.[83] It is a response to an inquiry from Pepperell regarding the state of the Stockbridge school, and in particular, relates to the "proper plan of a school for Indian girls in this place."[84] In this context, education is seen as

---

81. WJE 16:280. These phrases, while not written by Edwards, were forwarded by him to Rev. James Robe as evidence of the efforts of others "earnestly to invent means for the promoting [sic] religion." Given that the lengthy statement from this association of ministers comprises the bulk of this letter to Robe, Edwards's endorsement of its contents is obvious.

82. WJE 16:653.

83. WJE 16:406–14.

84. So Claghorn notes in WJE 16:406; the quote is on p. 407. Unusual for the time, Edwards states plainly in this letter that "girls as well as boys" should be educated. WJE 16:411.

closely connected to not only religion, but to a vital family devotional life. Edwards's program of education is decidedly out of touch with modern conceptions of a full-orbed educational program. In short, the single dominating concern for Edwards is spiritual development—all other subjects, while of use, should serve this greater end. The following particulars in this lengthy letter warrant note.

Edwards laments as a chief defect in typical educational programs that they teach by rote, without seeking to engage the reason: "children, when they are taught to read, are so much accustomed to reading, without any kind of knowledge of the meaning of what they read, that they continue reading without understanding, even a long time after they are capable of understanding."[85] Similarly, Edwards writes elsewhere, "The art of teaching, and more especially little children at the first opening of their understanding, requires superior talents. And the cultivating and new forming the minds of those that come out of such great wildness will require great prudence, faithfulness, and constant application."[86]

Edwards underscores that the same watchfulness would be necessary in teaching the catechism: "In like manner they are taught their catechism, saying over the words by rote.... [I]f the question were put in phraseology somewhat new, to which they have not been accustomed, they would not know what to answer."[87] So also, teachers are to ensure that their students are interacting with the material and understanding it, rather than merely reproducing forms and words. But what subject matter should be taught? What would Edwards want home and school to teach? In particular, the Bible, "scriptural history," "great successive changes and events in the Jewish nation and world of mankind that connect the history of the Old and New Testaments," geography (that is, of the biblical lands), and music, "especially sacred music" were to be taught.[88] Brief mention is made of the necessity of the basics of reading and arithmetic, but these are subservient to Edwards's chief aim:

> In order to promote the salvation of the children, which is the main design of the whole Indian establishment at this place, I think that, beside their attending public worship on the sabbath, and the daily

85. WJE, 16:407.
86. WJE, 16:433.
87. WJE 16:407–8.
88. WJE 16:409–11.

worship of the family, and catechizing in the school . . . the duty of secret prayer, and the duty pressed and enforced on every one; and care should be taken, that all may have proper opportunity and convenience for it.[89]

It is impossible to miss that for Edwards, these are the basics that every child should know. One must conclude that these elements comprise only the beginnings for what should be taught even the most ignorant of children. By contrast, it is not difficult to surmise that in the Edwards home the bar would be considerably higher. Knowledge of the Bible, catechism, the singing of Psalms, and the history and geography of the Bible would all be ingrained in the fabric of daily life. Singing rises to prominence periodically in Edwards's correspondence, and this practice must be featured as well in the home.[90] Still more, secret and family prayer, and frequent questioning and interaction, would be regular practices. In the school at Stockbridge, "each child should, from time to time, be dealt with singly, particularly, and closely, about the state and concerns of his soul."[91] It appears highly likely, then, that this would all routinely take place under Edwards's own roof.

In speaking of their new home at Stockbridge, Edwards writes to his father regarding his own family's assessment of the new situation: "They like the place far better than they expected. Here, at present, we live in peace; which has of long time been an unusual thing with us."[92] He writes, though, with stern disapproval regarding the manner in which a teacher at the Stockbridge school has failed to submit to her husband: "Mrs. Sergeant is undoubtedly a woman of very considerable abilities, and her natural temper disposes her much more to dominion than subjection. She loves to have a hand in the management of public affairs and she had a vast ascendance over Mr. Sergeant." While a power struggle at the Stockbridge encampment

---

89. WJE 16:411–12.

90. Edwards writes, in a letter to Rev. Benjamin Colman dated May 22, 1744, and with a perspective that was comparatively novel for this period in New England, "It has been our manner in this congregation, for more than two years past, in the summer time, when we sing three times upon the sabbath, to sing an hymn, or part of a hymn of Dr. [Isaac] Watts' . . ." WJE 16:144. In a Thanksgiving Day sermon, Edwards instructed, "Parents ought to be careful that their children are instructed in singing, that they may be capable of performing that part of divine worship. This we should do, as we would have our children trained up for heaven; for we all of us would have our children go to heaven." *Works*[2] 2:917.

91. WJE 16:412.

92. WJE, 16:420.

serves as the backdrop for these comments, they are nevertheless a reflection of Edwards's broader concern that women take a subservient role.

The hardships of life against which all of these spiritual and family concerns were set were very real, as has been noted. Severe illnesses were common in the Edwards home, although this was a familiar problem to many families in the period.[93] But sickness was by no means the only threat to health and home. Both at Northampton and at Stockbridge, the Edwards family periodically had to board soldiers, owing to the persistent danger of attack: "Here we have been in much fear of an army suddenly rushing in upon the town in the night to destroy it."[94] Particularly at Stockbridge, Edwards expressed strong concern that their lives were in grave danger.[95] Such realities may help explain why Edwards often, and with urgency, set life and death, and the imminence of heaven and hell, before his family, his congregation, and his readership.

Implications: The Theologian's Paternal Interest

On the whole, the emphasis in Edwards's personal correspondence, then, appears eminently consistent with the emphasis found in his sermons and theological treatises. He writes, "Every Christian family is a little church, and the heads of it are its authoritative teachers and governors." Similarly, Edwards avers, "Every family should be a little church, a family of Christ. Means are appointed to this end. Baptism. Family worship. Let parents use them. Heads of families see to it that they are so. Use endeavors one with another. Husbands with wives, and wives with husbands. Improve their society to that end."[96] Two vignettes drawn from this correspondence will perhaps help bring this into sharper relief. While his son was not yet ten years old, Edwards allowed, and probably encouraged, Jonathan Jr. to go on a months-long missions trip with Gideon Hawley. As a result, when Jonathan Jr. received a letter from his father, he was off in the rugged wilderness at the

---

93. See comments regarding illness in WJE vol. 16, for example, on pp. 543–44, 548, 595, 598, 668, 672, 673, 681, 691, and 731.

94. WJE 16:215.

95. See WJE vol. 16, letters 207, 208, and 218. In letter 218, to Rev. Gideon Hawley, dated October 9, 1756, Edwards comments, "What will become of us, God only knows." WJE 16:691.

96. WJE 4:487; and Edwards, *Glory and Honor of God*, 171.

"Indian settlement" at Onohquaga.[97] Edwards's letter to his son sublimates any temporal concerns to those more essentially spiritual. He urged, "Always set God before your eyes, and live in his fear, and seek him every day with all diligence: for 'tis he, and he only can make you happy or miserable, as he pleases; and your life and health, and the eternal happiness of your soul, and your all in this life and that which is to come, depends on his will and pleasure."[98] Edwards's thoughts for his son, in the midst of genuine physical hardships, are heavenward. We might well infer that there were two principal reasons Jonathan Jr. was even with Gideon Hawley at Onohquaga: for his personal spiritual growth, and as an outgrowth of his father's desire for the spread of the gospel to the ends of the earth—this was suitable training for life as a missionary.

So also, Deborah Hatheway was a young convert who lived in Suffield, Massachusetts, who wrote to Edwards for advice and counsel when Suffield was without a pastor.[99] Edwards responds with nineteen points at which Hatheway might examine her life in order to "conduct [herself] in [her] Christian course."[100] As will be seen in the section on Christian conference that follows later in this chapter, it is a thorough, well-rounded, almost paternal communication, as Edwards sets out his perspective on how a young Christian woman should organize her life.

It is odd, then, to observe how just over three weeks later Edwards, in a letter to his own twelve-year-old daughter Sarah, offers very little spiritual counsel, with the exception of a typical warning about the brevity of life and the necessity of following hard after God.[101] Is this indicative of a lack of love or concern for Sarah, or even of a preference for the work of the ministry over against Edwards's responsibilities to his own children?

Very likely, the reason for this apparent favoritism is that the nineteen points of counsel Hatheway received would be nothing new to Sarah, even at the age of twelve. Self-examination, counsel with other Christians, the call to exhort other young people to a serious and devout life, warnings about pride and deadness of spirit—these themes in the letter to Hatheway were regular

---

97. WJE 16:666–67.

98. WJE 16:667. As editor George Claghorn notes, even at this early age, "The Indians welcomed him and were especially pleased at his proficiency with their language."

99. Claghorn in WJE 16:90.

100. WJE 16:91.

101. See WJE 16:95–96.

elements among others not only in Edwards's preaching, but clearly in his own home and his family's worship. So, for example, when Edwards counsels Hatheway that when she hears sermons that are evidently directed toward others (such as the unconverted) she consider "in what respects is this that I hear spoken, applicable to me."[102] Sarah, and all the Edwards children, would find this familiar fare.

In sum, then, we can discern a number of features that would be elements of morning and evening family devotions within the Edwards's home. There would be prayers, certainly—for the home, for relatives, for the church, with respect to circumstances, and for countless other matters. There would be catechism. There would likely be frequent opportunities for self-examination. There would be concerns for revival. And if his children, when far from home, were consistently urged to draw near to God even more intimately than their own family relations, surely in the home itself this same emphasis would have also been likely.[103]

The unsettling question some might still have, even at this juncture, is just this: Was there love in the Edwards home? With all the emphasis on spiritual rigor, and self-examination, and catechism, and early morning worship, was there love? When Jonathan Edwards died, his wife Sarah

---

102. WJE 16:92.

103. Numerous sermons could have been included here that would bolster these conclusions substantially. Notable among them are the following:

"Youth and the Pleasures of Piety," preached first in May 1734 and on at least five more occasions, and devoted to Prov 24:13–14: "My son, eat thou honey, because it is good; and the honeycomb, which is sweet to thy taste: so shall the knowledge of wisdom be to thy soul: when thou hast found it, then there shall be a reward, and thy expectation shall not be cut off." WJE 19:78, 81–90.

"The Danger of Corrupt Communication Among Young People," preached in July 1740, on Eph 4:29: "Let no corrupt communication proceed out of your mouth, but that which is good to the use of edifying, that it may minister grace unto the hearers." WJE 22:158–66.

"Children Ought to Love the Lord Jesus Christ above All," preached in August 1740, on Matt 10:37: "He that loveth father or mother more than me is not worthy of me." WJE 22:170–80.

"Youth Is Like a Flower That Is Cut Down," preached in February 1741 upon the sudden death of a child in his congregation, centered on Job 14:2: "He cometh forth like a flower, and is cut down." WJE 22:319–38. See 319–21 for the historical backdrop of this sermon, which Edwards preached again on February 21, 1748, at the funeral of his own daughter Jerusha.

"The Importance of Revival among Heads of Families," preached in August 1741, on Luke 1:17: "And he shall go before him in the spirit and power of Elias, to turn the hearts of the fathers to the children, and the disobedient to the wisdom of the just; to make ready a people prepared for the Lord." WJE 22:451–54.

and daughter Susannah wrote a joint letter to Esther Burr, another of the Edwards's daughters and the recent widow of the Rev. Aaron Burr. In such a time, their deepest affections were on display. Sarah wrote,

> What shall I say? A holy and good God has covered us with a dark cloud. O that we may kiss the rod, and lay our hands on our mouths! The Lord has done it. He has made me adore his goodness, that we had him so long. But my God lives; and he has my heart. O what a legacy my husband, and your father, has left us! We are all given to God; and there I am, and love to be.[104]

And to this, Susannah added the note, "My father took leave of all his people and family as affectionately as if he knew he should not come again. On the sabbath afternoon he preached from these words,—We have no continuing city, therefore let us seek one to come.... When he had got out of doors he turned about,—'I commit you to God,'—said he."[105] If there was not genuine love in the Edwards home, could such tributes be possible?

Private Reading of Scripture

Jonathan Edwards somewhat famously distances himself from the theological roots of Calvinism with these words: "I should not take it at all amiss, to be called a Calvinist, for distinction's sake: though I utterly disclaim a dependence on Calvin, or believing the doctrines which I hold, because he believed and taught them; and cannot be justly charged with believing in everything just as he taught."[106] And, while Edwards speaks approvingly of how it was that "God began gloriously to revive his church again" during the Reformation, and mentions Luther, Melanchthon, Zwingli, and Calvin as he reviews the history of the work of redemption, the Reformer's emphasis on the five "solas"—*Sola Fide, Sola Christus, Sola Gratia, Soli Deo Gloria*, and *Sola Scriptura*—are not emphasized by him per se.[107]

It might be surprising to many that while Edwards certainly believed in the concept of *Sola Scriptura*, in his preaching an emphasis on the private reading of Scripture—as frequent as it is—is less pronounced than, say, the practice of self-examination and perhaps also prayer. There is certainly much

---

104. *Works²* clxxix.
105. Ibid.
106. From Edwards's preface to *Freedom of the Will* in WJE 1:131.
107. See WJE 9:421–22.

he has to say about the value and importance of Scripture reading, as will be seen.[108] But given the prominence of the Scriptures to the Reformers and others, in the application of the preached Word that he offers to his congregation, unexpectedly, his direction that they read the Scriptures is insistent and intense, but not overwhelmingly frequent. Since the sermon "Christian Knowledge," considered previously, includes the admonition to "be assiduous in reading the holy Scriptures," another vantage point is warranted to consider Edwards's approach to this topic.

Edwards's view on the private reading of Scripture is best understood by a careful consideration of his extraordinary—and nearly obsessive—personal practice. Resolution 28 serves as a credible starting point, and offers a window into his world: "Resolved, to study the Scriptures so steadily, constantly and frequently, as that I may find, and plainly perceive myself to grow in the knowledge of the same."[109] It was his own aim, then, to "steadily, constantly and frequently" be engaged in this spiritual discipline of the private reading of Scripture. How was this general aim worked out in the specific realities of Edwards's life?

By virtue of the vast volume of writings by Edwards, published and unpublished, consider how it was that he must have been constantly putting pen to paper in an effort to carry out the aim of studying the Scriptures. His sermons and lectures, of course, necessitated frequent and in-depth preparation, as he unpacked the doctrine of a particular text of Scripture. But the whole of his life was consumed with such activities. Sereno Dwight, one of his earliest biographers, offers the following portrait:

> His most usual diversion in summer, was riding on horseback, and walking; and in his solitary rides and walks, he appears to have decided, before leaving home, on what subjects to meditate. He would commonly, unless diverted by company, ride two or three miles after dinner, to some lonely grove, where he would dismount and walk awhile. At such times, he generally carried his pen and ink with him, to note any thought that might be suggested, and which promised some light on any important subject.[110]

---

108. It must be emphasized that Edwards taught that "The knowledge and understanding of the Word of God is the root and foundation of fruitfulness." See his sermon entitled "Profitable Hearers of the Word" in WJE 14:246–77.

109. WJE 16:755.

110. *Works*² 1:xxxviii.

The outcome of this habit of life is seen in a few of the artifacts that remain from that prolific pen. There are the 1,360 "miscellanies" that record his thoughts on the full range of theological topics, several of which span the length of full treatises. There is his "Blank Bible," containing more than 5,500 notes written on the interleaved pages, which complements his "Notes on Scripture," a notebook in which are contained more than 500 comments on specific passages.[111] Similarly, Edwards recorded several hundred types, as for example "Images of Divine Things" and "Types of the Messiah."[112] One sees in these voluminous notes and other extended writings, which span the whole of Edwards's adult life, the realization of the goals of his early "Resolutions."

Given this, it is no surprise that Edwards admonishes and encourages his congregation to be sedulous in their reading of the Scriptures. He warns "those who live careless and vicious lives" to no longer "neglect duties of religion such as secret prayer and reading the Scriptures."[113] The assurance of Christ as Redeemer will make the Bible "a sweet book to you."[114] Christians are to exert themselves in its study. He preached, "Diligently use those means that God has appointed for our instruction and conversion. The Word of God was given to us to be read and doubtless is what is above all things adapted to obtain those great ends."[115] Those who are "true converts" will "have new eyes, that instead of being employed to seek the objects of their lusts are employed in reading God's holy Word and beholding the wondrous works of God."[116]

These few quotes, all drawn from one volume comprised of twenty-two of Edwards's sermons, certainly make the point that the private reading of

---

111. For further historical details on these artifacts see the editors' introductions to the various volumes of the Yale works.

112. So for example, "The extreme fierceness and extraordinary power of the heat of lightning is an intimation of the exceeding power and terribleness of the wrath of God." WJE 11:59. Anderson and Watters write, "For Edwards, types were found not only in the Old Testament; the phenomenal world also declared divine truths." WJE 11:3.

113. BL 42.

114. BL 62.

115. BL 105.

116. BL 305. A fifth sermon in this volume also makes brief mention of Scripture reading; Edwards's concern in this instance is that if the reading is done without genuine devotion, it is done for naught: "They can read in the Bible and pray in their families and yet take no care in those things." BL 229.

Scripture is no inconsequential matter for Edwards. But the fact that only a few of the twenty-two sermons in this volume offer this counsel helps to set the matter in an unexpected light: while Scripture reading was important, and essential, there were other aspects of personal religion that potentially warranted emphasis to an even greater degree. Another sermon from this same volume helps sharpen this point. One can have all of the externals of a spiritual life, and can participate in public and private acts of devotion, and yet worship in vain. Conversely, "Consider that to live in love to the Lord Jesus Christ is the way to live the most pleasant life in the world. That will be the way to enjoy sweet communion with Jesus Christ. It is the most delightful entertainment to the soul to spiritually view the beauties and glories of such a beloved. It is a pleasant exercise to have the heart going forth in love to such a blessed one."[117]

The Scriptures are the means by which one may learn about God and about life, but in effect, they remain the means but not the end—the aim is a knowledge of God that touches the whole of life. In describing the revival at Northampton, Edwards expressed this connection clearly: "While God was so remarkably present amongst us by his Spirit, there was no book so delighted in as the Bible, especially the Book of Psalms, the Prophecy of Isaiah, and the New Testament. Some by reason of their esteem and love to God's Word, have at some times been greatly and wonderfully delighted and affected at the sight of a Bible."[118] As such, while Edwards would have unflinchingly supported the Reformers' notion of *Sola Scriptura*, one wonders if even in this matter he might have averred that he might not be "justly charged with believing in everything" just as they taught. The Scriptures, as precious as they were to Edwards, were therefore not the goal, but the source of the knowledge and wisdom that will draw the reader to God himself. He writes,

> In order to judge what sort of difficulties are to be expected in a revelation made to mankind by God, such as Christians suppose the Scriptures to be, [we should remember that it is] a revelation of what God knows to be the very truth concerning his own nature; the acts and operations of his mind with respect to his creatures; the grand scheme of infinite wisdom in his works, especially with respect to the intelligent and moral world; a revelation of the spiritual and invisible world; a revelation of that invisible world which men shall belong

---

117. BL 294.
118. WJE 4:184.

to after this life; a revelation of the greatest works of God, the manner of his creating the world and of his governing it, especially with regard to the higher and more important parts of it; a revelation delivered in ancient languages.[119]

As such, the Scriptures remained utterly vital to Edwards as the means by which one might draw near to and know God. Edwards emphasized this practice of reading the Scriptures, as with so many other aspects of private devotion, as an indispensable dimension of the Christian experience. In an early sermon, he preached, "We must be much in reading the Scriptures, if we would get spiritual and saving knowledge. They are the means by which ... God communicates this knowledge. Except we diligently and frequently read the Scriptures, therefore, we cannot reasonably expect to be enlightened, except we can expect that God will work without means; which is most unreasonable."[120]

Conference with Another Christian

Christian conference was a substantial component of private devotion to the Puritans. This counsel was to take place with a minister, with other mature Christians, with one's parents, or with peers.[121] Edwards's letter to Deborah Hatheway, written in June of 1741, was composed in response to the young convert's request for advice. George Claghorn comments in connection with this letter, "The town of Suffield, Massachusetts, had experienced revivals in 1734 and, later, as a result of Whitefield's visit in 1740 and a visit from Edwards in early 1741, before the famous preaching of *Sinners in the Hands of an Angry God*. So it was natural for Deborah Hatheway, an eighteen-year-old convert who was without a pastor, to turn to a known, trusted adviser for counsel."[122] He adds, "the letter, often reprinted, has become a classic of Christian devotion." Near the end of the correspondence, Edwards draws attention to some of the ways in which this "dear child" might engage in conference with others:

---

119. WJE 23:367.
120. WJE 14:94.
121. For some of the background associated with this practice, see Hambrick-Stowe, *Practice of Piety*, 150–55.
122. See WJE 16:90.

12. You ought to be much in exhorting and counseling and warning others, especially at such a day as this, Heb. 10:25. And I would advise you especially, to be much in exhorting children and young women your equals; and when you exhort others that are men, I would advise that you take opportunities for it, chiefly when you are alone with them, or when only young persons are present. See 1 Tim. 2:9, 11–12.

13. When you counsel and warn others, do it earnestly, affectionately, and thoroughly. And when you are speaking to your equals, let your warnings be intermixed with expressions of your sense of your own unworthiness, and of the sovereign grace that make you differ; and if you can with a good conscience, say how that you in yourself are more unworthy than they.

14. If you would set up religious meetings of young women by yourselves, to be attended once in a while, besides the other meetings that you attend, I should think it would be very proper and profitable.[123]

In this counsel, a number of features are immediately evident. The particular text cited from the book of Hebrews warrants consideration: "not neglecting to meet together, as is the habit of some, but encouraging one another, and all the more as you see the Day drawing near." This verse has been characteristically appropriated as a text that encourages Christian gatherings for public worship. It is cited in the Westminster Confession, for example, in support of the assertion that God is to be worshipped "so, more solemnly in the public assemblies, which are not carelessly or willfully to be neglected, or forsaken, when God, by His Word or providence, calleth thereunto."[124] Edwards here expands the application of this text to encompass the private counsel of the individual Christian, and moreover, that "you ought to be *much*" engaged in this activity.[125] It should be noted, though, that in reflecting elsewhere on Heb 10:25, Edwards believes that "the exhorting here spoken [of] is not private exhorting in conversation, but public exhorting of their assemblies, as seems manifest by the connection of this latter part of the verse with the former part."[126] Supremely, then, such counsel is to be done "earnestly, affectionately, and thoroughly."

---

123. WJE, 16:94.
124. Presbyterian Church in America, *Westminster Confession*, 72.
125. Emphasis added.
126. WJE 24:1152.

In these private interactions, it is worth observing that Edwards instructs the young Hatheway to "exhort," "counsel," and "warn," but there is not a counterbalancing advocacy in these specific instructions to offer something akin to "encouragement" or "affection." There is a seriousness intended, and warning appears to be set forth as a key hallmark of such relationships. It is not that love is not featured in this letter to Deborah Hatheway—specific instruction appears shortly before the passage cited that "when love is in lively exercise, persons don't need fear"—but there is an apparent intensity intended for Christian conference.[127] One's own focus, and likely the impulse that would attenuate the sharpness of any warnings, was to be the consideration of one's own unworthiness to receive the grace of God.

In the portion of this letter to Deborah Hatheway quoted above, Edwards moves from what appears to be a description of one-on-one counsel to the practice of "religious meetings" as a closely related matter. And so, while it can not be said that the discipline of Christian conference was a common point of emphasis in Edwards's preaching, "religious meetings" sometimes were, and seemingly, they rose more naturally to mind when Edwards addressed youth:

> And I should think it advisable not only that there should be sometimes private meetings, wherein both sexes and all ages do meet together; but that there should be also other religious societies, wherein persons of a particular sex and age are associated by themselves, to seek and wait upon their Creator; as young men by themselves, and young women by themselves.[128]

In this same sermon, Edwards encouraged his congregants to not only be willing to give counsel to other Christians in private—counsel that was to be serious, and earnest, and full of warning—but to be willing to receive it as well: "If your neighbors at any time are putting you in mind of the danger and dreadfulness of your condition, and the need you have to improve your opportunities, and the danger of backsliding, don't scornfully reject it; but listen to it, and labor to get good at it."[129] Similarly, Edwards averred, "Let all private societies be filled with praises. Whereas private companies used to in times past to be filled up much with unprofitable discourse, now they

---

127. WJE 16:94.
128. WJE 19:404.
129. WJE 19:408. In this sermon Edwards touches on this topic in several points of application.

should be filled with praises. Let God be praised in your private meetings for religion, and let your tongues praise the Lord in your occasional meetings with your companions and neighbors."[130]

As a concluding point of contrast to this section, it might be noted that while Edwards advocated conference with other Christians, he did not seemingly practice this to any great degree in his own life. This may explain in part why this discipline was not a frequent point of application in his sermons.[131] We do see Edwards correspond periodically with other ministers, although even this was not typically to seek counsel so much as to describe a situation in the congregation (such as a period of dryness or revival) or to detail a personal struggle (such as the communion controversy).

The closest friendships outside the bonds of blood, then, particularly with other men, would likely have been those Edwards had with those he was mentoring in his home or supporting in some other way, as exemplified by David Brainerd or Samuel Hopkins. And, while Edwards's bonds to his family were indisputably closer still, Edwards's own "conference" was likely elsewhere:

> Men generally seek very much for the friendship of those that have power in their hands, and can manage things for or against us as they list; they are generally careful how they fall out with them, that have either their goods or their lives in their hands, and love to make friends with those whose friendship they hope to be profited by. And yet, they are such fools as to neglect to make friends with him who holds the universe in his hands; who has them and all other men every moment in his power.[132]

And so, while Edwards was often isolated, and almost ostracized, during his time at Yale, and although he experienced strong bonds of friendship seemingly only during his brief New York pastorate, Edwards did enjoy conference, divine conference: "There is no other love so advantageous as love to Christ, and therefore none so pleasant.... the love of Christ has the tendency to fill the soul with an inexpressible sweetness."[133]

---

130. WJE 19:469. As a point for more in-depth study on this topic, one might explore the possibility that this theme of conference with another Christian, private meetings, and religious meetings as a point of application increased during periods of revival, as Edwards recognized their effectiveness in encouraging personal evangelism.

131. For an exception, see "Perpetuity and Change of the Sabbath," WJE 17:249.

132. WJE 10:431.

133. WJE 10:617.

A Comprehensive Observance of the Sabbath

Beginning with the earliest days of the Pilgrims, strict laws were set in place in order to protect the sanctity of the Sabbath. New England law records reveal a wide range of ostensibly innocuous offenses that were committed in violation of the famous blue laws, which generally began on Saturday afternoon around 3 p.m. and continued through the end of Sunday afternoon worship.[134] Alice Morse Earle describes the ideal of Puritan worship:

> Sweet to the Pilgrims and to their descendants was the hush of their calm Saturday night, and their still, tranquil, Sabbath,—sign and token to them, not only of the weekly rest ordained in the creation, but of the eternal rest to come. The universal quiet and peace of the community showed the primitive instinct of a pure, simple devotion, the sincere religion which knew no compromise in spiritual things, no half-way obedience to God's Word, but rested absolutely on the Lord's Day—as was commanded. No work, no play, no idle strolling was known; no sign of human life or motion was seen except the necessary care of the patient cattle and other dumb beasts, the orderly and quiet going to and from the meeting, and at the nooning, a visit to the churchyard to stand by the side of the silent dead. This absolute obedience to the letter as to the spirit of God's Word was one of the most typical traits of the character of the Puritans, and appeared to them to be one of the most vital points of their religion.[135]

Jonathan Edwards would have been reared in a home that meticulously practiced such an observance of the Sabbath, and he eventually settled in his grandfather's church at Northampton, where such patterns were simply an unquestioned part of the normal fabric of life.[136] By Edwards's day, "Strict observance of Sunday (that is, attendance at divine worship and abstinence from all secular business and public recreations) had become something of a badge of Puritanism in the Anglo-American world."[137]

For his own part, Edwards vigorously reinforced this ideal in his own writings. He saw in the Scriptures clear justification for the continuance of the practice: "That saying of our Savior to his disciples, 'But pray ye that

---

134. Earle, *Sabbath in Puritan New England*, 245–49.
135. Ibid., 257–58.
136. For example, Solomon Stoddard lamented the fact that despite the many laws that were on the books, there remained a great many sins for which the "profaning of the Sabbath is not punishable by law." See Stoddard, *Fear of Hell*.
137. See Valeri's editorial comments in WJE 17:217.

your flight be not in the winter, nor on the sabbath day' (Matt. 24:20), is a very great evidence of the Christian sabbath."[138] During times of revival, he believed that the improvement in the people's observation of the Sabbath was particularly noteworthy, and a vital evidence of the Spirit's work: "God's day was a delight, and his tabernacles were amiable [Ps. 84:1]. Our public assemblies were then beautiful; the congregation was alive in God's service, everyone earnestly intent on the public worship, every hearer eager to drink in the words of the minister as they came from his mouth."[139] In a letter to Benjamin Colman, Edwards described how the effect of revival had resulted not only in a transformation of the youth in terms of their attentiveness in public worship, but that Sabbath-day nights—which had long been an occasion when the youth of the congregation would spend time with one another in one form of revelry or another—were at last being reformed, and had been replaced by religious meetings at his urging.[140]

From Edwards's preaching we gain perspective on how he taught from the pulpit that the Sabbath was to be observed. As a basic starting point, the following assertion represents very nearly a terse definition of Edwardsean Sabbitarianism: "Keep the sabbath: not to hunt nor to work nor to play a sabbath, but spend the time in praying, going to meeting, and thinking and talking about the things of religion."[141] It was God himself who had ordained such practices, for the good of the church and society as a whole:

---

138. WJE 23:288. This is taken from miscellany 1320 on the Lord's Day. Mark Valeri notes that Edwards employs fourteen biblical references in justification of the practices of the Christian Sabbath in his sermon entitled "The Perpetuity and Change of the Sabbath." This sermon offers a key statement of Edwards's understanding of the Sabbath, and will be considered further in the conclusion to this section. Valeri also observes, "He writes on the sabbath as integral to the order of creation in 'Miscellanies' no. 45 and 'Notes on the Apocalypse' no. 16. Edwards also addresses the question of the sabbath in several 'Miscellanies' from the early 1730s (e.g., nos. 464, 466, 495 and 500), and, later, during the mid-1730s (nos. 531, 536, 551, 691, and especially 693)." WJE 17:217–18.

139. WJE 4:151.

140. WJE 16:49.

141. WJE 25:573. Edwards offered this counsel to the Stockbridge Indians in what was possibly his first sermon to them, preached in January of 1751 in a sermon entitled "The Things That Belong to True Religion," which was based on Acts 11:12–13: "And the spirit bade me go with them, nothing doubting. Moreover these six brethren accompanied me, and we entered into the man's house: and he showed us how he had seen an angel in his house, which stood and said unto him, Send men to Joppa, and call for Simon, whose surname is Peter." As was noted previously, Edwards affirmed a basic agreement with the Westminster Confession of Faith (which would include the Larger and Shorter Catechisms, from which

God also is the author of all the ordinances of the gospel by means of which he communicates grace. 'Tis he who appointed prayer and the preaching of the Word and sabbaths and public assemblies and sacraments and church discipline. These are very necessary in order to the salvation of men's souls. You may easily conceive of what a sorrowful case religion would be in if there were no sabbaths and no public assemblies, no public ministry and no discipline. Religion would soon run to utter ruin.[142]

Edwards was often upbraiding the congregation for a failure to live up to this ideal. And, as was so often the case regarding all matters of personal and private worship, Edwards distinguished between an external, perfunctory observation of the day, and a vital, inner union with Christ: "Now therefore," he preached to the mission outpost at Stockbridge, "let everyone look into and search his own heart and see whether he does truly believe in the Lord Jesus Christ. Don't think it enough that you come to meeting, that you are honest, that you keep the sabbath days, that you don't get drunk. You must do these things, must keep the sabbath, but these things alone won't do. You must give your whole heart to Christ."[143] The consequences for contentment with a mere appearance of spirituality were damnable: "A way of sabbath-breaking and of profaning God's worship is a sure way to hell. Is not this a common thing amongst us? Are there not many amongst us, especially young people, that have no regard to holy time, but in their talk and actions do trample God's sabbath under foot and make no difference between holy time and other time."[144]

More positively, a comprehensive observance of the Sabbath was to be less a duty than a delight. God's people would naturally desire to be in his presence, to hear his Word preached by his chosen ministers, and to pray for the deepest possible impressions of his Spirit. A godly man "will exalt God amongst men by endeavoring all that possibly he can in his place and station,

---

he occasionally quoted). The Westminster Confession represents among the more strident Sabbitarian statements in existence. It is noteworthy that in his sermon "The Perpetuity and Change of the Sabbath," Edwards explicitly refers to "our catechism," making apparent reference to question 43 of the Shorter Catechism. See WJE 17:237. It is difficult to imagine he would positively affirm this question in the catechism in the context of a sermon on the Sabbath, while being opposed to the numerous other questions that relate to the Sabbath (e.g., questions 57–62).

142. BL 216.
143. BL 245.
144. WJE 10:328.

that sin and wickedness may decay, and holiness and religion may flourish and prosper.... He with delight will exalt God amongst them by showing his regard unto the worship and ordinances of God, by his regard to his public worship, his holy sabbath, and his ministers."[145] The Sabbath, having been ordained by God, was supernaturally equipped: "That word *sanctify* as it is used in Scripture is of extensive signification. Sometimes it signifies making holy as persons. Or things may be sanctified or set apart to a holy use, whereby they may be said in a sense to become holy things. Thus God is said to have sanctified and hallowed the sabbath. He has set it apart for our holy use."[146] The net effect was to produce joy:

> The external duties of religion are made easy and pleasant by true love to God. Duties toward God, such as prayer, singing God's praises, hearing the Word and the like, are his delight. How doth the wicked man hate to come into God's presence, especially in secret, closet prayer, which is so great a duty of a Christian; with how little taste and relish doth he hear the Word of God, and when shall we ever hear him speaking of heavenly things? But it is far otherwise with him that truly loves God; he is never so well pleased as when his heart is engaged in such duties.[147]

Edwards commanded, "Therefore, above all, improve your sabbaths; and especially improve the time of public worship, which is the most precious part of holy time."[148]

Virtually all of these themes are reechoed in the important three-part sermon entitled "The Perpetuity and Change of the Sabbath."[149] As Mark Valeri remarks, "this sermon is not a typical New England Jeremiad against immoral behavior on the Sabbath. Rather, it is largely an exegetical and theological defense of Sunday worship."[150] Edwards's interest is not so much centered on defending Puritan traditions so much as on defending a strict observance of the day on biblical grounds.[151] And indeed, the vast preponderance of his concerns in this sermon are doctrinal, as he expends substantial

---

145. BL 77.
146. BL 298; emphasis original.
147. WJE 10:639.
148. WJE 19:259.
149. WJE 17:220–50.
150. Valeri in WJE 17:217.
151. Various forms of the word "strict" appear repeatedly throughout the sermon.

energy defending two points from Scriptural principles: that one day in seven has been decreed by God for worship, and that this day of worship is now the first day of the week—Sunday—for the Christian. In his points of application, however, Edwards has much to say about what a spiritually minded observation of the Sabbath would entail.

The Sabbath is something for which man should be thankful, given that it is a day of rest ("outward, but especially spiritual, rest") and a day of joy, and as a consequence, they are "exhorted to keep holy this day" by "strictly and conscientiously" observing it.[152] In this way, God is greatly honored, and man is greatly blessed, as on this day God is wont to favor the prayers of his people, to draw men to himself, and to be active in "conferring his graces and blessed gifts on his people on this day."[153] He directs his hearers to studiously avoid sin, given that such sin is even more heinous on the Lord's Day, to avoid work and recreation, to perform "works of mercy and charity," and to spend "the time in religious exercises" and "especially to meditate upon and celebrate the work of redemption."[154] How might the whole of the day be spent? Edwards proclaims,

> We should take care, therefore, to employ our minds on a sabbath day on spiritual objects, by holy meditation, improving for our help therein the holy Scriptures and other books that are according [to] the Word of God. We should also employ ourselves outwardly on this day in the duties of God's worship in private and public. It is proper to [be] more frequent and abundant in secret duties on this day than on other days, as we have time and opportunity, as well as to attend on public ordinances on this day.
>
> It is proper not only on this day to be especially promoting the exercises of religion in ourselves, but also in others: to be assisting them and endeavoring to promote their spiritual good on this day by religious conversation and conference. And especially those that have the care of others ought on this day especially to endeavor to promote their spiritual good. Heads of families should be instructing and counseling their children, and quickening them in the ways of religion, and should see to it that the sabbath be strictly kept in their houses. A peculiar blessing may be expected upon those families where there is due care taken that the sabbath be strictly and devoutly observed.[155]

152. WJE 17:242–43.
153. WJE 17:246.
154. WJE 17:248–50.
155. WJE 17:249.

This notion that the Sabbath "be strictly and devoutly observed," while one that others might have viewed as an ideal, was for Edwards a point of practice that was to reflect the norm. One was to prepare the night before for the day of public and private worship to come, a kind of holy anticipation; the Sabbath in this way was to come to reflect the regular pinnacle of the Christian experience, a time carefully set apart for joyful, yet sober, spiritual service.

For Edwards, all the external elements of public worship, and particularly the preaching of the Word, were to be met with an unvarnished inward reality, the unfeigned stirring of the heart, soul, and mind.[156] This experience of true worship was to overflow in ongoing self-examination, taking advantage of the full range of tools available in private devotion. Preparation for the Christian Sabbath, then, and the right observation of the day itself, were necessary ingredients to ensure that from week to week this spiritual rhythm, this communion with God himself, could continue unabated. In many ways, this desire to inculcate a life of constant worship can be seen as the culmination of Edwards's aims with respect to public and private acts of devotion—a life consumed by, and preoccupied with, virtually uninterrupted reverence for the almighty God.

---

156. Cf. Matt 22:37.

five

Conclusion

It is no small challenge to succinctly capture the multifaceted life and thought of Jonathan Edwards, rather like trying to describe the roar of a lion—some things have to be experienced to be rightly understood. Still, many have tried. Marilla Ricker wrote in 1918 that Edwards "believed in the worst God, preached the worst sermons, and had the worst religion of any human being who ever lived on this continent."[1] Rather more typically, he has been heralded as "America's Theologian," "America's Evangelical," "America's Augustine," and "arguably America's greatest religious genius."[2] George Marsden proposes a "central theme for understanding Edwards . . . encapsulated in the phrase, 'the divine and supernatural light.'"[3] M. X. Lesser regards Edwards's thought to be "an extended meditation on divine sovereignty."[4] John Piper, "the most influential popularizer of Edwards for evangelicals today," summarizes Edwards's legacy with the phrase, "God is most glorified when we are most satisfied in him."[5] And Iain Murray, whose biography of Edwards has been labeled as "uncritical," "filiopietistic," and "hagiography," may however be nearest the essence of the matter when he states plainly that Edwards is "first of all, a Christian."[6]

1. Stout et al., *Jonathan Edwards at 300*, vii.

2. See Jensen, *America's Theologian*; Gura, *Jonathan Edwards: America's Evangelical*; Marsden, "Jonathan Edwards: American Augustine"; and Kimnach, Minkema, and Sweeney, eds., *Sermons of Jonathan Edwards*, ix.

3. Marsden, "Quest for the Historical Edwards," 13. Josh Moody touches on this theme often as well; see Moody, *Jonathan Edwards and the Enlightenment*, 119–54.

4. It is this succinct description that Lesser uses to review his own work. See Lesser, *Jonathan Edwards: An Annotated Bibliography*, 104.

5. See Lewis, "Jonathan Edwards between Church and Academy," 233.

6. Murray, *Jonathan Edwards: A New Biography*, xxvii. For the characterization "uncritical," see Marsden, *Jonathan Edwards: A Life*, xvii; for "filiopietistic" see Lewis, "Jonathan Edwards between Church and Academy," 231; for "hagiography" see Guelzo's review of Murray in *Fides et Historia*. See also Stein's review of Murray.

A portrait of even the one dimension of Edwards's thought here explored—his views on public and private worship—must therefore be acknowledged as only partial. Many of Edwards's published sermons and private letters have been reviewed, but others could have easily been included that would have added further insight and texture, and the sermons and letters that have been included could also have been considered in far greater detail. His many unpublished sermons have only been superficially explored. And what of his many theological and philosophical writings? While some effort has been expended to include key touchpoints from these writings on the subject of worship, much work remains to adequately flesh this out. But one thing is clear even at this juncture: Edwards at worship is "first of all, Christian."

Beyond this, however, it is easy to see that the differences between the ideal of Christian worship Edwards that taught and practiced, and virtually all contemporary approaches to worship, are staggering. Consider some of the aspects of public and private worship that Edwards was familiar with that have basically fallen from the Christian landscape. Fast days are essentially unknown, especially in response to such natural phenomenon as droughts or earthquakes. Whole days set aside for prayer and thanksgiving, on days other than Sundays, are rare or non-existent. Infant baptism is no longer the de facto standard. Church discipline in almost any form is uncommon. Aspects of private devotion espoused by Edwards, such as the keeping of a private journal or family worship, have largely fallen out of fashion. Certainly, the overriding centrality of self-examination in public and private worship is almost entirely passé.[7] And even the content of Edwards's preaching must be acknowledged as essentially different from contemporary norms—while it must be recognized that Edwards did not routinely preach "fire and brimstone messages" (despite the characterizations of many), the fact that he preached *any* such sermons would be troubling to many. Can you imagine a contemporary sermon title on a roadside sign promoting "The Justice of God in the Damnation of Sinners"? Couple this with his propensity for almost never using illustrations or humor, and one begins to recognize how different his approach was to preaching. Finally, the comprehensive observance of the Sabbath advocated by Edwards also stands in vivid contrast to contemporary norms.

---

7. But see Church, "Self-Examination as Preparation."

Conversely, what might Edwards think of various aspects of worship that were not in vogue in his day, but are now? What would he think of such practices as "children's church," where the youth in some congregations are brought out for a service intended to speak to their particular needs and interests—which also happens to keep the sanctuary quiet? What might he think of hands lifted up during church services? What would he think of mime, or drama, in the context of worship? What would he have to say about the so-called "emerging" church?[8] What would he have to say about ministries aimed at promoting financial prosperity? What might he say about speaking in tongues and the exploding Charismatic movement? What would Edwards say about the increasingly egalitarian approach to involving women as leaders in worship? What would he make of "invitations," common in various circles, where unbelievers (the "wicked," in Edwards's parlance) are urged to come forward and publicly profess faith in Christ? Could such invitations allow for adequate proof of conversion, or would they potentially lead many to a premature assurance of salvation? What would he think of "seeker-sensitive" services, aimed at drawing the unconverted into church in a relaxed atmosphere? What would he think of the use of humor, or extended illustrations, in preaching? What would he think of attending movies on Saturday nights or shopping at Wal-Mart on Sunday?[9]

While some of these questions are easy to answer, more challenging is the question how it is, since Edwards was undisputedly a biblicist, that worship as taught and practiced by Edwards is so very different from virtually all contemporary Protestant worship, which one would assume would rise from the teachings of the same Bible. Edwards's attitude toward Roman Catholicism was consistently negative, even vitriolic. As Gerald McDermott notes, "In his private notebooks he compiled lists of commercial, political, social and military setbacks for the Roman Catholic church in order to document what he was already convinced would take place, the downfall of the papacy."[10] Can the substantial variations be attributed solely to cultural factors, or to efforts on the part of contemporary congregations to adapt the message of the Bible to a new age? Are the concerns, needs, and interests of contemporary Christians so markedly different from the Christians

---

8. See, for example, Kimball, *Emerging Church*.
9. Along these lines, see Lundin, "What Would They Think," 49–50.
10. See McDermott, *One Holy and Happy Society*, 178.

of Edwards's day? Can it be sustained that the Christian church has simply learned more about the true intent of the Bible?

One key difference between Edwards's approach to worship and contemporary Christian worship will help sharpen the matter considerably. It may be surprising to many that virtually nothing has been said throughout the course of this work on the subject of music, given its often extraordinary place of prominence in Christian worship at present. In some quarters, the word "worship" is in fact now virtually synonymous with music. When music leaders stand in many Protestant churches, they will often lead "worship sets" or say simply, "Let's worship."[11]

While Alice Morse Earle's description of music in New England slightly predates the time of Edwards, her characterization is so stark as to provide an essential point of understanding. In describing Puritan church music, she writes, "Of all the dismal accompaniments of public worship in the early days of New England, the music was most hopelessly forlorn—not alone from the confused versifications of the Psalms which were used, but from the mournful monotony of the few known tunes and the horrible manner in which those tunes were sung."[12] Ola Winslow cites some improvement in this situation in the latter days of Solomon Stoddard: "By the Old Way each male worshipper sang without reference to the time and pitch of all the others. The women remained silent. By the New Way, or Singing by Rule, the entire congregation arrived at the same point in the hymn at approximately the same time and in approximately the same key."[13]

For his own part, Edwards must be seen as favoring the "New Way," and to have endorsed various innovations so far as singing is concerned. One of his rare diary entries, written in 1722, recounts his desire to "praise God, by singing psalms in prose, and by singing forth the meditations of my heart in prose."[14] In 1736, "at a singing meeting," he preached a sermon entitled "That a public singing of God's praises is an ordinance instituted by Christ to be observed in the Christian church."[15] In the midst of his *Faithful Narrative* he remarked that a key aspect of the revival of the religion could be observed in the congregation's music:

11. See the interesting perspective on worship sets in Best, *Unceasing Worship*, 148.
12. Earle, *Sabbath in Puritan New England*, 202.
13. Winslow, *Jonathan Edwards: 1703–1758*, 104.
14. WJE 16:781.
15. WJE 19:805.

> Our public praises were then greatly enlivened; God was then served in our psalmody, in some measure, in the beauty of holiness [Ps. 96:9]. It has been observable that there has been scarce any part of divine worship, wherein good men amongst us have had grace so drawn forth and their hearts so lifted up in the ways of God, as in singing his praises. Our congregation excelled all that ever I knew in the external part of the duty before, generally carrying regularly and well three parts of music, and the women a part by themselves. But now they were wont to sing with unusual elevation of heart and voice, which made the duty pleasant indeed.[16]

In May of 1744, Edwards wrote to the Rev. Benjamin Colman, "It has been our manner in this congregation, for more than two years past, in the summer time, when we sing three times upon the sabbath, to sing an hymn, or part of a hymn of Dr. [Isaac] Watts', the last time, viz.: at the conclusion of the afternoon exercise. I introduced it principally because I saw in the people a very general inclination to it."[17] And, more than seven years later, Edwards commented, "Music, especially sacred music, has a powerful efficacy to soften the heart into tenderness, to harmonize the affections, and to give the mind a relish for objects of a superior character."[18] Still later, he sought "somebody at Stockbridge to teach the Indians to sing."[19]

But for all of this, the case cannot be made that music or singing was a common point of emphasis in the preaching and teaching of Jonathan Edwards.[20] Instead, in a sermon considered briefly previously, "They Sing a New Song," his aim is not primarily to emphasize the value of music in worship, but to underscore the necessity of genuine spiritual vitality. He proclaims,

> In vain will all our singing be if we han't learned to sing this song [the song of the redeemed]. We may sing psalms sabbath after sabbath, we may keep thanksgiving days; but no song is acceptable to God but this. Without this, all our learning the rule of singing and endeavors

---

16. WJE 4:151.
17. WJE 16:144.
18. From a letter to Sir William Pepperrell dated November 28, 1751, in WJE 4:411.
19. From a letter to an unidentified singing teacher dated June 4, 1753, in WJE 4:597.
20. So for example, Edwards makes rare passing reference to singing in a sermon entitled "True Love to God," which was preached at some point between the summer of 1722 and the spring of 1723. See WJE 10:639.

to perfect ourselves in all that art will be in vain. We shall make no melody to God.[21]

And so, while it is evident that Edwards saw music as an important and fitting part of worship, it would appear, given the rarity of the topic in his writings and its subjugation to the Word preached, that he might also be out of step with contemporary Christianity in this crucial matter.

It is unquestionably the case that a dramatic resurgence of interest in Jonathan Edwards has taken place since the advent of Perry Miller's "intellectual biography" and the emergence of the *Works of Jonathan Edwards* published by Yale.[22] What is more, a long-standing rise in research on Edwards has resulted in significant numbers of scholarly and popular works. Stephen Nichols indicates that "the number is fast approaching 4,000."[23] Even in 1994, M. X. Lesser wrote,

> In his keynote address to the Wheaton conference on Jonathan Edwards in the fall of 1984, Henry F. May cites the doubling of dissertations about him in the decades since 1940 as "intriguing" evidence of his durability. By that calculation, Edwards is alive and well, if graying. Not surprisingly, the number of dissertations has fallen off—to fifty or so in each of the decades since the sixties from the eighty of geometric forecast—but interest has not.[24]

Given this obvious energy, one is necessarily struck by the fact that virtually nothing has been written about Edwards on worship, an act he considered central to the purpose of human life.

Perhaps the matter is simple. As was considered at the outset, many will likely ask how Edwards, the preacher of such sermons as "Sinners in the Hands of an Angry God" and "The Eternity of Hell Torments," can be relevant in *any* contemporary theological discussion, much less a discussion of worship—a motif that has begun to enjoy such freedom and variety of expression. Jonathan Edwards has been presented repeatedly as a thoroughgoing biblicist. It therefore seems reasonable that those who would claim to be biblically motivated Christians would be compelled to consider his conclusions. Furthermore, given the radical divergence of his perspectives on worship from contemporary practice, it seems appropriate to engage in

21. WJE 22:242.
22. Miller, *Jonathan Edwards*.
23. Nichols, "Jonathan Edwards: His Life and Legacy," 36.
24. Lesser, *Jonathan Edwards, An Annotated Bibliography*, xiii.

renewed dialogue in order to confirm or reject his preaching and teaching on public and private devotion to God. Edwards proclaimed, "'Tis in your power to attend all ordinances, and all public and private duties of religion, and to do it with your might."[25] Is this no longer true?

As has been intimated at a number of points, much more study is yet possible on Edwards and worship. A review of unpublished sermons could yield much fruit, as well as a closer examination of many published sermons. Additional texture could be provided by a careful review of the miscellanies. More detail can be culled from his major treatises. Scriptural studies associated with key biblical passages on worship can be reviewed to gather Edwards's perspective on these texts. Further detail from Edwards's Puritan forebears would provide needed context at many points. Even more fundamentally, however, similar studies are called for with a strong biblical orientation. Biblical commentaries could be developed with Edwards's insights. Book-length treatments of Edwards on missions, or evangelism, or prayer or other themes are clearly possible. One suspects, however, that each of these efforts will ultimately fail to rightly apprehend Edwards if they fail to affirm that which drove Edwards himself—that an individual earnestly strive to bring glory to God. "So, whether you eat or drink, or whatever you do, do all to the glory of God" (1 Cor 10:31, ESV).

---

25. WJE 19:283. This is taken from a sermon preached in February of 1735, entitled "Pressing into the Kingdom of God," which was based on Luke 16:16: "The law and the prophets were until John: since that time the kingdom of God is preached, and every man presseth into it."

Bibliography

Puritans

Alleine, Joseph. *A Sure Guide to Heaven*. 1671. Reprint, Edinburgh: Banner of Truth, 1959.

Barker, William. *Puritan Profiles: 54 Contemporaries of the Westminster Assembly*. Geanies House, Scotland: Mentor, 1996.

Bayly, Lewis. *The Practice of Piety: Directing a Christian How to Walk, That He May Please God*. Morgan, PA: Soli Deo Gloria, n.d.

Beeke, Joel R. *Puritan Reformed Spirituality*. Grand Rapids: Reformation Heritage, 2004.

Bickel, R. Bruce. *Light and Heat: The Puritan View of the Pulpit*. Morgan, PA: Soli Deo Gloria, 1999.

Bolton, Robert. *The Carnal Professor*. 1632. Reprint, Morgan, PA: Soli Deo Gloria, 1992.

Bolton, Samuel. "Sin: The Greatest Evil." In *The Puritans on Conversion*, edited by Don Kistler, 6–14. Ligonier, PA: Soli Deo Gloria, 1990.

Brook, Benjamin. *The Lives of the Puritans*. Pittsburgh: Soli Deo Gloria, 1994.

Brooks, Thomas. *Heaven on Earth: A Treatise on Christian Assurance*. 1654. Reprint, Edinburgh: Banner of Truth, 1961.

Burgess, Anthony. *Spiritual Refining: The Anatomy of True and False Conversion*. 2 vols. 1652. Reprint, Ames, IA: International Outreach, 1996.

Burroughs, Jeremiah. *The Evil of Evils, or, The Exceeding Sinfulness of Sin*. 1654. Reprint, Ligonier, PA: Soli Deo Gloria, 1992.

Caiger, J. A. "Preaching—Puritan and Reformed." In *Puritan Papers*, edited by J. I. Packer, 2:161–85. Phillipsburg, NJ: Puritan & Reformed, 2000.

Calvin, John. *Institutes of the Christian Religion*. Edited by John T. McNeill. Translated by Ford Lewis Battles. Philadelphia: Westminster, 1960.

Church, Keith D. "Self-Examination as Preparation for the Lord's Supper in Light of the New Covenant." PhD diss., Southeastern Baptist Theological Seminary, 2007.

Crook, Samuel, et al. *Ta diapheronta, or, Divine Characters: In Two Parts, Acutely Distinguishing the More Secret and Undiscerned Differences* . . . London: printed for Adoniram Byfeild, 1658.

Davies, Horton. *The Worship of the American Puritans*. New York: Peter Lang, 1990.

———. *The Worship of the English Puritans*. Morgan, PA: Soli Deo Gloria, 1997. Doolittle, Thomas. *Love to Christ: Necessary to Escape the Curse at His Coming*. Pittsburgh: Soli Deo Gloria, 1994.

Durham, James. *The Unsearchable Riches of Christ*. Morgan, PA: Soli Deo Gloria, 2002.

Earle, Alice Morse. *The Sabbath in Puritan New England*. New York: Scribner's, 1891.

Firmin, Giles. *The Real Christian, or, A Treatise of Effectual Calling: Wherein the Work of God in Drawing the Soul . . .* Boston: printed by Rogers & Fowle, 1742.

Goodwin, Thomas. *Christ Set Forth*. Morgan, PA: Soli Deo Gloria, 1992.

———. *Works*. Edited by J. Miller. London: James Nicholl, 1861.

Guthrie, William. *The Christian's Great Interest*. 1658. Reprint, Edinburgh: Banner of Truth, 1994.

Hambrick-Stowe, Charles E. *The Practice of Piety: Puritan Devotional Disciplines in Seventeenth Century New England*. Chapel Hill: University of North Carolina Press, 1982.

Hemming, G. A. "The Puritans' Dealing with Troubled Souls." In *Puritan Papers*, edited by J. I. Packer, 1:31–43. Phillipsburg, NJ: Puritan & Reformed, 2000.

Johnson, Stephen M. "'The Sinews of the Body of Christ': Calvin's Concept of Church Disciple." *Westminster Theological Journal* 59.1 (1997) 87–100.

Johnston, O. R. "Thomas Shepard's 'Parable of the Ten Virgins.'" In *Puritan Papers*, edited by J. I. Packer, 1:122–27. Phillipsburg, NJ: Puritan & Reformed, 2000.

Kistler, Don. *The Puritans—On Conversion*. Ligonier, PA: Soli Deo Gloria, 1990.

———, ed. *The Puritans on the Lord's Supper*. Morgan, PA: Soli Deo Gloria, 1997.

Love, W. Deloss, Jr. *The Fast and Thanksgiving Days of New England*. Boston: n.p., 1895.

Manton, Thomas. *The Works of Thomas Manton*. London: James Nisbet, 1874.

Mead, Matthew. *The Almost Christian Discovered*. 1661. Reprint, Morgan, PA: Soli Deo Gloria, 1993.

Mingard, D. "William Guthrie on the Trial of a Saving Interest in Christ." In *Puritan Papers*, edited by J. I. Packer, 1:203–211. Phillipsburg, NJ: Puritan & Reformed, 2000.

Morgan, Edmund S. *The Puritan Family: Religion and Domestic Relations in Seventeenth-Century New England*. Rev. ed. New York: Harper & Row, 1966.

———. "The Puritans and Sex." *The New England Quarterly* 15.4 (1942) 591–607.

Packer, J. I. "The Puritan Conscience." In *Puritan Papers*, edited by J. I. Packer, 2:237–57. Phillipsburg, NJ: Puritan & Reformed, 2000.

———. "The Puritan View of Preaching the Gospel." In *Puritan Papers*, edited by J. I. Packer, 1:255–69. Phillipsburg, NJ: Puritan & Reformed, 2000.

———. *A Quest for Godliness—The Puritan Vision of the Christian Life*. Wheaton, IL: Crossway, 1990.

———, editor. *Puritan Papers*. 4 vols. Phillipsburg, NJ: Puritan & Reformed, 2000.

Rutherford, Samuel. *The Letters of Samuel Rutherford*. 1664. Reprint, Edinburgh: Banner of Truth, 1984.

Ryken, Leland. *Worldly Saints: The Puritans as They Really Were*. Grand Rapids: Zondervan, 1986.

Scholes, Percy Alfred. *The Puritans and Music in England and New England*. New York: Russell & Russell, 1962.

Sedgwick, Obadiah. *The Anatomy of Secret Sins*. Morgan, PA: Soli Deo Gloria, 1995.

———. *The Doubting Believer*. Morgan, PA: Soli Deo Gloria, 1993.

Shepard, Thomas. *Parable of the Ten Virgins Opened and Applied*. 1660. Reprint, Whitefish, MT: Kessinger, 2003.
Solberg, Winton U. *Redeem the Time: The Puritan Sabbath in Early America*. Cambridge, MA: Harvard University Press, 1977.
Stoddard, Solomon. *The Defects of Preachers Reproved in a Sermon Preached at Northampton, May 19th, 1723*. New London, CT: n. p., 1724.
———. *The Safety of Appearing on the Day of Judgment in the Righteousness of Christ*. Morgan, PA: Soli Deo Gloria, 1995.
Stoddard, Solomon, and Increase Mather. *A Guide to Christ, or, The Way of Directing Souls That Are under the Work of Conversion*. Whitefish, MT: Kessinger, 2003.
Vincent, Nathaniel. "The Conversion of a Sinner." In *The Puritans on Conversion*, edited by Don Kistler, 88. Ligonier, PA: Soli Deo Gloria, 1990.
Vincent, Thomas. *Fire and Brimstone*. 1670. Reprint, Morgan, PA: Soli Deo Gloria, 1999.
———. *God's Terrible Voice in the City*. 1667. Reprint, Morgan, PA: Soli Deo Gloria, 1997.
———. *The True Christian's Love to the Unseen Christ*. Ligonier, PA: Soli Deo Gloria, 1993.
Watson, Thomas. *Heaven Taken by Storm*. 1810. Reprint, Morgan, PA: Soli Deo Gloria, n.d.
———. "The One Thing Necessary." In *The Puritans on Conversion*, edited by Don Kistler, 192–202. Ligonier, PA: Soli Deo Gloria, 1990.
Weld, Thomas. *Brief Narration of the Practices of the Churches in New England*. London: printed by Matthew Simmons, 1645.

Selected Works by Jonathan Edwards and Related Topics

Bailey, Richard A. and Gregory A. Wills, editors. *The Salvation of Souls: Nine Previously Unpublished Sermons on the Call of Ministry and the Gospel*. Wheaton, IL: Crossway, 2002.
Hickman, Edward, editor. *The Works of Jonathan Edwards*. 2 vols. 1834. Reprint, Edinburgh: Banner of Truth, 1974. [Though this two-volume set bears the same title as the Yale critical edition below, they are unrelated.]
Kimnach, Wilson H., Kenneth P. Minkema, and Douglas A. Sweeney, editors. *The Sermons of Jonathan Edwards: A Reader*. New Haven: Yale University Press, 1999.
Kistler, Don, editor. *Jonathan Edwards: Containing 16 Sermons Unpublished in Edwards' Lifetime*. The Puritan Pulpit. Morgan, PA: Soli Deo Gloria, 2004.
———. *To All The Saints of God: Addresses to the Church*. Morgan, PA: Soli Deo Gloria, 2003.
———. *The Wrath of Almighty God: Jonathan Edwards on God's Judgment Against Sinners*. Morgan, PA: Soli Deo Gloria, 1996.
Lesser, M. X. *Jonathan Edwards: An Annotated Bibliography, 1979–1993*. Westport, CT: Greenwood, 1994.
McMullen, Michael D. *The Glory and Honor of God: Previously Unpublished Sermons of Jonathan Edwards*. Nashville: Broadman & Holman, 2004.
———, editor. *The Blessing of God: Previously Unpublished Sermons of Jonathan Edwards*. Nashville: Broadman & Holman, 2003.

Miller, Perry (vols. 1–2), John E. Smith (vols. 3–9), and Harry S. Stout (vols. 10–25), editors. *The Works of Jonathan Edwards*. 26 vols. New Haven, CT: Yale University Press, 1957–2006. Volumes listed below.
1. *Freedom of the Will*. Edited with an introduction by Paul Ramsey. 1957.
2. *Religious Affections*. Edited with an introduction by John E. Smith. 1959.
3. *Original Sin*. Edited with an introduction by Clyde A. Holbrook. 1970.
4. *The Great Awakening*. Edited with an introduction by C. C. Goen. 1972.
5. *Apocalyptic Writings*. Edited with an introduction by Stephen J. Stein. 1977.
6. *Scientific and Philosophical Writings*. Edited with an introduction by Wallace E. Anderson. 1980.
7. *The Life of David Brainerd*. Edited with an introduction by Norman Pettit. 1985.
8. *Ethical Writings*. Edited with an introduction by Paul Ramsey. 1989.
9. *A History of the Work of Redemption*. Edited with an introduction by John F. Wilson. 1989.
10. *Sermons and Discourses, 1720–1723*. Edited with an introduction by Wilson H. Kimnach. 1992.
11. *Typological Writings*. Edited with an introduction by Wallace E. Anderson and Mason I. Lowance Jr., with David H. Watters. 1993.
12. *Ecclesiastical Writings*. Edited with an introduction by David D. Hall. 1994.
13. *The "Miscellanies": A–Z, AA–ZZ, 1–500*. Edited with an introduction by Thomas A. Schafer. 1994.
14. *Sermons and Discourses, 1723–1729*. Edited with an introduction by Kenneth P. Minkema. 1997.
15. *Notes on Scripture*. Edited with an introduction by Stephen J. Stein. 1998.
16. *Letters and Personal Writings*. Edited with an introduction by George S. Claghorn. 1998.
17. *Sermons and Discourses, 1730–1733*. Edited with an introduction by Mark Valeri. 1999.
18. *The "Miscellanies," 501–832*. Edited with an introduction by Ava Chamberlain. 2000.
19. *Sermons and Discourses, 1734–1738*. Edited with an introduction by M. X. Lesser. 2001.
20. *The "Miscellanies", 833–1152*. Edited with an introduction by Amy Plantinga. 2002.
21. *Writings on the Trinity, Grace, and Faith*. Edited with an introduction by Sang Hyun Hung Lee. 2002.
22. *Sermons and Discourses, 1739–1742*. Edited with an introduction by Nathan O. Hatch, Harry S. Stout, and Kyle P. Farnley. 2003.
23. *The "Miscellanies": 1153–1360*. Edited with an introduction by Douglas A. Sweeney. 2004.
24. *The "Blank Bible."* Edited with an introduction by Stephen J. Stein. 2006.
25. *Sermons and Discourses, 1743–1758*. Edited with an introduction by Wilson H. Kimnach. 2006.
26. *Catalogues of Books*. Edited with an introduction by Peter J. Thuesen. 2008.

Minkema, Kenneth J., and Richard A. Bailey, editors. "Reason, Revelation and Preaching: An Unpublished Ordination Sermon by Jonathan Edwards." *The Southern Baptist Journal of Theology* 3.2 (1999) 27.

Smith, John E., Harry S. Stout, and Kenneth P. Minkema. *A Jonathan Edwards Reader*. New Haven, CT: Yale University Press, 1995.

Selected Works on Edwards

Bailey, Richard. "Driven by Passion; Jonathan Edwards and the Art of Preaching." In *The Legacy of Jonathan Edwards,* edited by Hart, Lucas, and Nichols, 67. Grand Rapids: Baker, 2003.

Brown, Robert. *Jonathan Edwards and the Bible*. Bloomington: Indiana University Press, 2002.

Burns, Sherard. "Trusting the Theology of a Slave Owner." In *A God Entranced Vision of All Things: The Legacy of Jonathan Edwards*, edited by Piper and Taylor. Wheaton, IL: Crossway, 2004.

Chamberlain, Ava. "The Grand Sower of the Seed: Jonathan Edwards's Critique of George Whitefield." *New England Quarterly* 70.3 (1997) 368–85.

Church, Keith D. "Self-Examination as Preparation for the Lord's Supper in Light of the New Covenant." PhD diss., Southeastern Baptist Theological Seminary, 2007.

Davies, Ronald E. "Jonathan Edwards: Missionary Biographer, Theologian, Strategist, Administrator, Advocate—and Missionary." *International Bulletin of Missionary Research* 21 (April 1997) 60–66.

Dwight, Sereno Edwards. *The Life of President Edwards*. New York: G. & C. & H. Carvill, 1830.

Ehrhard, Jim. "The Preaching of Jonathan Edwards: A Critical Analysis of the Tradition of Edwards as a Manuscript Preacher." Online: http://www.teachingresources.org/insights/Jonathan%20Edwards/02.01%20Edwards%20Preaching,%20Ehrhard.htm.

Gelernter, David. "Puritanism Lives." *The American Enterprise* 17.4 (2006) 25–27.

Gerstner, John H. "Jonathan Edwards and God." *Tenth* 10 (January) 2–71.

———. *The Rational Biblical Theology of Jonathan Edwards*. 3 vols. Powhatan, VA: Berea, 1991.

Guelzo, Carlos. Review of *Jonathan Edwards: A New Biography*, by Iain H. Murray. *Fides et Historia* 21 (June) 81–83.

Gura, Philip F. *Jonathan Edwards: America's Evangelical*. New York: Hill & Wang, 2005.

Hart, D. G., et al. editors. *The Legacy of Jonathan Edwards*. Grand Rapids: Baker, 2003.

Haykin, Michael A. G. *Jonathan Edwards: The Holy Spirit in Revival*. Webster, NY: Evangelical Press, 2005.

Holmes, Stephen R. *God of Grace and God of Glory: An Account of the Theology of Jonathan Edwards*. Grand Rapids: Eerdmans, 2000.

Hopkins, Samuel. *The Life and Character of the Late Reverend Mr. Jonathan Edwards*. Boston: Kneeland, 1765.

Jamieson, John F. "Jonathan Edwards and the Renewal of the Stoddardean Controversy." PhD diss., University of Chicago, 1967.

———. "Jonathan Edwards's Change of Position on Stoddardeanism." *Harvard Theological Review* 74 (January 1981) 79–99.

Jenson, Robert W. *America's Theologian: A Recommendation of Jonathan Edwards*. New York: Oxford University Press, 1988.

Johnson, Thomas H. "Jonathan Edwards and the 'Young Folks' Bible." *New England Quarterly* 5 (1932) 37–54.

Kimnach, Wilson H. "Edwards as Preacher." In *The Cambridge Companion to Jonathan Edwards*, edited by Stephen J. Stein, 122. New York: Cambridge University Press, 2007.

———. *The Brazen Trumpet: Jonathan Edwards's Conception of the Sermon*. Rutherford, NJ: Fairleigh Dickinson University Press, 1975.
Kling, David W. and Douglas A. Sweeney, editors. *Jonathan Edwards at Home and Abroad: Historical Memories, Cultural Movements, Global Horizons*. Columbia: University of South Carolina Press, 2003.
Kreider, Glenn R. "Jonathan Edwards's Theology of Prayer." *Bibliotheca Sacra* 160 (2003) 434–56.
Lee, Sang Hyun. "The Concept of Habit in the Thought of Jonathan Edwards." PhD diss., Harvard University, 1972.
———. "The Importance of the Family: A Reformed Theological Perspective." In *Faith and Families*, edited by Lindell Sawyers, 115–35. Philadelphia: Geneva, 1986.
———. *The Philosophical Theology of Jonathan Edwards*. Princeton: Princeton University Press, 1988.
———, editor. *The Princeton Companion to Jonathan Edwards*. Princeton: Princeton University Press, 2005.
Lee, Sang Hyun, and Allen C. Guelzo, editors. *Edwards in Our Time: Jonathan Edwards and the Reshaping of American Religion*. Grand Rapids: Eerdmans, 1999.
Lewis, Sean Michael. "Jonathan Edwards between Church and Academy." In *The Legacy of Jonathan Edwards*, edited by Hart, Lucas, and Nichols, 234. Grand Rapids: Baker, 2003.
Logan, Samuel T., Jr. "The Hermeneutics of Jonathan Edwards." *Westminster Theological Journal* 43 (1980) 85–90.
Lundin, Roger. "What Would They Think of the 90s? Jonathan Edwards." *The American Enterprise* 10.6 (1999) 49–50.
Marsden, George. *Jonathan Edwards: A Life*. New Haven, CT: Yale University Press, 2003.
———. "Jonathan Edwards: American Augustine." *Books and Culture* 5 (November–December 1999) 10–12.
———. "The Quest for the Historical Edwards." In *Jonathan Edwards at Home and Abroad: Historical Memories, Cultural Movements, Global Horizons*, edited by David W. Kling and Douglas A. Sweeney, 3–15. Columbia: University of South Carolina Press, 2003.
McDermott, Gerald R. "Jonathan Edwards, Theologian for the Church." *Reformation and Revival Journal* 12.3 (2003) 11–23.
———. *One Holy and Happy Society: The Public Theology of Jonathan Edwards*. University Park, PA: Pennsylvania State University, 1992.
Miller, Perry. *Jonathan Edwards*. New York: Sloane, 1949.
Minkema, Kenneth. "Jonathan Edwards on Slavery and the Slave Trade." *The William and Mary Quarterly* 54 (1997) 823–34.
Moody, Josh. *Jonathan Edwards and the Enlightenment*. Lanham, MD: University Press of America, 2005.
Murray, Iain H. *Jonathan Edwards: A New Biography*. Edinburgh: Banner of Truth, 1987.
———. "Thirteen Hours, Every Day." *Banner of Truth* 271 (April 1986) 18–25.
Nichols, Stephen J. "Heaven Is a World of Love, Congregations Can Be Full of Strife: The Life of Jonathan Edwards and Handling Conflict." *Reformation and Revival Journal* 12.3 (2003) 25–42.
———. *Jonathan Edwards: A Guided Tour of His Life and Thought*. Phillipsburg, NJ: Puritan & Reformed, 2001.

———. "Jonathan Edwards: His Life and Legacy." In *A God Entranced Vision of All Things: The Legacy of Jonathan Edwards*, edited by Piper and Taylor. Wheaton, IL: Crossway, 2004.

Niebuhr, H. Richard. "The Anachronism of Jonathan Edwards." *The Christian Century* 113 (May 1996) 480–85.

Noll, Mark A. *America's God*. Oxford: Oxford University Press, 2002.

———. "And the Winner Is . . . . Jonathan Edwards?" *Reformed Journal* 39 (March 1989) 5–6.

Parkes, Henry Bamford. *Jonathan Edwards, the Fiery Puritan*. New York: AMS, 1979.

Piper, John, and Justin Taylor, editors. *A God Entranced Vision of All Things: The Legacy of Jonathan Edwards*. Wheaton, IL: Crossway, 2004.

Piper, John. *God's Passion for His Glory: Living the Vision of Jonathan Edwards* Wheaton, IL: Crossway, 1998.

———. *A Godward Life*. Sisters, OR: Multnomah, 1997.

———. *Let the Nations Be Glad: The Supremacy of God in Missions*. Grand Rapids: Baker, 1993.

———. *The Supremacy of God in Preaching*. Grand Rapids: Baker, 1990.

Pauw, Amy Plantinga. *The Supreme Harmony of All: The Trinitarian Theology of Jonathan Edwards*. Grand Rapids: Eerdmans, 2002.

Rivera, Ted. "Jonathan Edwards's 'Hermeneutic': A Case Study of the Sermon 'Christian Knowledge.'" *Journal of the Evangelical Theological Society* 72 (2006) 273–86.

Simonson, Harold P. *Jonathan Edwards, Theologian of the Heart*. Macon, GA: Mercer University Press, 1974.

Smith, John E. *Jonathan Edwards: Puritan, Preacher, Philosopher*. Notre Dame, IN: University of Notre Dame Press, 1992.

Spohn, William C. "Spirituality and Its Discontents: Practices in Jonathan Edwards's *Charity and Its Fruits*." *Journal of Religious Ethics* 31 (2003) 253–76.

Stein, Stephen J., editor. *The Cambridge Companion to Jonathan Edwards*. New York: Cambridge University Press, 2007.

Stout, Harry S. "The Puritans and Edwards." In *The Princeton Companion to Jonathan Edwards*, edited by Sang Hyun Lee, 274–91. Princeton: Princeton University Press, 2005.

———, et al. *Jonathan Edwards at 300: Essays on the Tercentenary of His Birth*. Lanham, MD: University Press of America, 2005.

Stuart, Robert Lee. "'Mr. Stoddard's Way': Church and Sacraments in Northampton." *American Quarterly* 24 (1972) 243–53.

Sweeney, Douglas A. "The Church." In *The Princeton Companion to Jonathan Edwards*, edited by Sang Hyun Lee, 167–68. Princeton: Princeton University Press, 2005.

Sweet, Leonard I. *The Minister's Wife: Her Role in Nineteenth-Century American Evangelism*. Philadelphia: Temple University Press, 1983.

Tracy, Patricia J. *Jonathan Edwards, Pastor: Religion and Society in Eighteenth-Century Northampton*. New York: Hill & Wang, 1980.

Turnbull, Ralph G. *Jonathan Edwards the Preacher*. Grand Rapids: Baker, 1958.

Waanders, David W. "The Pastoral Sense of Jonathan Edwards." *Reformed Review* 29 (Winter 1976) 124–32.

Wheeler, Rachel. "'Friends to Your Souls:' Jonathan Edwards Indian Pastorate and the Doctrine of Original Sin." *Church History* 72 (2003) 241.

Winslow, Ola Elizabeth. *Jonathan Edwards, 1703–1758: A Biography*. New York: Collier, 1940.

Yarbrough, Stephen R., and John C. Adams. *Delightful Conviction: Jonathan Edwards and the Rhetoric of Conversion*. Westport, CT: Greenwood, 1993.

Other

Ames, William. *Marrow of Theology*. Translated and edited by John Dykstra Eusden. Grand Rapids: Baker, 1969.

Barth, Karl. *Church Dogmatics*. Edited by G. W. Bromiley and T. F. Torrance. Vol. 4, Part 1: *The Doctrine of Reconciliation*. London: T. & T. Clark, 1956.

Baxter, Richard. *The Practical Works of Richard Baxter*. Edited by William Orme. Vol. 7. London: J. Duncan, 1830.

Best, Harold. *Unceasing Worship*. Downers Grove, IL: InterVarsity, 2003.

Derrida, Jacques. *The Problem of Genesis in Husserl's Philosophy*. Translated by Marion Hobson. Chicago: University of Chicago Press, 2003

Engelsma, David. "Assurance for All the Children." *The Standard Bearer* 80.9 (Feb 1, 2004). Online: http://www.prca.org/standard_bearer/volume80/2004feb01.html.

Frei, Hans. *The Eclipse of Biblical Narrative: A Study in Eighteenth and Nineteenth Century Hermeneutics*. New Haven, CT: Yale University Press, 1974.

Gadamer, Hans Georg. *Truth and Method*. Translated by J. Weinsheimer and D. G. Marshall. 2nd ed. New York: Crossroad, 1989.

Hirsch, E. D. *Validity in Interpretation*. New Haven, CT: Yale University Press, 1967.

Hodges, Zane C. *The Gospel Under Siege*. Dallas: Redención Viva, 1981.

Kimball, Dan. *The Emerging Church*. Grand Rapids: Zondervan, 2003.

M'Cheyne, Robert Murray. *Memoir and Remains of R. M. M'Cheyne*. Edited by Andrew Bonar. Edinburgh: Banner of Truth, 1987.

MacArthur, John. *The Gospel According to Jesus*. Grand Rapids: Zondervan, 1988.

Miller, Perry. "The Rhetoric of Sensation." In *Errand into the Wilderness*. Cambridge, MA: Belknap, 1956.

Munzer, Stephen R. "Self-Abandonment and Self-Denial: Quietism, Calvinism, and the Prospect of Hell." *Journal of Religious Ethics* 33.4 (2005) 747–81.

Osteen, Joel. "Find Your New Beginning." Online: http://www.lakewood.cc/resources_find_beginning.htm.

Owen, John. *The Glory of Christ*. Edinburgh: Banner of Truth, 1994.

The Presbyterian Church in America. *The Westminster Confession of Faith*. 1654. Reprint, Glasgow: Free Presbyterian, 1994.

Ricoeur, Paul. *Hermeneutics and the Human Sciences: Essays on Language, Action and Interpretation*. Translated by John B. Thompson. Cambridge: Cambridge University Press, 1981.

Rubin, Julius H. *Religion Melancholy and Protestant Experience in America*. Oxford: Oxford University Press, 1994.

Selement, George, and Bruce C. Woolley, editors. *Thomas Shepard's Confessions*. Boston: Collections of the Colonial Society of Massachusetts, 1981.

Stein, Stephen J. Review of *Jonathan Edwards: A New Biography*, by Iain H. Murray. *Church History* 59 (1990) 564–65.

Steinmetz, David. "The Superiority of Pre-Critical Exegesis." *Theology Today* 37 (1980) 27–38.

Vanhoozer, Kevin J. *Is There a Meaning in This Text?: The Bible, the Reader, and the Morality of Literary Knowledge*. Grand Rapids: Zondervan, 1998.

———, editor. *Dictionary for Theological Interpretation of the Bible*. Grand Rapids: Baker, 2005.

Whitefield, George. *Sermons*. 3 vols. New Ipswich, NH: Pietan, 1991.

Wittgenstein, Ludwig. *Philosophical Investigations*. Translated by G. E. M. Anscombe. 3rd ed. New York: Macmillan, 1968.

www.ingramcontent.com/pod-product-compliance
Lightning Source LLC
Chambersburg PA
CBHW052058230426
43662CB00036B/1691